MURRAY'S

BERKSHIRE GUIDE

Already published in this series:

BUCKINGHAMSHIRE

Among titles in preparation the next to be published is:

LANCASHIRE

MURRAY'S
BERKSHIRE

Architectural Guide

EDITORS

JOHN BETJEMAN

JOHN PIPER

LONDON

JOHN MURRAY

50 ALBEMARLE STREET, W.1

FIRST EDITION - - - - 1949

MADE, PRINTED AND BOUND IN GREAT BRITAIN
BY W. S. COWELL LTD, IPSWICH AND LONDON
HALF-TONE BLOCKS BY GEE AND WATSON LTD

CONTENTS

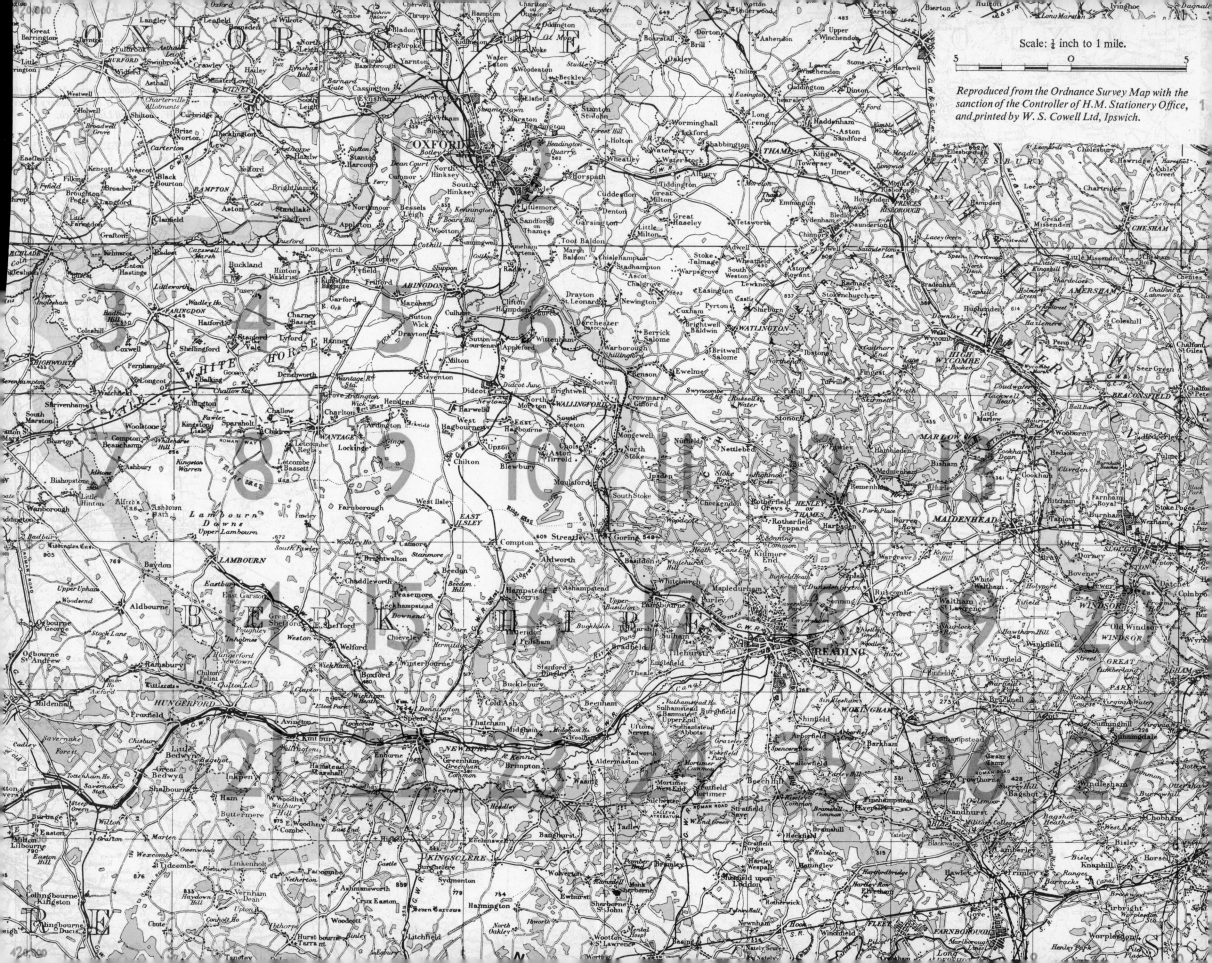

BERKSHIRE has long been a battleground. The Neolithic, Bronze, and early Iron ages studded the downs from Streatley to Ashbury with camps, settlements and burial places. The Romans seem to have made use of the Thames and Kennet valleys, particularly at Reading and Speen. Wessex fought Mercia, Saxon fought Dane, the Normans built castles, King Stephen besieged Matilda, Barons besieged one another, Parliament fought King, and all in Berkshire and for longer and harder than they fought their battles and fortified themselves in other parts of the South of England. Today Berkshire is a prominent battleground between industry and agriculture. The eastern half of the county with Reading as headquarters represents industry with the huge forces of Slough and London behind it and that sinister vanguard, the Harwell Atomic Research Station, advanced far into the agricultural territory. The western half of the county is still agricultural though over-mechanized farming with its wire fences, concrete milking sheds and other hideous paraphernalia, has turned too many farms into fifth columnists on behalf of industry. The race-horse trainers preserve parts of the downs and to them we must be grateful for much that is still beautiful in the county, to them and to the few surviving great estates such as His Majesty the King's at Windsor and the Benyon's at Englefield. They may be described as last outposts of agriculture almost encircled by industry.

When Berkshire was not a battleground, it seems generally to have been considered as on the way to somewhere. That ancient nomadic road, Bronze age or earlier, the Ridgeway, ran from Oxfordshire and Buckinghamshire along the top of the north downs into Wiltshire. Its grass track is now much ruined by farm tractors. The Romans drove three great roads through Berkshire from Silchester in Hants to London, Gloucester and Bath. The middle ages used the Thames, which is the northern border from Surrey to Gloucestershire of this long sausage of a county, as a highway. In the eighteenth century, Berkshire was on the way from London to Bath, in the next century it was on the way from Paddington to Bristol. In this century it is on the way to the West of England.

This battleground, scored with traffic routes, has little early architecture. There is no great cathedral, its Benedictine monastery at Reading, once the third biggest in England, is shapeless scattered masonry; its many castles are mostly reduced to earthworks except for Windsor and a gateway at Newbury. Where medieval architecture does survive, it is in the undisturbed spaces of country between the great traffic routes away from warring barons or main-road motorists. Shottesbrook, Uffington, Lambourn, Faringdon, Wantage, the well-defended chapel of St George at Windsor, and Great Coxwell tithe barn alone compare in size and splendour with the medieval architecture of most other English counties. This paucity of ancient buildings is not wholly due to Berkshire's troubled history. Much of the county is chalk and flint or sandy heath, away from the great rivers up which cut stone could be brought. Medieval buildings are therefore generally of flint and, since cut stone for quoins, window tracery and vaulting was expensive, the churches are small and humble. Indeed, they were so small and humble, so patched with wood and brick in the seventeenth and eighteenth centuries, that they excited the contempt of tidy-minded Tractarians who generally pulled them down and started again in the last century.

It is chiefly as a county of domestic architecture that Berkshire stands out. The fifteenth-century manor house Ockwells is as magnificent as any timbered house of the date in England. There is a distinct and beautiful Elizabethan style, with gabled and projecting upper storeys, stone or wooden mullions and transoms to the leaded windows, plaster or brick between the structural timbers and red-tiled roofs. The two show houses in this style are Ufton Court (mostly 1568) with its secret passages and E-shaped plan and spreading, three-storeyed front, and Shaw House, Donnington, of brick with stone dressings and first traces of Renaissance detail. But the county is full of smaller examples.

Berkshire's domestic architecture came into its own in the late sixteenth century when the cloth trade prospered and local brick kilns were busy. The county was, moreover, by then well served with roads from London and country seats were improved and rich Londoners could build themselves new ones, a practice that they continued into the present century. Consistent grandeur and creativeness is found in buildings from the seventeenth to nineteenth centuries and for this reason we have devoted a good deal of space to them. The magnificence of Abingdon Town Hall and the great houses at Hamstead Marshall, Coleshill and Ashdown set a standard which was afterwards remembered, though it was not, as in many counties, raised still higher in Georgian times. The eastern part of the county, the heathery and sandy landscape, was beautified by Thomas Sandby for William Augustus Duke of Cumberland, the Victor of Culloden, when he made Virginia Water in the middle of the eighteenth century. Sandby also planted mostly beech trees and oaks in picturesque groups to suggest the landscape of Claude. Later in the century the Prince of Wales (George IV) became enamoured of the Great Park and planted many sweet chestnuts and was also responsible for a Swiss Cottage, now demolished, on the edge of Virginia Water. To heighten the Swiss effect, he had the sandy, heathery land towards Sunninghill planted with conifers. Near Virginia Water and Windsor Great Park were built many of the grandest late eighteenth- and early nineteenth-century houses of the county. They were mostly plain Grecian or Gothic houses with landscaped gardens, and Berkshire became, as it still is, a great county of private parks whose owners delighted to convey variety and distance within a small compass.

The best town architecture is a fairly equal blend of seventeenth and eighteenth century. All the towns, except Faringdon, are brick built. Abingdon, Newbury and Reading display a wide range of types of brick and ingenious use of them for varying and decorating plain surfaces. Sir John Soane who was born at Whitchurch, near Pangbourne, spent his early years in Reading and his severely original style left its mark on later Georgian builders in that town.

The railway age brought new people and a new type of architecture to Berkshire, wedding its eastern half to London. First came public institutions like Broadmoor Criminal Lunatic Asylum (1863) designed by Sir Joshua Jebb and Wellington College (1856–9) by John Shaw and various hospitals, barracks and sanatoria. They chose the coniferous districts of east Berkshire, not for the picturesque reasons that appealed to George IV, but because the land was cheap and near London. By the 'eighties, sandy soil was considered healthy, as well as Swiss, Scottish and beautiful. Brick kilns were plentiful and many large houses, half-timbered, or turretted or towered and spired sprung up, to live a short time as country estates, and in our own time to sink from the status of 'country club' to a branch office of a Government department where clerical grade officers may be seen carrying trays of tea down corridors once carpeted to deaden the sound of the footmen's feet. The popularity of the Thames at the end of the century brought much gay timbered and turretted architecture to Maidenhead and Bray. In the agricultural parts of the county, still mostly undisturbed, several distinguished Victorian architects, among them Street and Woodyer, left strong marks of their talent which in the past has been dismissed or too grudgingly appreciated. No other county in the south of England is so profitable a one for the study of pre-Raphaelite stained glass.

The present century has left its architectural mark, as does every age, along the wake of traffic. The main roads of Berkshire are more built up than open. From London, through Maidenhead to Reading and Newbury, it is semi-detached villas and factories for most of the way. Reading has spread tentacles of villas, lessening to bungalows and finally to shacks for miles in all directions. Extremely ugly council houses of concrete deface most of the villages in the western half of the county. Clumsy poles and wires stretch over miles of skyline.

He who would see Berkshire must explore the places between the main roads and far from the main railway stations. If there is one part of the county that can safely be described as Berkshire and not partaking of the characteristics of the bordering counties, it is that triangle with Tidmarsh as its eastern apex and Wantage to Hungerford as its western base line. Here are small villages with large fields, tidy beech and oak copses, winding lanes through chalk or sand, hedges with holly trees, occasional heathy commons with larch and chestnuts and bracken, and many box hedges in cottage gardens. The beautiful descriptions of such scenery to be found in Miss Mitford's *Our Village* (1819) are true of many places in this triangle, though it would be hard to find their like today in Shinfield where they were written. The Vale of the White Horse with its willows and elms, chalk-built or timber-framed thatched cottages, streams and meadows lying under the high northern ridge of the chalk downs is another beautiful kingdom of its own.

The downs themselves grow more magnificent as they roll westwards from Streatley until at White Horse Hill itself they are more awe-inspiring and ancient-looking than any part of them in Wiltshire. But the western part of the downs on the Wiltshire borders from Ashbury, the grand heights in that remote south-western corner of Inkpen Hill (1,011 feet), are characteristic Wiltshire. The northern half of the county from Cumnor to Shrivenham, with villages and big country houses overlooking the upper Thames, is all a warm grey limestone. Faringdon is the capital of this part of Berkshire which seems to belong to the Cotswolds. Between Abingdon and Wallingford there is a flat orchard land of the Thames Valley with many seventeenth-century timber-framed farms and cottages, and the ever-present outline of Wittenham Clumps (alternatively known as The Berkshire Bubs and Sinodun Hill) with their Iron Age camp. This is a little-spoiled part best seen from the river. Along the southern border from Newbury to Finchampstead, the gravelly soil, pine trees and occasional stretches of heath suggest Hampshire. The pines and lakes and heather of the Bracknell area, now villa-sprinkled and served by Southern Electric, are indistinguishable from north-west Surrey. The clay country between Reading and Windsor has a look of Middlesex. But that part of the Thames which flows through chalk from Reading to Wallingford has a grandeur of its own. The flint and brick houses in the milder meadows of the upper reaches of the Kennet and Lambourn rivers seem to be a foretaste of the chalky streams of Wiltshire and Dorset.

This book follows the general plan of our Architectural Guide to Buckinghamshire in the same series published last year. There are minor differences and, we think, improvements. More prominence has been given to the gazetteer of parishes, this is longer and fuller; and we ourselves are jointly responsible for a larger proportion of the photographs—'jointly', in that we both approved the subjects and compositions, whichever of us afterwards may have opened and closed the shutter. Also, we have attempted in the written information on the picture pages to give a countywide index of objects of the same kind as those illustrated there—brasses, painted glass, almshouses, Victorian churches and so on—so that these pages in themselves provide a rough index of architectural beauties. The gazetteer may then be referred to, under the parish names, for fuller information.

We still believe in the virtue of making clear our reactions to buildings and to towns and villages. We believe that houses and churches do, and should, inspire love and hate, and that it is worth while recording the reactions of two observers, instead of making a cold catalogue. We are aware that this puts us in some bad company; also that occasionally our remarks, made after only one or two visits to places, will very likely offend people who know those places better and have looked at them longer: but we shall be content if we succeed in inspiring love for a few buildings which might otherwise receive neglect, or a cold, impartial revaluation. We have illustrated only those buildings or parts of buildings that seem to us beautiful or full of character, except on the last pages. This is a guide to the architecture of Berkshire; but, since buildings are often meaningless without an understanding of their purpose and surroundings, many of the photographs and descriptions will be found to take account of the setting, and an anecdote here and there in the gazetteer has been added to humanize them.

JOHN BETJEMAN
JOHN PIPER

1949

ACKNOWLEDGMENTS

THE EDITORS are indebted to the authors of many Berkshire books which they have consulted, especially *Kelly's Directory*, several late Victorian editions of *Murray's Handbook*, the volumes of the *Victoria County History, Berkshire*, 1906–27, certain volumes of *Country Life* and the *Berkshire Archaeological Journal, The Little Guide* (1934 edn.), Morley's *Monumental Brasses of Berkshire*, 1924, Summer's *Congregational Churches in the Berks., South Oxon and South Bucks. Association*, 1905, and Beard & Co's *Seats and Mansions of Berkshire photographically illustrated, c.* 1870.

Among countless incumbents of churches and owners of houses who have assisted them they wish particularly to thank the Vicar of Hurst, the Vicar of Christ Church, Reading, Lord Berners, Lord Faringdon and Mr Geoffrey Berners. For information and help they are also indebted to Sir Owen Morshead, Librarian at Windsor Castle, Mr Eric Savill, Deputy Ranger of Windsor Great Park, Miss M. M. Swadling of the Reading Public Library, the Librarian of the Royal Military College, Sandhurst, the Abbot of Douai, the Headmaster of Bradfield College, Mr T. D. Kendrick, Mr H. S. Goodhart-Rendel, Mrs Arundell Esdaile, Mr E. Ravenscroft, the Town Clerk of Maidenhead, Mr Oliver Brown of Newbury, Mr E. W. Munford of Hungerford, The Hon Sherman Stonor, Sir Arthur Curgenven, and Prof Stuart Piggott. The Hon Mervyn Horder and Mr Howard Colvin again generously assisted with the proofs.

The Editors wish to thank those who have kindly given permission for the use of the photographs listed below, and particularly Mr Avery Colebrook for his exciting photographs of Windsor (unless here acknowledged, the photographs are by ourselves):—

Anthony Ayscough (from *Country House Baroque*, Heywood Hill, Ltd.) Photograph No. 90.

Avery Colebrook. Photograph Nos. 34–42.

Country Life. Photograph Nos. 80, 92, 93, 166.

Daily Mirror. Photograph No. 118.

Major L. Dent. Photograph No. 81.

A. Hartridge (via National Buildings Record). Photograph No. 83.

Percy Hennell. Photograph No. 147.

T. Huntley (from *A Victorian School: Wellington College*, by R. St C. Talboys. Basil Blackwell, Oxford). Photograph Nos. 1, 156.

Jay. Photograph Nos. 20, 82.

A. F. Kersting. Photograph Nos. 26, 48.

N. Lloyd (via National Buildings Record). Photograph Nos. 21, 46B.

National Buildings Record. Photograph Nos. 10, 31, 70, 126.
  H. Owen Vaughan (Courtauld Institute). Photograph No. 67.

Staniland Pugh. Photograph No. 100.

Ramsey & Muspratt. Photograph Nos. 2, 119.

Kenneth Rittener. Photograph No. 33.

Royal Commission on Historical Monuments. (O. G. S. Crawford via National Buildings Record). Photograph No. 133.

Reece Winstone. Photograph Nos. 71 (via National Buildings Record), 124

  Brass illustrations on page 6 are reproduced from *Monumental Brasses of Berkshire* by H. T. Morley.

  Fig. 3, page 8, is reproduced from *A History of Design in Painted Glass* by N. H. J. Westlake.

TWO EXTREMES OF SCENERY

1. These are two of the several kinds of contrasting scenery of Berkshire. In the southern, and especially the south-eastern, section of the county is much sandy and gravelly heath-covered country. On the edge of Windsor Great Park, George IV, as Prince Regent, planted birches, larches and firs. Early in the last century, this romantic scenery was favoured for country-houses. There are several late Georgian buildings in Sunningdale and Sunninghill. Later in the century, the land being poor and cheap and near London, it was taken over by the Army and by Institutions, such as Broadmoor Criminal Lunatic Asylum, hospitals and schools. Still later, as transport to London improved, it became suburban. WELLINGTON COLLEGE (built 1856–9) whose towers and spires are shown here is at Crowthorne in the heart of this country.

2. At the foot of the chalk downs from Streatley on the east to Ashbury on the west are numerous villages and hamlets with thatched cottages built of clunch, sarsen, plaster and brick, or a combination of these. Where clear chalk streams spring from the foot of the downs, there are often watercress beds, as here at LETCOMBE BASSETT.

NOTE
The numbers in heavy type in the text of the illustrated pages refer to the photographs

3

ROMANESQUE

There are few Norman churches in Berkshire and the only one at all complete is AVINGTON (**3, 5**), in a remote part of the Kennet valley, between Newbury and Hungerford. Plastered and weather beaten outside, it is dark and richly carved within. It is wholly twelfth century, except for the vestry. Other churches keeping their narrow Norman proportions are Hurley by the Thames, Upton, Catmore and Farnborough in the Downs, Frilsham Tidmarsh and Padworth. For the rest, there are towers, windows and doorways, sometimes with tympana, as at CHARNEY BASSETT (**4**), Brimpton chapel and Stanford Dingley. Of the overlap into Transitional Norman, the best, pure examples in the county are to be seen in parts of the churches at Blewbury, Lambourn, Cholsey, Faringdon and Beedon (chancel), and there are many arcades and doorways of the period.

6

EARLY GOTHIC

Of Early English churches, the best and most complete in the county—and it is an almost complete building of the period—is UFFINGTON (South transept door, 6). Other Early English architecture: the carefully-rebuilt spire at WELFORD (7); the chancels at Faringdon, Buckland, Cholsey and Tidmarsh, the last apsidal. There are details elsewhere.

The most complete Decorated church is the cruciform SHOTTESBROOK (8). Others, or parts of others, are Steventon, Aldworth, Sparsholt (with wooden roof and screens); Warfield (chancel); Greyfriars Reading (much restored); Chieveley (tower); Wantage (arcading and tower arches); Ashbury (chancel); North Moreton; and there are features at Cumnor, Stanford-in-the-Vale, West Hanney, Harwell and elsewhere.

BRASSES

Berkshire has merely an average number of brasses for a southern English county, and on the whole they are not of outstanding beauty. The best collections of brasses are at Blewbury, Bray, Childrey, West Hanney, Lambourn, Shottesbrook, Sonning, Sparsholt, Wantage, St George's Chapel Windsor, and Little Wittenham. Those figured on these two pages are among the least stereotyped brasses. *Fig. 1*, details, slightly enlarged, of animals which appear at intervals in the marginal inscription of the brass to John Estbury, *c.* 1485, at LAMBOURN. *Fig. 2*, the shroud effigies of Richard Yate and his wife Johane, 1498, at LONGWORTH. (Effigies, 27 inches. The children at the base omitted.) *Fig. 3*, the brass of Sir John de Foxley and his two wives, 1378, at BRAY. (Effigies, 29 inches). At Hurst, on a rectangular brass of 1600, a woman is shown in a four-poster bed.

This is a list of Berkshire churches containing figure brasses, the numbers following the names indicating the centuries to which the brasses belong:

Fig. 1.

Fig. 2.

Fig. 3.

Abingdon: 15, 16	Letcombe Regis: 15
Aldermaston: 15, 16, 17	Lockinge: 17
Appleton: 16	Longworth: 15, 16
Ashbury: 14, 15	Marcham: 16
Basildon: 15	North Moreton: 15
Binfield: 14, 16	Newbury: 16
Bisham: 16	Reading—St Giles: 16
Blewbury: 15, 16	Reading—St Lawrence: 15, 16
Bray: 14, 15, 16	Remenham: 16, 17
Brightwalton: 16	Sandhurst: 17
Brightwell: 16	East Shefford: 16
Buckland: 16	Shottesbrook: 14, 15, 16
Burghfield: 16	Sonning: 15, 16, 17
Buscot: 16	Sparsholt: 14, 15, 16, 17
Childrey: 15, 16	Stanford Dingley: 15, 17
Cholsey: 15	Stanford-in-the-Vale: 14
Compton: 16	Steventon: 15, 16
Cookham: 15, 16	Stratfield Mortimer: 15
Great Coxwell: 16	Streatley: 16, 17
Cumnor: 16	Swallowfield: 15, 16
Denchworth: 16	Tidmarsh: 15, 16
Easthampstead: 15	Tilehurst: 15
Faringdon: 15, 16	Ufton Nervet: 17
Fawley: 17	White Waltham: 15, 16
Finchampstead: 17	Wantage: 14, 15, 16, 17
East Hagbourne: 17	Warfield: 16
West Hanney: 16, 17	Welford: 15, 16, 19
Harwell: 16	Old Windsor: 17
Hatford: 17	Windsor—St George's Chapel: 14, 15, 16, 17
East Hendred: 15, 16	Winkfield: 17
Hurst: 16, 17	Little Wittenham: 15, 16, 17
Kintbury: 17	Wokingham: 16, 17
Lambourn: 15, 16	Wytham: 15

9. Late fourteenth-century brass of vested priest and layman at SHOTTESBROOK. The inscription is missing.

Fig. 1

Fig. 2

Fig. 3

PAINTED GLASS (PRE-VICTORIAN)

The glass here shown: This page, *Fig.* 1: The Annunciation at ALDERMASTON, thirteenth century. On a blue ground, the Archangel has a green robe and yellow mantle, the Virgin a yellow robe and red mantle. The inscription on the scroll, *Ave Maria Grat*, has blackened. Mounds of green grass are shown below the feet. *Fig.* 2: The Nativity in the private chapel at MILTON House, in yellow, white and green on a ruby ground. This glass has recently been reset, and in some places rearranged. There is a tradition that it was originally at Steventon. *Fig.* 3: part of the fifteenth-century armorial glass at OCKWELLS Manor House, Bray. The Crucifixion in yellow and white stain of the fourteenth century in the quatrefoil at the head of a contemporary window at NORTH MORETON (**10**).

The best ancient glass: Aldermaston, where are two thirteenth-century panels—the Annunciation and the Coronation of the Virgin. West Court, Finchampstead, where is a collection of thirteenth-century, fourteenth-century and later glass. North Moreton, where is a five-light window entirely glazed with fourteenth-century glass. This is of beautiful colour, though some of the drawing has gone. In other windows here are St Christopher, and the Crucifixion pictured opposite. There is fine fourteenth-century glass in the private chapel at Milton House (Fig. 2 and **96**). At Ockwells Manor, Bray, there is domestic armorial glass set up by Sir John Norreys, builder of the house between 1446 and 1466; at Radley there is much fifteenth and sixteenth-century Royal and Episcopal heraldry against dark and glowing backgrounds; at Childrey are panels with figure subjects in yellow and white with delicate drawing and detail, set up by the Fettiplace family in 1547. There is splendid glass in St George's chapel, Windsor (**38, 39**).

Considerable remains (entire figures, panels or more): *Fourteenth century:* Buckland, Compton Beauchamp, East Hagbourne, Long Wittenham, Sparsholt (and later), Warfield (and later). *Fifteenth century:* Goosey, Letcombe Regis (and earlier fragments), East Shefford, Stanford-in-the-Vale and (earlier), Wytham. *Sixteenth century:* Aldermaston. *Seventeenth century:* Abindon Town Hall, Aldermaston, Wokingham Lucas Hospital, Manor House Chapel, East Hendred, Stratfield Mortimer (and earlier), Bucklebury, Greenham (Jesse Tree), Wootton, Wasing, Coleshill.

More than vestigal fragments: *Fourteenth century:* Brightwell, Charney Bassett, Harwell, Old Windsor. *Fifteenth century:* Abingdon St Nicholas, Didcot, East Challow, East Hendred, West Hendred, Inkpen, Shellingford. *Sixteenth century:* Shrivenham. *Eighteenth-century* glass exists at Arborfield (enamelled), Wytham. Early *nineteenth-century* enamelled and 'transparency' glass at Abingdon, St Helen's (the last Berkshire window in the eighteenth-century tradition), Hungerford, St George's Windsor (Princess Charlotte chapel), Wasing, and in the original chapel of Douai Abbey at Woolhampton.

10. The crucifixion in fourteenth-century glass at NORTH MORETON.

12

MEDIEVAL STONE CARVING

Good stone being scarce, the carving of capitals and other details after the twelfth century is not on the whole remarkable, nor does it show much elaboration, nor unusual characteristics, except at Uffington, in the chalk carving at Warfield and Shottesbrook (**15**), at St George's chapel, Windsor, and perhaps in capitals of a rustic version of the stiff-leaf type, which are to be seen at EAST HENDRED (**11**), Steventon, North Moreton and one or two other churches. There is a simply carved stone screen at Baulking of the thirteenth century.

Nor is the window tracery on the whole inventive, but windows at the following churches would be worth measuring and drawing. *Fourteenth century:* Shottesbrook, North Moreton, Sparsholt and Warfield. *Fifteenth century:* St George's Windsor, St Helen's Abingdon, Old Windsor (square headed), DIDCOT (**12**), and Hagbourne—in the rustic examples named here a local style with some character has crept in. There are effigies of stone at Didcot (thirteenth century), Cumnor, Coleshill and the private chapel at East Hendred (fourteenth century) and the well-known series at Aldworth. Fyfield, Englefield and St George's Windsor also have fourteenth-century effigies.

In alabaster, there is the elaborate carved reredos at Drayton (late fourteenth century), and there are alabaster effigies at Wantage (1361), East Shefford (1440), Windsor (1513, 1526), Aldermaston (1539), and Lambourn (1558). (For later tombs carved in stone, alabaster or marble, see pp. 24, 25, 60–63).

13

MEDIEVAL WOODWORK

The county is not rich in this. Far the best of it is in the three carved effigies at SPARSHOLT of the fourteenth century, clearly the work of a considerable artist. Each is carved from a single trunk of an oak tree. The best and the most complete is of a widow (13, 14). There are other wooden effigies at Barkham and Burghfield.

The only extensive and beautiful screen and stall work is that in St George's chapel, Windsor (39, 42).

At Sparsholt there is a fourteenth-century parclose screen which is one of the earliest in England. There is fifteenth-century screen and stall work at Wantage and Sutton Courtney and screens at Blewbury, Hagbourne, Harwell, Sonning and Warfield. There are fourteenth-century roofs at Sparsholt and Little Coxwell. A painted fifteenth-century roof survives at the east end of the inner aisle of St Helen's church, Abingdon. The Litton chapel, Newbury, has a sixteenth-century roof, and Catmore a seventeenth-century one. The most attractive timber porches are at Long Wittenham (fourteenth century), East Hagbourne and West Challow (fifteenth century). At Bray there is a fifteenth-century half-timber gate-house.

The best domestic woodwork is in Charney Bassett Grange (thirteenth century), Abingdon Abbey (fifteenth century), Bisham Abbey, and Ockwells (21). Timber-roofed barns form separate sections (see pp. 18, 19, 46, 47).

Chalk carving on the canopy o
the mid-fourteenth-century foun
der's tomb in the north transept a
SHOTTESBROOK (15). Th
tomb is vaulted in miniatur
fashion under the canopy and ha
a panelled stone base. Simila
work in hard chalk is to be foun
near, at Warfield.

The towers of Berkshire, excep
for a few in towns, and in the lime
stone area near Faringdon (Coles
hill is notable among these) show
like the rest of the churches them
selves, ingenuity and enjoyment o
the use of poorish materials, rathe
than any sort of architectura
grandeur. There is an exception—
the fifteenth-century limeston
tower of FARNBOROUGI
(16) in the flint district of th
Downs. LITTLE or EAS'
SHEFFORD (18), a downlan
tower, has its two lower stages o
thirteenth-century flintwork, cir
cular, Norfolk fashion, becaus
cut stone for corners was not avai
able. The upper stage is fifteent
century and later, and uses cu
stone.

STANFORD-IN-THE-VAL
(19) is a Perpendicular completio
of an Early English design.

CHARNEY BASSETT (17
tower is part of the genera
stylizing of an earlier church tha
took place at the end of th
seventeenth century. Stanford an
Charney churches are of lime
stone faced with plaster.

15

17

19

20. This late fourteenth-century chantry of St Nicholas on the south side of NORTH MORETON church is an unexpectedly rich building to find added to a Berkshire church. It was built, like most of the rest of the church, by Miles de Stapleton, who was steward of Edward II's household and was slain at Bannockburn. He filled its windows with glass, of which that in the east window survives almost intact. There is other fourteenth-century glass here, too **(10)**.

OCKWELLS MANOR HOUSE **(21)**, near Bray, was built between 1446 and 1466. It is an almost perfect (though, of course, restored) house of the time, and has rich bargeboards to the dormer windows. The large hall remains, with roof and bay, and one side of the room consists of a large panelled window, which this picture shows from the outside. For glass in this window see page 8, fig. 3. There is a courtyard beyond with a double cloister round it.

Of other early houses in the county, there are remains of Appleton Manor (early thirteenth century), of three houses at Sutton Courtney — 'Norman Hall', (late twelfth century) with later open roof and gallery, the remnants of a mid-fourteenth-century manor house, and the abbey (a grange of Abingdon), also with fourteenth-century remains. At Charney Bassett was another grange of Abingdon, and there are parts of this, of the thirteenth century and later, incorporated in a comfortable modern house. At BISHAM (22) the Elizabethan manor house was built on to the remains of the late fourteenth-century priory. At East Hendred and Brimpton are domestic chapels. urley Priory and Fyfield have fourteenth-century and Wadley, by Faringdon, has fifteenth-century, remains. The bled mansion of Ufton Court, though in the main Elizabethan, belongs in its details more to medieval than to enaissance times.

The tithe barn at GREAT COXWELL (23, 24, 25) was built in the fourteenth century. It is 150 feet long, and more than 50 feet high to the apex of the stone-tiled roof. With its transepts, and its great roof timbers on stone bases, it looks like a cathedral inside. It was built by monks of Beaulieu, who owned the manor here. It was often visited and much admired by William Morris.

23

24

25

26. DONNINGTON CASTLE gatehouse, near Newbury, 1386. The rest of the castle was pu
down after the Civil wars. Except for Windsor, this is the only castle left in the county which has m
more than earthworks to show.

7. SHAW HOUSE, DONNINGTON, finished 1581. 'Lord have mercy on us miserable sinners!
Thomas Dolman has built a new house, and has turned away all his spinners.' Dolman was a Newbury
clothier, and his house was a merchant's mansion of the new age.

28

ASHBURY MANOR FARM (28, 29), a country manor house of the fifteenth century, under th
Downs, with chalk and sarsen walls, limestone dressings and a stone roof. In 1697 the brick upper store
to the porch was added, and the brick chimney stacks. Inside the house is a stone staircase, much ol

29

woodwork and seventeenth-century plasterwork. Though not complete, it is as beautiful a country manor house as can be found, both in its site and contrasting materials. For a neighbouring cottage, see (72).

30

31

32

EARLY RENAISSANCE MONUMENTS

At BISHAM: (30) In the Hoby Chapel, erected by Sir Edward Hoby in memory of his first wife, 1605.
(31, 32) Details of one of the two other seventeenth-century tombs in the Hoby Chapel.

The most original of the other early Renaissance tombs are at Coleshill (Pratt monument, with beautiful carving of details, especially hands); Sonning (Rich monument, with enormous urns); Faringdon; Shinfield (desk kneelers, and a monument with pretty girls drawing back curtains); Shottesbrook (1714, but earlier in style); Hurst (two sumptuous seventeenth-century tombs). At Waltham St Lawrence and Shrivenham are good collections of decorative tablets, and there are individual examples elsewhere.

33. WINDSOR CASTLE, from the Home Park.

34. WINDSOR CASTLE, looking down Castle Hill from the roof of the Grand Hall.

35. St George's Gate, WINDSOR CASTLE. Toy-fort architecture by Sir Jeffry Wyatville.

WINDSOR CASTLE has been the possession of the kings of England, with the Forest to the south of it, since the time of William I. This king saw the value of its site, on a steep chalk cliff above a bend in the Thames. The only prominent part of the castle built by the early kings is the Round Tower, which was built by William of Wykeham for Edward III, and even this was heightened and refaced in the nineteenth century, for George IV. The other considerable medieval building is St George's Chapel, which was started by Edward IV and completed by Henry VII and Henry VIII. This, with its choir school, deans' and canons' residences, is the nearest equivalent to a cathedral which Berkshire possesses. The delicate

(*continued on page* 32)

36. St George's Chapel, WINDSOR CASTLE. Detail of north wall showing the angel cornice below the clerestory windows.

37. St George's Chapel, WINDSOR CASTLE. The north aisle.

38. St George's Chapel, WINDSOR CASTLE. The great west window. Seventy-five figures of kings, popes and saints. Fifty-one are of 1503–9, eighteen are eighteenth-century designs by B. West and executed by Forest, six are by Thomas Willement, 1842, when E. Blore rebuilt the window.

. St George's Chapel, WINDSOR CASTLE. Fifteenth-century choir stall-work and the Banners of
e Knights of the Garter.

(*continued from page* 27)

elaboration of its glass and stone walls makes
strong and effective contrast to the grim, defen
sive castle. Though it may not be up to suc
masterpieces of perpendicular architecture a
King's College Chapel or St Mary Redcliff
Bristol, it compares favourably with most othe
large churches of the period. It is also mor
impressive than most buildings of its kind becaus
it is the burial place of many English kings, ric
with carved tombs and carved screens, canopie
stalls, armorial glass and the banners of th
Knights of the Garter (**39**). All round the insid
of the building below the clerestory is a mos
delicate carved cornice of angels (**36**), and th
vistas of fan-vaulting are particularly rich whe
seen from the aisles (**37, 42**). Most kings of Eng
land have exercised their taste inside the castle
notably Charles II in the State Apartment
Verrio and Grinling Gibbons having enriche
them for him; but most of the additions an
alterations were screened and overwhelmed b
the work of Sir Jeffry Wyatville, inaugurate
by George IV in 1824 and continuing into th
early years of Queen Victoria.

The distant effect of Wyatville's alteration
including the heightening of the Round Towe
and the adding of turrets to the Sovereign's res
dence in the upper ward is extremely picturesqu
whether seen from the Great Park or the rive
But on close examination, especially above th
East Terrace, the whole appears in a differen
light, with large and childish mouldings, an
numberless mock-defensive loopholes and battle
ments, carried out expensively and withou
any shoddiness, but giving an effect of clums
ness. Wyatville refaced most of the old wall
with white stone and black cement, dressin
windows and doors with yellow stone. This help
to give the impression of an enlarged toy fort t
close-range views.

The seventeenth and eighteenth-centur
canons' houses and deanery buildings in re
brick and plaster with tiled roofs are huddle
like a small town (**41**) to the north of St George'
Chapel. In the Dean's cloister there is thirteenth
century arcading and in the Canon's cloister
other medieval work. All this, together with th
Horseshoe cloister, picturesquely rebuilt by Si
Gilbert Scott in red brick and half timber
manages to assert itself in the vast, grey-walle
enclosure.

40. The Round Tower, WINDSOR CASTLE,
from St George's Chapel roof.

41. St George's Chapel cloisters, WINDSOR
CASTLE.

. St George's Chapel, WINDSOR CASTLE. Fan-vaulting over the screen. The nearest banner is
at of H.M. Queen Mary.

43. SUNNINGWELL. Bishop Jewel's porch, at the west end of the church. It was built in or about 1562. It is unexpectedly elaborate, and was probably the work of Oxford masons. It is an example of that blend of Gothic and Renaissance that is to be found in many of the older Oxford colleges.

ALMSHOUSES

There are more almshouses in Berkshire than in any other English county of like size. They are mostly o-storeyed brick buildings of the seventeenth and eighteenth centuries. The most famous is Jesus Hospital, ay, founded in 1627 — famous because it is in a riverside haunt and because it forms the setting for ederick Walker's well-known painting *The Harbour of Refuge*. It had a contemporary chapel, the inside which has been entirely gutted and renewed. The most beautiful group is that forming a close round the st end of the churchyard of St Helen's, Abingdon (**46A**, **46B**). Another town with several different collec-ns grouped together is Newbury, where are Raymond's buildings, 1678, and St Bartholomew's Hospital, 98 (**48**), both with later additions in the neighbourhood. There are also village almshouses as at Lyford 5), Harwell and Donnington.

4. ABINGDON, Tompkins' Almshouses, unded 1733.

45. LYFORD, Ashcombe Almshouses, 1611.

6A. ABINGDON, Christ's Hospital, founded 553.

46B. ABINGDON, additions of 1797 to Christ's Hospital.

47

48. St Bartholomew's Hospital, NEWBURY, 1698.

Other attractive almshouses are at (in chronological order) Shaw-cum-Donnington, The Donnington Hospital, *c.* 1570; Maidenhead, Salter's Almshouses, 1659; Wokingham, Lucas Hospital, founded 1663; Hurst, 1664; Wantage, Stiles Almshouses, *c.* 1680; Wallingford, 1681; Aldermaston, 1706; Twyford, 1707; Abingdon, Twitty's Almshouses, 1707, Tompkins' Almhouses, 1733 (**44**); Harwell, 1723; Blewbury, 1738 (and Charity School, 1709); Sutton Courtnay, 1818; Tilehurst, 1851; Lambourn, Victorian; Reading, Gothic, 1864–5.

Lucas Hospital, WOKINGHAM (**47, 49**), was begun in 1667, and was built for old men, inhabitants of Windsor Forest. It is managed by the Draper's Company. The chaplains' room, in the flanking wing opposite the chapel, has seventeenth-century armorial glass similar to that in the east window of the chapel. The building, apart from its satisfying proportions, is a particularly good specimen of rich red brickwork enhanced by white-painted woodwork, contemporary leaded windows and tiles.

49

50. ABINGDON TOWN HALL. This Wren-ish building is magnificent public architecture of Charle[s] II's reign. It was started in 1678. Christopher Kempster of Burford, one of Wren's masons at St Paul'[s] cathedral, was the sole mason-constructor of this town hall. The lantern and gables are in the advance[d] style of Coleshill and Ashdown (**56–60**), but the pilastered elevations are signs of a less revolutionar[y] Renaissance manner.

Other Berkshire Town Halls of the seventeenth century are at Windsor—not so imposing a building, thoug[h] its completion is attributed to Wren—and, of a country character, those at Faringdon and Wallingford. All have[,] or had, pillared market spaces on the ground floor.

51. HAMSTEAD MARSHALL, gate pier (see also following pages).

53

HAMSTEA⟩

Stone gate piers, and de⟩
tails of their carving, a⟩
Hamstead Marshall (51–55⟩
It is probable that they wer⟩
all designed by Edward Pierc⟩
who built them; he was ⟩
mason-architect employed b⟩
Wren. There are eight pai⟩
here, standing in fields or ga⟩
den walls. Another pair wa⟩

52. Detail of gate pier above⟩

54

MARSHALL

removed to serve as entrance
to Benham Place, and is beside
the Bath Road between Speen
and Stockcross. The house itself has disappeared. It was
the work of two Dutchmen,
Balthazar Gerbier and his
pupil, Captain Wynne or
Wynde.

55. Detail of gate pier above.

56

57. COLESHILL HOUSE is said to be an innovation in English country house building. Sir Roger Pratt was almost certainly its architect. Inigo Jones may have approved the plans. It is thought to be the first house in a classic manner to dispense with pilasters or columns on its main façades. Its architectural elegance depends on the grouping of the windows and their proportions in relation to wall space. The first floor is slightly set back from the ground floor above the dividing line of the cornice. The outer decorated chimney stacks have an affinity with the gate piers (56) and are, in their turn, set back from the first floor. The inner pairs of chimney stacks are related to the blank spaces between the windows. The interior carries on the old manorial plan of a large entrance hall: from it rises a double staircase (detail 58). The rooms are somewhat heavily decorated with plaster ceilings and stone chimney pieces, and one room has eighteenth-century hand-blocked wallpaper.

58

60

ASHDOWN HOUSE (59) is strangely foreign looking. It was designed for Lord Craven, possibly by John Webb, soon after the Restoration, is built of white chalk with stone dressings, and stands alone on the Downs among beech plantations. The staircase, of chestnut, running right up to the lantern, is the only impressive feature of the interior.

Other seventeenth-century 'builders' houses are Milton (with later additions, **94–96**), Kingston Bagpuize (**83**), what remains unrestored of West Woodhay Manor, and the mansion at Swallowfield, much altered in the eighteenth century. There are smaller houses of the period at Hanney (**80**), BUSCOT rectory (**61**), and in many other country parishes, and in the streets of Wallingford, Abingdon, Windsor (Wren House, and others) and Newbury.

61

62

63

64

BARNS

Old barns with timber or brick walls, and roofs heavily thatched with straw, are a prominent feature f the western agricultural half of the county, which was a region of large farms and correspondingly large arns, with oak or brick or clay floors and internal rafter construction which went on in the same style from edieval times until the last century. he biggest range of them is at EEDON (65), but almost every ownland and White Horse Vale llage has big barns near the old rms beside the churches. There are ther large wheat barns, built before e depression of 1879, in isolated ositions on the Downs: there is a ood example near LOCKINGE 2, 63, 64).

65

FARM BUILDINGS

Farm buildings near the Thames, west of Abingdon, and in the Vale of the White Horse are largely of stone, and partake of the character of Cotswold limestone buildings. Stone-built and stone-tiled barns and dovecote at MARCHAM (66) are an example. Not many cob and thatch orchard and garden walls, characteristic of all chalk valleys of England, survive. The best are at BLEW-BURY (67).

67

68

COTTAGES (A)

Types of Berkshire cottages: Weston, WELFORD (**68**), in the Lambourn Valley; brick and thatc
UFFINGTON (**69**), chalk and thatch. EAST HAGBOURNE (**70**), timber and plaster, thatched,
a brick ground storey with a tile-hung gable (flanked by a cob and thatch garden wall). WYTHAM (7
limestone and thatch.

70

71

COTTAGES (B)

72. ASHBURY, chalk and thatch. In this western area, near the Downs, sarsen is often used as a foundation, sometimes for whole walls, or as an infilling between brick or stone quoins.

73. STEVENTON, one of many timber, plaster and brick houses of the seventeenth century beside the mile-long raised causeway.

74

SHOP-FRONTS

Two Georgian shop-fronts: a general
stores at LAMBOURN (74) and a
saddler's and ironmonger's at HUNGER-
FORD (75). Others are: a cobbler's at
Wantage; a restaurant at Windsor; an
electrical showroom in Ock Street and the
County Fire Office near the Town Hall,
Abingdon; W. H. Smith & Son, Ltd, at
Wokingham; an imported example at
Heathfield School, Bracknell.

Passages between shops in country
towns often lead to courtyards of condemned old cottages, as at NEWBURY
(76), from which one is able to see the old
roofs, walls and chimneys of houses which
have been refaced on the main street.

BRICKWORK

Bricks have been better and longer used
than anywhere else except in Oxfordshire,
near Berks. and Bucks. borders, Kent and
East Anglia. There have been brickfields in
Berkshire since the fourteenth century and
there are local bricks of this date in the
tower of Letcombe Bassett church. The
whole county has deposits of clay suitable
for making bricks and there are, or have
been, brickfields at Reading (Katesgrove,
Coley), Pinkney's Green, Knowle Hill,
Ruscombe, Shaw, Tilehurst, Basildon,
Kintbury, Curridge, Wickham, Bracknell,
Wokingham, Cumnor, Faringdon, Drayton, Uffington, Childrey Challow, Hermit-

age and Frilsham. At the last named in the 1930's bricks when damp were sprinkled with salt and sand
before firing, producing multi-coloured grizzles from grey to purple.

77

Indeed, the county is primarily a brick one. At ABINGDON (79) in St Helen's are this and other eighteenth-century examples. Newbury too has a great variety of brick cornices, friezes and labels to show above the shop-fronts of Northbrook Street and its other main streets, full of diversity and delicacy. The richest example of brickwork in the county is the seventeenth-century gabled house in Northbrook Street, NEWBURY (78), though only its upper stages survive. But the whole street is full of brickwork, and the house above a chain shoe shop on the opposite side of the street to the example shown, is rich mid-eighteenth-century work.

It was late in the eighteenth century that the Berkshire brickworkers gave up making the specially small bricks for the radiation pattern of the voussoirs of windows, as at FARNBOROUGH (77) (a detail from the house shown in 81). Such bricks were difficult to set in the kiln, and had to be treated like pottery. At this time a glazed brick, either blue-black or grey then came to be used to diversify façades. The customary procedure was to put glazed bricks in stripes between the windows as again, at Farnborough, and many examples may be seen in Wantage, Newbury, Hungerford, Wallingford and Abingdon. Later, glazed bricks were used alternately for entire walls, and at the end of the eighteenth century some houses, e.g. Donnington Grove, were built entirely of grizzles, or grey glazed bricks. Panels in parapets, bands of string-courses and labels under windows were generally of 'place' bricks, that is, entirely red, made to contrast with the 'sandels' or partially red brick

d glazed bricks of the rest of a façade (an
ımple in the house at Hanney, **80**.)
Excellent local brick-making went on until
ıe end of the nineteenth century and many
:ctorian architects, such as William White
St Stephen's, Orts Road, Reading (**132**), did
ıir best to show up this local material in all
; variety.
TILES are made at many of the brick kilns,
ıd, though the county is less favoured with
ı-hung houses than Kent, Surrey or Wilts,
ıwbury has several seventeenth-century ex-
ıples, and tile-hanging was common enough
: villages of the Downs and the Vale (e.g. East
ıgbourne, **70**). Sometimes in the early eigh-
nth century, as in the roof of the farm beside
ı church at East Garston in the Lambourn
ılley, the tiles were arranged in patterns
:cording to their colours; this practice also
ıs noted and imitated by some Victorian
:hitects. Here and there tiles and bricks form
ı floors of churches, barns and farmhouse
ıssages and kitchens.
The bricks and tiles of Berkshire are seen at
ıir best in crisp winter sunlight, when they
ım to glow like fires and, as the sun goes
ıwn, to hold the light more warmly than the
ıset.

78

79

80. The Old Rectory, WEST HANNEY, *c.* 1740.

81. The Old Rectory, FARNBOROUGH, 1749. Central projection, *c.* 1840.

82. WELFORD PARK.

83. Kingston House, KINGSTON BAGPUIZE.

84

EAST or LITTLE SHEFFORD (**84**), the disused medieval church in a meadow of Lambourn valley
WASING (**85**), a 1761 and 1826 rebuilding of a small fifteenth-century church. Most old churches in the
southern part of the county were small unpretentious rustic buildings of this sort, patched and added to
in each century until the mid-nineteenth, when Victorian Gothic Revivalists, disgusted by such flimsy
looking masonry and carpentry, either took them down altogether and rebuilt or so added to them and
enlarged them as to create new buildings incorporating a few old features which took their fancy.

LATE RENAISSANCE MONUMENTS

The stately monument in variegated marbles at PUSEY to Jane Pusey, 1742, is by Peter Scheemakers
(**86**). The bust above, in a grey roundel recess, is of her husband.

Besides this, there are splendid eighteenth-century monuments with figures in the round, busts or bas-relief
carving at Coleshill (Rysbrack); Abingdon St Helen's (John Hickey); Kintbury (Scheemakers: busts on two monuments); Bascot (Robert Cooke); Padworth (J. Wilton, 1776); Faringdon, and Englefield (probably by Sir Robert
Taylor (**99**). Of architectural compositions without figures the best perhaps are at White Waltham (W. Palmer,
1723), Faringdon, Swallowfield (severe Russell monuments), East Garston (Seymour tablet, 1731). There are wall
tablets of beauty or dignity of the eighteenth century at Abingdon, Ashbury, Compton, Beauchamp, Eaton Hastings,
East Hagbourne, Harwell, Hurley, Kintbury, Inkpen, Lambourn, Reading, St. Mary, Shinfield, Shottesbrook,
Steventon, Sutton Courtney, Tidmarsh, Wallingford, Waltham St Lawrence and White Waltham. (This is not a
complete list, but mentions some churches with distinguished examples).

Among the best nineteenth-century figure compositions are those at St George's chapel, Windsor (Princess
Charlotte monument, by Chantrey), Sonning (Westmacott, jr.), Cookham, Basildon and Purley. The last three
churches have relief carvings by Flaxman. That at Cookham shows Sir Isaac Pococke being 'suddenly called from
this world to a better state whilst on the Thames, near his own house', 1810. There are grand black marble floor
ledgers with arms at Hurst, Shrivenham, Coombe, and elsewhere.

87

88

TOMBSTONES

The eighteenth-century tombstones at
[GR]EENHAM (**87, 88**) are the most
[or]iginal and deeply carved in the county
[w]hich is not remarkable for its churchyard
[to]mbs.

That at COLESHILL (**89**) is in the style
[of] the neighbouring Cotswolds. Individual
[ex]amples with beauty, or collections, will be
[fo]und at Stanford-in-the-Vale, Letcombe Bas-
[se]tt, Faringdon, Great Coxwell, Uffington,
[S]haddleworth, Shottesbrook, Bray, Marcham,
[H]urley, Cookham. At the last named, a series
[of] fancifully shaped slabs stand to the south of
[th]e church. A table tomb in the Egyptian style
[is] a prominent nineteenth-century feature in
[K]ingston Bagpuize churchyard. At the begin-
[n]ing of the nineteenth century, too, the table
[to]mbs of wealthier farmers were painted pale
[gr]ey or white with lettering and rules in black.
[A] restored example may be seen at Compton
[B]eauchamp. Simple stones, treated in the same
[w]ay, may be seen at Hurst.

89

90

PLASTERWORK

There is no remarkable early plasterwork, except that at Ufton Court (*see* Gazetteer). A cottage
Appleton has a porch delightfully decorated in its pediment with parget-work of the seventeenth centur
Of the same period, on a grand scale, there are the ceilings and staircase decorations at Coleshill (5
which are heavy, elaborate and well-preserved. There is a miniature variant on the Coleshill ceilings in
room at Milton Manor House. The most sumptuous seventeenth-century plasterwork is in the Sta
apartments at Windsor Castle, especially in the Van Dyck room. The ceiling paintings are mostly I
Verrio. Of grand eighteenth-century work there are several examples. The William Kent-ish stucco wo
on a background of scagliola at HALL PLACE, Hurley (**90**) may be by the Anglo-Danish artist Charl
Stanley (1703–61), and it was executed about 1734. There is other stucco work in this room, including t
chimney-piece.

1. At BASILDON PARK there is plasterwork of two dates: the original Carr of York building (1767) as partly decorated at that time. In 1839–44 it was completed and further decorated, this work including overmantels and ceilings, one of which, on the first floor, is shown here (**91**) by John Papworth. Other houses that have plasterwork of the eighteenth century are Faringdon House, where there are ceilings and an overmantel with an urn in light scroll work of beauty; Pusey; Buckland, where the saloon ceiling was designed by Cipriani, and executed by him and by Biagio Rebecca; Monkey Island, Bray; Buscot, where there is original work as well as expert reconstructive work of the twentieth century; Padworth House (by Rose); Calcot Park and Swallowfield. There is also mid-eighteenth-century plasterwork in the church at Wasing.

92. FARLEY HILL PLACE. Classical deities in a perspective setting are painted on the (flat) ceilin of the hall gallery. The work was done about 1730, perhaps by Amigoni. This photograph looks upward into the lantern, in whose apex can be seen a wind indicator, connected with an outside weathervan

Other painted ceilings in Berkshire of similar date are at Bradfield Hall and (by François Clermon in one of the pavilions on Monkey Island, Bray, and the library at Buckland whose ceiling was painted by Cipriani.

3. PADWORTH HOUSE. A chimneypiece and overmantel in coloured marbles, plaster and wood.
This was once in the banqueting room of the Fishing, or Boating Lodge, which is to the north of the
house, on the edge of the now dried-up lake, and was moved to the house in 1922. Padworth House (by
. Hobcraft) was built in 1769, the Fishing Lodge a few years later.

MILTON MANOR HOUSE is of two dates. The original house—the main block in the centre—is of about 1680, and is in brick and dressed stone with some plaster details (95). It is a 'builder's' house of fine type, with interior details reminiscent of Coleshill and Ashdown. In 1764 (completion 1772) two wings were added by the purchaser, a Roman Catholic merchant from London. Externally, these wings agree in style and material with the building to which they were added. Internally, their architect—Stephen Wright, the mason, being 'Mr Morris of London'—embellished the chapel (96) and library (94) below it in a Gothic style, as befitted what the owner saw as the ancientness of his religion.

Roman Catholic chapels in country houses at this date were often decorated in a Gothic style—e.g. Stonor and Mapledurham, Oxon. The internal arches of the windows in Milton library show how the 'Pointed' interior was adapted from a Classic exterior.

97

UCKLAND HOUSE, *c.* 1759 (**97**) and FARINGDON HOUSE, 1780 (**98**). These, along with uscot and Pusey, all stand on the 'Golden Ridge' above the Upper Thames. All except Buscot have een attributed to J. Wood of Bath the Younger. At Buckland there is a central block communicating with ctagonal pavilions (one originally the chapel) by vaulted passages. The immense recessed addition behind e central block is of the early twentieth century—a clever enlargement done by W. Romaine-Walker. aringdon House was built for Pye, the poet Laureate. Curved blind walls with niches flank the south front.

98

Near this Place is interred the Body of
Mrs MARY BENYON, daughter of FRANCIS TYSSEN Esqr
and RACHEL his Wife of *Hackney* in the County of Middlesex
She was twice Married, first in 1737, to POWLETT WRIGHTE Esqr
of *Englefield House* in this Parish
who died 8th January 1740, leaving only one Son POWLETT,
and secondly in 1745, to RICHARD BENYON Esqr of *Gidea Hall*
in the County of Essex by whom She had one Son RICHARD
who caused this Monument to be erected
She died 18th September 1777, Aged 62 Years.

SOME ARCHITECTS OF THE LATE EIGHTEENTH AND EARLY NINETEENTH CENTURIES WHO WORKED IN BERKSHIRE:

ATKINSON, WILLIAM: Beckett Park, *c.* 1834. Gothic.

BASEVI, G.: Titness Park, Sunninghill (one tower only remains). Gothic.

BLORE, E.: Holy Trinity, Windsor, 1843. Gothic.

BRIANT, HENRY: Reading, Royal Berkshire Hospital, 1839. Classic.

BROWN, 'CAPABILITY': Benham Park, 1765 ('completed 1775 under Lady Craven's direction'). Classic.

CARR OF YORK: Basildon Park ('on principle of Wentworth Woodhouse'). Classic.

EMLYN, H. OF WINDSOR: Beaumont, 1790. 'British'.

FISHER OF OXFORD: Marcham Church, 1837. Gothic.

GARBETT, EDWARD: Theale Church, 1822 (**134, 135**). Gothic.

HOBCRAFT, JOHN: Padworth House, 1769. Classic.
                (?) Wasing, *c.* 1770. Classic.

HOLLIS, C.: Windsor Parish Church (under Wyatville). Gothic.

PAPWORTH, J. B.: Basildon Park, additions, 1839–44. Classic.

PILKINGTON, WILLIAM: Chilton Foliat, c. 1800. Classic.

PINCH OF NEWBURY: Donnington Grove (**104, 105, 106**). Gothic.
             Hungerford Church, 1814–16. Gothic.
             (?) Churchyard Gates, Newbury. Gothic.
             (?) House in Newbury (Bath Road), *c.* 1812. Gothic.

SOANE, SIR JOHN: Greyfriars Parsonage, Reading. Classic.
             Obelisk, Market Place, Reading. Classic.
             And possibly other Reading houses. All Classic.

STUART, 'ATHENIAN': (?) Grecian Ruins, Park Place. Classic.

TAYLOR, SIR R.: Maidenhead Bridge, 1772. Classic.
             Wallingford Church and Parsonage, 1769. Gothic. This page.
             (?) Monument, Englefield, 1777, opp. Classic.

WOOD, J. OF BATH, the younger: Buckland House, *c.* 1759 (**97**). Classic.
             Faringdon House, 1780 (**98**). Classic (probably).
             (?) Pusey House, *c.* 1743. Classic.

WYATT, JAMES: Works at Windsor, including Frogmore ruin (Gothic) and restoration of Frogmore House. Classic.
             Sunningdale Park, alterations. Classic.
             Sandleford Priory, 1781 (**101, 102**). Gothic.
             Purley Park, *c.* 1795. Classic.
             Royal Military Academy, Sandhurst, *c.* 1808 (**112**). Classic.

WYATT, T. H.: Woolley, alterations. Classic.

WYATVILLE, SIR J.: Wodley Park alterations, 1799.
             Windsor Castle transformations, 1824–40 (**33**, etc.). Gothic.
             Denford House (Classic) and Church (Gothic), 1832 (**135**).

Sir Robert Taylor, who was apprenticed to Cheere, the sculptor, as a young man, probably designed the monument at ENGLEFIELD, 1777 (**99**), and certainly designed the steeple of St Peter's, WALLINGFORD, 1769 (**100**). He also designed Bridge House beside it.

Gothic Survival is found in the church of Shrivenham, which was rebuilt round a fifteenth-century central tower, in 1638. Medieval construction survived, too, in the timber-roofs of large barns (**25, 63**) into the nineteenth century.

The county was early in consciously reviving the ancient and, as it was then thought, Romantic style. The first attempts are in surface decorators' work, generally applied to interiors as at P A D W O R T H (**93**) (Fishing Lodge (**103**)) and Milton (**94, 96**). This manner may fairly be written as Gothick. It was started by Batty Langley, whose book of engravings wherein he invented five orders of Gothic architecture, appeared in 1742. Horace Walpole used the style, rather more in the ancient manner, at Strawberry Hill, Middlesex, in 1747, but still only plaster deep. Its example was followed in Berkshire, mostly in lodges and gates, as those to Newbury Parish Church (*c.* 1780), to Purley Park (1795), and to Kintbury House (*c.* 1810); in eyecatchers such as Strattenborough Castle (*c.* 1790), near Coleshill, and Toll-houses as that between N E W B U R Y and H U N G E R F O R D (**108**).

One of the earliest complete Berkshire houses to be built (1781) in a Gothic style was SANDLEFORD PRIORY (**101, 102**) by James Wyatt, for the blue stocking Mrs Elizabeth Montagu. Wyatt here attempted to blend the Classic and Gothic externally by using round and square headed windows and castellating the parapets, adding crocketed spirelets and crosses as pinnacles, running attenuated Gothic niches into buttresses and applying Gothic motives in glazing bars and iron-work, and doors. The interior (now a girls' school) is less of a compromise. The hall is frankly Gothic and the round music room and 'Punch's Room' leading to it form a graceful extent of Adam style interior, chaste and Classic.

At about this time William Brummell, father of Beau Brummell, bought DONNINGTON GROVE (**104–106**) and entirely remodelled it in a Gothic style. The architect was probably John Pinch, a local man, who must in that event also have been responsible for the house in the same style on the Bath Road, Newbury, next to the Queen Anne Dower House. The interior of Donnington Grove (**105, 106**) is Gothic through almost all its extent and has lately been decorated in carefully chosen colours which show off the thin delicacy of its mouldings and inventive decorative detail. Columns, when they appear, as in the front porch (**104**) come almost straight from Batty Langley's *First Order of Gothick Architecture*. The windows throughout are in a Tudor style with pronounced hoodmoulds and all the external brickwork is of grizzle bricks. The figure in the niche was introduced by the present proprietor. Other work in this Gothic style, but less accomplished, is to be seen in the neighbourhood.

Inventiveness in style reached its climax in Berkshire with the building of Beaumont, near Windsor, by a local architect, Henry Emlyn. To the main fronts of this otherwise classically-proportioned building, he added columns in what he called the British style. These are twin pillars meant to resemble beech-trunks, the join at their base being hidden by a cartouche, their capitals being in a leaf motif. They resemble long pairs of legs upside down, with the cartouche looking rather like a fig leaf.

(*continued on page* 75)

104. DONNINGTON GROVE, probably by John Pinch, of Newbury; *c.* 1785.

continued from page 73)

New styles whether they were Batty Langley's attempt to classicize Gothic, or Wyatt's to combine Gothic and Classic in one façade, or Emlyn's invention of a new order, were drowned in the wave of antiquarianism which succeeded the publication of Scott's *Waverley Novels* (1814 onwards). Berkshire, being near to London, was as usual, early to catch the tide of fashion. Perpendicular and Tudor were the most popular styles. There were more original examples of these throughout the country than of any other, and their proportions adapted themselves easily to the Classic architecture which still prevailed. Perpendicular and Tudor buildings were measured and correctly copied.

Eighteenth-century brick houses, such as SHOTTESBROOK PARK (107), were given Tudor exteriors (*c.* 1830). Beckett Park, Shrivenham, was built in a Perpendicular style under William Atkinson in 1834. Sir Jeffry Wyatville's Gothic transformation of Windsor Castle (1824–40) undoubtedly had an influence on domestic work. But the Classic did not die out, as may be seen in the list on page 71.

Somewhere about the middle of the nineteenth century one of the last Romantic reconstructions was made in the grounds of ABINGDON ABBEY (109), where sham ruins, consisting of genuine fragments from the Abbey buildings, together with carved stones and statues of various styles and dates, are arranged amid winding paths and rockeries. A Perpendicular window was reconstructed to complete the churchlike effect of genuine arcades which may be seen beyond it.

105

106

DONNINGTON GROVE, the gallery round the top storey of the staircase well (**105**).

DONNINGTON GROVE, the entrance hall (**106**).

107. SHOTTESBROOK PARK, from the south-west.

108. A tollhouse near HALFWAY, on the Bath Road between Newbury and Hungerford.

109. The ruins in the ABINGDON ABBEY gardens.

CLASSICAL REVIVAL

The church at KINGSTON BAGPUIZE (110) was built 1799–1800. Possibly it is by J. Fidel c
Faringdon, and certainly it was modelled on a church by Sir Robert Taylor, built at Ditton, in Surrey
now destroyed. The interior of Kingston Bagpuize church was altered for the worse and entirely refurnishe
in 1882, when galleries and high pews were removed. The church at PUSEY (111) was originally buil
about 1753 and may be—as the house may be—by J. Wood, Junior, of Bath. It had transepts, nave an
narrow chancel, and about 1840 the tower was added. This tower is by some architect such as Hakewil
Goodrich of Bath, or Charles Parker, author of Italianate copy-books.

112. The original Royal Military College, SANDHURST, on the Surrey border, 1807–12. It wa
designed by James Wyatt in a severely classical manner. Here he shows himself a master of the long, low
two-storey front to which is added a portico of exactly the right relative proportion. The chimney behin
is *not* by Wyatt!

NONCOMFORMIST CHAPELS

The Baptist Chapel in Ock Street, ABINGDON (113), was built in 1841. The interior was altered n 1882.

Nonconformity was prosperous in Berkshire in the nineteenth century, so that older interiors have almost all een altered. Attractive chapels are still to be found at these places—a selection only:

(Country) — *Aston Tirrold:* Presbyterian, 1778, restored; *Buckland:* Baptist, brick, among fields, *c.* 1830, restored; *Grove:* Strict Baptist, cottage character, *c.* 1830; *Mortimer West:* Lady Huntingdon's, 1798, box pews.

(Town) — *Abingdon:* Primitive Methodist, architect, Wilson of Bath, 1845, Gothic; Congregational, 1862, talian; Baptist, 1841 (above); *Faringdon:* Wesley, 1837; Congregational, 1840; *Hungerford:* Congregational, 840, Italian; *Newbury:* Waterside Chapel, Unitarian, 1697 (altered inside for secular purposes and all original urniture and fittings sold or destroyed, 1947); Congregational, 1822; *Reading:* Methodist, London Street, grand, alleried, Classic; Congregational, Broad Street, grand, galleried, Classic; *Thatcham:* Congregational, 1804, brick; *Wallingford:* Congregational, 1799, brick, now the Roman Catholic church, after having served secular purposes ince the beginning of the present century; *Windsor:* Congregational, 1832, Classic.

The small Quaker meeting houses in *Faringdon, Uffington* and *Wantage* are no longer used for their original urpose. Of Victorian box-of-coloured-bricks-style chapels there are several in the west of the county. There is a rominent example at *Stanford-in-the-Vale.*

114

115

ROMANTIC COTTAGES

At the same time that they were makin
Gothic the Classic fronts of their country house
or building new mansions in the Gothic style
Berkshire landowners delighted to build estat
cottages in the same manner, especially wher
they could be seen from the house or the publi

116

ay, such as the fashionable Bath Road. The
most complete picturesque village with church
o match, is at Sulham (1838). Lodge to
ULHAM House (**114**), cottages in the village
16), post office (**115**), a forester's house,
USEY Common Wood, c. 1835 (**117**).

117

118

119

TRANSPORT

The Kennet and Avon Canal at NEWBURY, 1794 (**118**), EAST GARSTON Station, Lambourn Valley line, 1898 (**119**). Bath Road villas at MAIDENHEAD, *c*. 1840 (**120, 121**). *The Air Balloon* public house; Ock Street, ABINGDON (**122**).

120

121

122

READING

Reading is a medieval town and had a castle and a rich abbey. But most of it is late Georgian, and nine-teenth and twentieth century, and an epitome of the architecture of those periods. Most of its handsome buildings are not to be seen in the shopping districts. Those illustrated here are representative of prevailing types of Reading building. Furthermore, they are to a large extent representative of prevailing types of Berkshire building, except near its northern and western boundaries; brick, plaster and a sparing use of stone being the usual building materials. For further comments on Reading buildings *see* the gazetteer and for brickwork as seen in Reading and elsewhere, pp. 55–7.

123. Royal Berkshire Hospital, READING. Central block, by Henry Briant, 1839. The wings and colonnades were added in 1862.

124, 125. Brick and stucco architecture on Castle Hill, READING, a part of the Bath Road out of the west end of the town.

126. Miss Mitford's parents' town house, London Road, READING, *c.* 1800.

127. Eldon Square, Italianate. There are many examples of such stone-built Italianate houses in the eastern half of READING.

128. Ingenious late Victorian speculation in Pell Street, READING.

130. St Mary's, Castle Street, READING. A mid-nineteenth-century tower and portico added to a church of 1798.

129. A terrace in London Road READING.

132. St Stephen's, Orts Road, READING; architect, William White, 1865. An essay in local bricks.

131. The Pearl Assurance Building, Station Road, READING. F. Morris, architect.

The earliest revived Gothic churches are at HUNGERFORD (J. Pinch, 1814–16) and Windsor Parish Church (C. Hollis, 1820–22), both of which externally are Georgian versions of Perpendicular. Denford Church, 1832, by Sir Jeffry Wyatville, is a Georgian Gothic survival, incorrect, highly decorated Romantic, and designed to set off the extremely plain Classic mansion he built near it at the same time. THEALE (134, 135), by E. Garbett, 1822, though ten years earlier than Denford is far more 'correct', and was in fact the first church in England to be built in reasonably accurate Early English revival. It is of ashlar and the details are borrowed from Salisbury, but their proportions are extraordinary. The peculiar and striking effect is emphasized by the enormous size of all external mouldings which look big enough for a cathedral. The interior is vaulted and an apse was added by J. O. Scott in 1892. All pinnacles are in solid stone: many of them have been taken down lately. The tower is connected with the church by a large room whose entrance is from the tower arch under which goes the churchyard path.

From now on, as elsewhere in England, Berkshire church architecture became a matter of individual architects rather than of local styles. But even those tame essayers in the Middle Pointed Sir Gilbert Scott and Benjamin Ferrey were unexpectedly unusual in the county. Scott's restoration of Bradfield church, which amounted almost to a rebuilding, produces a most charming and mysterious interior. Ferrey (see p. 92), is wildly decorative at Wickham while that original and creative architect, G. E. Street, is at his earliest and best both in village schools and churches (see p. 93), Butterfield, a master of brick architecture, did not, unfortunately, have many opportunities in this brick county, but another Tractarian architect, with a style all his own, Henry Woodyer, did much of his best work here (see p. 99). S. S. Teulon at LECK-HAMPSTEAD (136, 137), 1859, was at his most original, using coloured bricks and flint for a building that is of North German character—so far as it has any precedent at all.

The final phase of the Revival, when in the 'seventies and 'eighties men like Bodley, the Seddings and G. G. Scott, junior, were trying to carry on Perpendicular from where the medievals left off, is to be found only in Bodley's chancel of St Bartholomew's, Reading, his Dedworth church, and in J. N. Comper's re-decoration of Stockcross.

136

LECKHAMPSTEAD Church (136, 137), by S. S. Teulon, 1856. Teulon also recast Windsor Parish Church internally in 1869 in a commonplace style compared with this eccentric effort at Leckhampstead.

WELFORD Church (138), a detail of the chancel arch and pulpit. The church was rebuilt, except for the medieval tower and spire (7), by T. Talbot Bury, 1852–5.

NINETEENTH-CENTURY CHURCH ARCHITECTS

ALBURY, F. W.: Reading, Coley, St Saviour's, '87
ARMSTRONG, R.: Stratfield Mortimer, '69–'96; Ufton Nervet, '62
ST AUBYN, J.P.: Reading, All Saints', '66–'74; Reading, St Giles', '73; Reading, St Luke's, '82–3
BEAZLEY, C. N.: Cold Ash, '65
BLOMFIELD, SIR A. W.: Windsor, All Saints', '63; Binfield, '67; Eddington, '67; Crowthorne, '73–'89; West Woodhay, '38
BLORE, E.: Windsor, Holy Trinity, '43
BODLEY, F. W.: Dedworth, '81; Reading, St Bartholomew's chancel, '81
BRANDON, D.: Windsor, St Mary's, '54; Little Wittenham (old tower), '61–3
BUCKERIDGE, J. C.: Streatley, '64–5
BUCKLER, J. C.: Knowle Hill, '40, chancel '71; East Hendred, R.C., '65; Windsor, St Edmund's, R.C., '68
BURY, T. TALBOT: see above: Lambourne Woodlands, '51; Ch:ch: Kintbury, '67; Braywood, '67.
BUSBY, C. A.: Maidenhead, St Andrew's and St Mary Magdalene's, '24–5, chancel '77–8
BUTTERFIELD, W.: Wantage, Charlton, '51; Marlston, '55; Newbury, St John Evangelist, '60, destroyed by bomb, 1944; Wokingham, St Sebastian's, '65; Beech Hill, '67
CARPENTER, R. C.: Cookham Dean, '44–5; Stubbings, '50–4
CLACY, J. B.: Burghfield, '43; Dry Sandford, '55
CLARKE, G. R.: Maidenhead, St Luke's, '66
COE & GOODWIN: Bracknell, '51
DIXON, W. A.: Reading, St John Evangelist, '74
DOLBY, E.: Garford, '80
FERREY, B.: see p. 92
FISHER, of Oxford: Marcham, '37
GARBETT, E.: Theale, '22 (ex. chancel)
GOOD, W., Jr.: Bear Wood, '46
HAKEWILL, L.: Wallingford, St Leonard's, '49
HANSOM, J. C.: Buckland, R.C., '46
HAYWARD, C. F.: East Shefford, '70

HOLLIS, C.: Windsor, Parish Church (under Wyatville), '20–2 (recast, Teulon, '69)
HOARE & WHEELER: Reading, St Mark's, 1903
HUGALL, J. W.: Winterbourne, '54; Fernham, '61; Bourton, '62; Chieveley, '73
JOHNSON, J.: Woolhampton, '57; Midgham, '69; Brimpton, '69–'72
PARRY, GAMBIER: Tilehurst, St George's, '84
PEARSON, J. L.: see p. 106
PICTON, J. A.: Arborfield, '63
PINCH, J.: Hungerford, '14–16 (arcades and porch later)
PUGIN, A. W. N.: Tubney, '46
ROBSON P. A.: Grove, 1901
RUSHFORTH, T. H.: Ascot, All Saints', '64
SCOTT, J. OLDRID: Sunningdale, '87–8 (with Street, earlier)
SCOTT, SIR G. J.: Moulsford, '47 (almost rebuilt); Bradfield, '48 (almost rebuilt); Shippon, '55; Abingdon, St Michael's, '67; Appleford (with Ewan Christian), '85–6
SHARP, J., Jr.: Shurlock Row, '70
SHREWSBURY, E. J.: Maidenhead, St Paul's, '87–9; Littlewick Green, '93; Furze Platt, '97
STEVENSON, S. R.: Sotwell, '84; Wallingford, St Peter's, 1904
STOKES, LEONARD: Maidenhead, R.C., '84
STREET, G. E.: see p. 93
TEULON, S. S.: see above
TURNER, J.: Earley, '44; Touchen End, '64
UNDERWOOD, H. J.: Littleworth, '39–'76
WARDELL, W.: Abingdon, R.C., '55–'65
WATERHOUSE, A.: Reading, St Bartholomew's, '79 (chancel Bodley
WHITE, WILLIAM: Reading, St Stephen's, '65 (p. 87)
WIGGINTON, W.: Hatford, '73–4
WIGLEY, G. J.: Woolhampton, St Mary's R.C. Church, '48
WOODMAN, J.: Reading, Greyfriars (old parts), '63; Pangbourne, '66
WOODYER, H.: see p. 99
WYBORN, —.: Windsor, St Saviour's, '75

138

140. The elaborately decorated west end of the church at WICKHAM, which was rebuilt with the exception of the tower in 1845 by Benjamin Ferrey.

There are other Berkshire churches by Benjamin Ferrey at Cranbourne, 1846; Twyford, 1847 (tower much later); Winkfield, 1847; Grazeley, 1856; and Brightwell, 1858—the last being a restoration amounting almost to a rebuilding.

139. One of the 'roof elephants' which occupy the places that roof angels occupy in churches in Norfolk and elsewhere. Eight of them gaze down from the roof of the north aisle at WICK-HAM. When originally brought from the Paris Exhibtion of 1863, four of these were intended for the decoration of the neighbouring, grand, parsonage; but they were found to be too big, and were presented to the church, for which more were made to match. They are of *papier maché*, painted and gilded.

41. The splendid village church interior at FAWLEY, a remote place on the Berkshire Downs; architect, G. E. Street, 1866.

There are other Berkshire churches by Street at Chavey Down, Bracknell (attached to Heathfield, now a girls' school), 1848; Eastbury, 1851; Boyne Hill, Maidenhead, 1854–65; Tilehurst, 1855; East Hanney, 1856; Watchfield, 1859; Sunningdale, parts, 1861; Brightwalton, 1862–3; Sandhurst, 1864; White Waltham, 1869; Purley (old tower), 1870–7; East Garston (almost rebuilt), 1872–82; Speenhamland, chancel, 1879. He restored many other churches in the county, and built many village schools. (*See also* **155**).

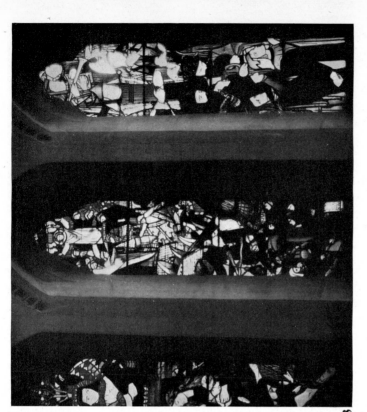

143

142. Belgian glass, *c.* 1850, in the south aisle at WICKHAM. The richest colours (the borders to the vessicas are in ruby glass) are used in complex geometrical patterns with good effect in this elaborate Gothic Revival church.

143. The west window of the original chapel, now the dining hall, at BRADFIELD College, 1849. The earliest pre-Raphaelite glass ever made. The drawing for the figures was by Burne Jones, the arrangement by William Morris. It was also one of the first undertakings of Messrs Powell and Sons, Whitefriars, who executed it.

144. The Crucifixion in the north transept, BRIMPTON; by Thomas Willement, *c.* 1856.

145. The east window at STEVENTON, by Warrington & Co, *c.* 1850. The two lower panels shown here represent (*left to right*) the Angel appearing to Manoah and his wife, and Jacob wrestling with the Angel.

145

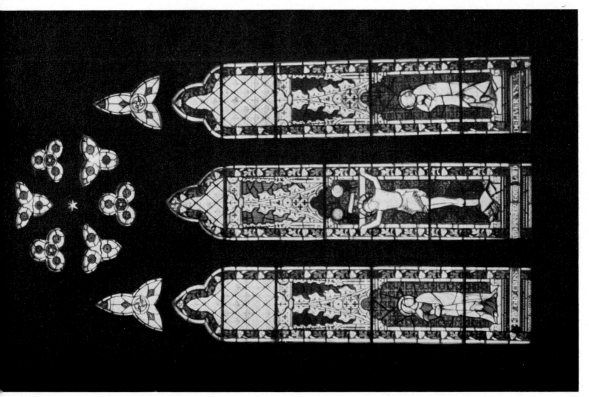

144

St·matthew

6. Glass by Sir E. Burne ... nes beside the pulpit at ... ATON HASTINGS.

147. Our Lord Blessing Children, by Ford Madox Brown, beside the font at BRIGHTWALTON.

SOME NINETEENTH-CENTURY STAINED GLASS

GIBBS: Binfield, Brightwell '58, St Sebastian's '65, Beech Hill, Uffington '50, Bray.

HARDMAN: E. Hendred, private chapel, Shottesbrook, Reading C.C., Wokingham St Paul's, Shippon (E.), Wasing (E.).

HEATON (Warwick): Wokingham.

O'CONNOR: Pusey '48, Sparsholt (grisaille), Woodlands St Mary, Stanford-in-the-Vale, Easthampstead, Milton, Grazeley, Maidenhead St Luke's '71 (moonlight), Drayton '53.

PRE-RAPHAELITE: Longcot (from Newbury), Bradfield College (**143**), Buscot, Eaton Hastings, Brightwalton (**147**), Dedworth, Fawley, Easthampstead, West Woodhay.

J. H. RUSSELL: Abingdon Town Hall, Lockinge.

WAILES: Pusey '48, Bear Wood '49, Buckland R.C., Bradfield, Faringdon '54, Sonning '53, Bradfield College dining-hall.

WILLEMENT: Windsor St George's, Hurst '38, Milton, Radley College, Lambourn '49, Brimpton (**144**), Twyford '47, Wantage '48, Woolhampton '53, Wallingford St Mary's '56.

148

Christ Church, READING (**149**), designed by H. Woodyer in 1862. The light, reticulated tracery that fills the tympanum of the chancel arch symbolizes the lifting of the Veil in the Temple.

149

GREENHAM Church (**150**), by H. Woodyer, 1875—88.

The church at Woodley, the restorations of Milton and Newbury, the village School at Sonning, some Convent buildings at Windsor and many other works in Berkshire were done by Woodyer.

For a note on Woodyer in relation to the Gothic revival, see p. 88.

For a note on Woodyer in relation to the Gothic revival, see p. 88.

Paul's, WOKINGHAM (**148**), signed by H. Woodyer, 1864.

150

151

152

153

54. King Alfred's School, WANTAGE;
Cirencester stone with Bath stone dressings.
Architect, J. B. Clacy, 1850. For Berkshire
churches by Clacy, see p. 90.

Shops in WANTAGE Market Place
(**155**). These are probably a reconstruc-
tion by G. E. Street, who started
private practice in Wantage.

(*Opposite*) THE MODEL VILLAGE

In connection with large Berkshire estates
several model villages were laid out and built
in the nineteenth century. The earliest is
EVERTON (**151**), near Hungerford, *c.* 1800.
LOCKINGE village (**152**), planted with
cypresses in balancing rows on a slope, was
built *c.* 1840 and later. STOCKCROSS (**153**)
is an early twentieth century layout, with pairs
of cottages in brick, half timber and thatch. To
these might be added Bear Wood, built by Mr
Walter of *The Times* in 1869, Buscot, an Edwardian Cotswold-style essay by Sir Ernest
George for Lord Faringdon, 1890, and Sulham
(**114–116**). All these villages except the last two
are conceived on the eighteenth-century principle
of *rows*, not on the irregular grouping principle.

155

156. WELLINGTON COL-LEGE, Sandhurst. Architect, John Shaw, 1855–9. This school building, the distant effect of whose roofs and cupolas may be seen in (**1**), is a pheno-menon for its date. It was built in the height of the Gothic Revival and its Baroque style must have been repugnant to many people at this time. When the school chapel was built, a few years later, dull and uncompromising Gothic by Sir Gilbert Scott was used. Whether regarded for its exuber-ant yet scholarly detail, its happy use of red brick, Portland stone and wood, or the general stately effect of its proportions standing out red and white behind black Wellingtonias and dark green banks of rhododendron, this huge quadrangular block is one of the best pieces of revived Renaissance architecture in the country. It was forerunner of the Queen Anne style to be revived nearly thirty years later by Norman Shaw.

157. The hall at **KINGSTON LISLE** House. It was built into the original house for the arch-æologist owner, for whom the figures, with their classical allu-sions, were also designed.

A detail of the saloon at **BUSCOT PARK** (**158**). It is an eighteenth-century room, decorated by Burne Jones with painted (canvas) panels in an elaborate gilt Adam-style setting. The first Lord Faringdon who commissioned them, was a patron of pre-Raphaelitism and caused Burne Jones to design glass at Eaton Hastings and Buscot. Across the river, at Kelmscott, was William Morris' house.

THIS SLE[...]

159

160. GREENHAM LODGE: architect, R. Norman Shaw, 1879. In this main façade it is modelled on the design of the entrance front of the Elizabethan Shaw House, Donnington, on the other side of Newbury, and is yet astonishingly original for the date. Inside, an immense hall with screens, a gallery and very high panelled and embossed overmantel are the main feature. In several of the rooms chimney-pieces are inset with elaborately patterned glazed and coloured tiles (159), designed by William de Morgan and made by Carter's Pottery at Poole.

161. The house at BOWDEN GREEN, architect, Arnold Mitchell, c. 1909 (enlarged later), is a characteristic example of the kind of country houses without property that were set down on the London side of Berkshire in the early years of the present century. The popularity of the Thames increased their number.

162. All Souls, SOUTH ASCOT: architect, J. L. Pearson, 1897. A large and fine church; the flat-capped tower still lacks its spire. Inside, the vaulting and vistas in which Pearson delighted are well displayed

REPRESENTATIVE PUBLIC AND DOMESTIC ARCHITECTURE, 1870-1920

COLE, A. ADAMS: Wargrave, Woodclyffe Hall, 1902. JOHN BELCHER: House, Pangbourne (now the Nautical College) 1898. EDWARD BURGESS: Marlstone House (now school), 1896–9. ERNEST GEORGE and YATES: Village Street Buscot, 1897. ERNEST GEORGE and PETO: House, Ascot, 1889. E. DOUGLAS HOYLAND: House, Winkfield, 1901. ROBERT KERR: Bear Wood Mansion, 1869. SIR EDWIN LUTYENS: Deanery, Sonning (**166**), 1900; Tyle House Mill, or the Kennet, restoration, c. 1920. C. E. MALLOWS: A riverside house, Abingdon, 1910. ARNOLD MITCHELL: House Bowden Green, Pangbourne (**161**), 1901. F. MORRIS & SON, McIlroy's shop, Reading; Pearl Assurance Buildings, Reading (early twentieth-century). REGINALD MORPHEW: Wallingford, a house. WEST NEVE: Fishery Estate, Maidenhead c. 1880. ERNEST NEWTON: Glebelands, Wokingham, 1898. S. GAMBIER PARRY: Frilsham House (now school), 1896. M. H. BAILLIE SCOTT: The White House, Wantage (**163, 164**), 1899. R. NORMAN SHAW: Greenham Lodge (**159, 160**), 1879. C. STEWARD SMITH: Bradfield College, Science block, 1913. LEONARD STOKES: Pangbourne, Church Cottage, lychgate and shops, 1897; Shooter's Hill House, Pangbourne, 1898; House, Cold Ash, 1899. A. H. RYAN-TENISON: Additional house, Radley College, 1904. WARWICK and HALL: The Berks County Hall, Reading, 1904.

The White House, WANTAGE (**163, 164**), was built for the chaplain of the community of St Mary the Virgin by M. H. Baillie Scott. It is a prototype of well-designed, craft-movement villas usually found in garden cities and garden suburbs. Its style is a popular architectural expression of the Morris movement. The architect has designed door-handles, grates, fender, fabrics, and even the stained-glass Madonna in the priests' private chapel, (**164**).

164

The Greek Theatre, BRAD-
FIELD College (**165**), constructed in an old chalkpit to
the east of the main buildings
in 1892.

166. The Deanery, SONNING, by Sir Edwin Lutyens, 1900. (There have been more recent additions). Built for
the founder of *Country Life*. This was one of the earliest of Lutyen's personal romantic country houses.

LATER BUILDING

167. A Riverside house at PANGBOURNE, *c.* 1890, survival of the time when boating on the Thames was fashionable. It is one of a group called 'The Seven Deadly Sins' by those who think decoration is immoral.

168. 'Queensmere', near WOKINGHAM, was designed by the owner, G. H. Gascoigne, 1927, and made from timbers of an old barn. The splendid garden of 'Queensmere' looks out on to the lake itself (**169**). By way of contrast, in the adjacent parish of Stratfield Mortimer, a colony of over seven hundred shacks among conifers by Longmore lake is known as 'California in England'.

169

170

The examples on the preceding pages, and the modernistical villas along the Bath road on the London side of READING (170), like many other small houses of the mid-wars period, are the last gasp of individualism. Post-war Berkshire's crowning state monument is HARWELL Atomic Research Establishment (171). It was built on the downs by order of the Ministry of Supply which overrode other ministries and local objections. It drains labour from the nearby agricultural villages; its imported workers swell the old towns of Wantage and Abingdon to impracticable size. Its prefabs and factories spread monthly farther over the Downs and higher into the skyline. Its service to Berkshire is that the scientists in it are engaged in splitting the material of which the world and its inhabitants are made.

171

GAZETTEER OF PARISHES

The map numbers after place names refer to the map squares
The word Gothic when spelt Gothik means Georgian Gothic
Page number references refer to illustrations and the additional information in their descriptions

ABINGDON [map 5], despite the fact that the huge industrial city of Oxford is only six miles away, remains resolutely Berkshire. Not even the presence of the MG motor works and a large, noisy aerodrome kills the essentially market and country quality of this meadow-set, river-bordered, old brick town. The town grew up around the great Abbey with which it was not always friendly, especially when the cloth industry in the fifteenth century gave the town a standing of its own. The Abbey, dissolved in 1538, was a large grey limestone building of various dates. The vaulted fifteenth-century gateway beside the small, over-restored church of St Nicholas, is prominent. But down by the river beside a mill, the old Prior's House (*c.* 1250) and long Guest House of two storeys (*c.* 1400) are picturesquely jumbled with seventeenth- and eighteenth-century brick cottages and look like an old watercolour. The interiors of Prior's and Guest House have been lately restored and are among the few genuine medieval interiors in the county. The stone chimney of the Prior's House with its lancet openings (*c.* 1250) was much copied by Victorian architects of the Gothic revival. In the gardens of a house called 'Abingdon Abbey' and of another house now used as Council Offices and behind the gateway, are various sham ruins (pp. 75, 77) constructed partly out of fifteenth-century remains of the Abbey, in a sylvan setting used as a public wandering place. On the south side of the gateway is the Jacobean hall of Roysse's Grammar School (1553). But the greatest medieval building as architecture in Abingdon is St Helen's church, whose tall spire with flying buttresses draws the Thames meadow scenery round it. The church inside is remarkable because it is broader than it is long and consists of five aisles. Seen from the entrance under the tower it seems to be a forest of stone columns; the most graceful are the latest in date, adorned with hollow chamfers. So much do these many arcades, originally made for guild chapels, dominate the church, that one hardly notices at first how variously and heavily the church was restored in the last century and cluttered with ranks of pews. Survivals from earlier times are the painted Perpendicular roof, only visible when electric light is switched on, over the east end of Our Lady's aisle; the baroque marble monument in the north wall to Elizabeth Hawkins, by John Hickey, 1780; the late Georgian window at the west end of the north aisle, a richly coloured four-light design combining enamelled glass in the eighteenth-century style with pot metal glass which was just being rediscovered for the making of church windows. Everywhere in the church the mouldings are deep and delicate, as though the fifteenth-century townsmen were determined to show they could produce as fine buildings as the Abbey. Round the churchyard of St Helen's is the most beautiful collection of buildings in a town which is full of good things. Its western end forms a sort of close flanked on the east by the broad extent of the church and on the other three sides by almshouses. The oldest of these is Christ's Hospital (p. 35), a long, low building with wooden cloister and brick and rough-cast walls and paintings over its entrance (1607). On the river side of the churchyard is a brick extension of the hospital (1797), ingeniously designed with arches and wooden balconies. Twitty's Almshouses (1707) are on the remaining side. Abingdon has other almshouses, notably Tompkin's (p. 35) in Ock Street. The prevailing architecture of the streets is seventeenth- and eighteenth-century roughcast and brick with red-tiled, uneven roofs. St Helen's Street (p. 57), which runs from the superb Town Hall (p. 38) to St Helen's church, is the least touched by modern commerce and contains a range of Georgian houses on its south-east side whose gardens go down to the river. Ock Street, which grows wider as its houses grow humbler at the west end of the town, has several noble Georgian houses and a Gothik shop front, now an electrical shop. But throughout the town there are many streets of modest old houses. The Market Place has much Victorian brickwork, notably the Queen's Hotel and the Corn Exchange (1885, C. Bell architect) in an Italianate manner, which does not clash with the Georgian and earlier styles of the town, such as the Baptist Church (p. 79) and the *Air Balloon* public house (p. 83). There is an imaginative layout of the mid-nineteenth century at Albert Park (1864) where Roysse's School was rebuilt in red brick in 1864 by a local Gothic revival architect, E. Dolby. A monument to Prince Albert, designed by John Gibbs of Oxford, stands in the park, and shrubs and conifers hide ample Gothic houses all round it, built in a North-Oxford style. A worthy stone church by Sir Gilbert Scott (1867) completes the Victorian effect. Contrasting with this, across the river and running parallel to the river Ock and Ock Street, is a dreary extent of modern council houses, stretching for a monotonous mile and more over flat meadow land.

ALDERMASTON [map 23]. A brick and tiled village with compact seventeenth- and eighteenth-century houses and cottages flanking a village street that slopes up to the lodges of the Court, with an inn at the bottom of the street congenial in style and date. The lodges are of brick and are Dutch gabled and were the wings of a house, the centre of which was pulled down, and the entrance thus formed was closed with the splendid iron gates from Midgham House. Aldermaston Court, an Elizabethan mansion, was burned down in 1845, and the present house (now offices) was designed and built by P. C. Hardwick five years after. It was much altered in 1894, and it is a highly elaborate and dull building. Part of the original staircase, illustrated in Nash's *Mansions of the Olden Time*, was rebuilt into the new house and there is some heraldic glass. The seventeenth-century stables survive. The church is a hotchpotch of medieval and new features, and has patched, leaning walls, irregular tiled roofs and shingled spire. The late twelfth-century west door has birds carved on the capitals. The building has been too much cossetted, and is darkened inside by glass by Kempe and Newman; but it is lucky in its possessions: two panels of thirteenth-century glass (p. 8, fig. 1), the alabaster tomb of Sir George Forster and his wife Elizabeth, 1539, and some beautiful eighteenth-century armorial glass probably restored. There are some old, among many new, wall paintings.

ALDWORTH [map 16]. An easterly Downs village of scattered cottages, old and renewed, near the Ridgeway. The church, which was fourteenth-century with the remains of a Norman tower, was hardened and had most of its interest and beauty removed, 1845–75, by J. P. St Aubyn. It has some old woodwork, including carved poppy-heads on four pews and a Jacobean pulpit from St Lawrence, Reading. But it is best known for its extraordinary effigies of the de la Beche family. These—six of them under elaborate canopies, three others disposed between arches of the arcade—were visited by Queen Elizabeth, and have been so much touched and jostled since that they are in a bad state and have lost limbs here and there. They are enormous, and locally called the giants, and are of the early fourteenth century.

In the churchyard there is a decrepit, knotted, white-trunked yew, held together by a chain with a girth of twenty-seven feet. Beche Farm stands on the site of the house, and a pond in a hollow marks the site of the moat.

APPLEFORD [map 6]. The village is an elm-shaded, untidy oasis of old brick and stone cottages in flat country which has been scarred with gravel workings and bisected by the Great Western Railway. The church contains some Norman work but was virtually rebuilt by Sir Gilbert Scott and Ewan Christian 1885-6. The tower is surmounted by an extraordinary spire of original and lumpy beauty, which looks like a heightened stone pyramid. It is a prominent and attractive feature of the flat landscape. The Victorian interior is graced by a Gothic organ, some tablets and other decent features.

APPLETON [map 1]. The village is high on the Cumnor hills and looking down into the Upper Thames Valley. Its limestone cottages are interrupted by bungalows and new villas, country retreats of Oxford citizens. The moated stone manor house of King John's reign is in trees west of the church. It has an Elizabethan porch, below which is a round-headed entrance door of four orders (c. 1200) with flowered capitals such as one expects to see in a church. Inside the house are Elizabethan panelling and screens.

The church is plastered on the outside and stone-roofed. A modern wooden cap to the tower provides space for extra bells, for the village is famous for bellringing and now has ten bells in the small tower. The church interior is spacious with a north chapel in classic style of 1821 to the Southby family with hatchments and modest wall tablets, and there are armorial shields in one window. The nave was skinned and the grand Transitional arcade has been tooled over. In the chancel is a rich Fettiplace monument (1593) and armoured recumbent figure. The electric lighting is too prominent.

ARBORFIELD [map 25]. The old church is in a split-up park, near a gutted Victorian–Jacobean house. It is a ruin, its final dereliction hastened by Army occupation of the house 1939-46. There are a few picturesque remains of seventeenth-century Arborfield Hall in the farm and outbuildings towards the Loddon. From the old church there is a good view of the new one with its spire, to the east, across fields. This, of nave with apsidal chancel, tower and south porch, is by J. A. Picton, 1863, built of stone-dressed flint, roofed with fish-scale tiles. The general effect is tall and spiky and not unattractive. The interior is oil-lighted, with ranks of poppy-heads up each side of a pale red and black tiled nave floor. The roofs are painted pale blue in the intervals of pitchpine rafters. There is a stone pulpit and a marble monument from the old church showing a reclining child at the feet of its parents, 1639. There is stained glass by Rowell of Wycombe (c. 1780), from the old church, a head of Aaron. Two windows in the apse are dated 1863 and have semi-transparency vessicas. There is a colourful window of 1873.

ARDINGTON [map 9]. At the foot of the Downs, among trim plantations. The cottages are almost all half-timbered in the 1880 style of the local Lockinge estate. Ardington House, an eighteenth-century brick building, is a marked contrast. The church has a beautiful north door of about 1200. The building was very expensively restored and over-furnished in 1887. In the north-west corner is the Vernon chapel, now nearly filled with an organ, built in the 1840's, and with stone vaulting, richly-tiled floor and glass of the

period. Here also is a kneeling marble figure of Mrs Vernon by E. H. Baily, R.A., 1830. (He did the figure of Nelson in Trafalgar Square.) The south chapel, unrestored compared with the rest of the church, is now used as a vestry and contains Jacobean Clarke monuments and hatchments.

ASCOT [map 27]. The race-course was formed in the eighteenth century, on a heath of Windsor Forest. The earliest part of the Grand Stand is 1839, and considerable additions were made in 1902. There are late eighteenth-century stables on the opposite side of the road. The nondescript architecture of the street has the seasonal look of buildings only in active use when the races are on. But looking on to the course on the road to Windsor and elsewhere are elaborate houses in half-timber in the riverside style, as seen at Pangbourne and Maidenhead. Conifers and birches abound. The church of All Saints, of red brick, by T. H. Rushforth (1864), is on the main Wokingham road. It is richly polychromatic within and has low brick arcades and a soaring chancel with gilded roof.

SOUTH ASCOT [map 27]. A red brick settlement of humble dwellings in sandy soil among conifers and birches, dominated by J. L. Pearson's All Saints' church. In other parts of the parish, on firry steeps, are larger late-Victorian houses, schools and priories, and smaller modern villas for Londoners.

ASHAMPSTEAD [map 16]. High up in copses. A few tasteful cottages in half-timber and tile-hanging, mostly modern. The little church, of nave and chancel only, is of twelfth-century origin. Above the chancel beam and on some of the walls are thirteenth-century wall paintings, retouched in the 1930's. They depict the Annunciation, Visitation, Shepherds, Nativity and Crucifixion.

ASHBURY [map 7]. Except for Coombe, this is the most beautifully situated village in Berkshire, and consists of Perpendicular church, late Georgian rectory, chalk cottages (p. 52) and manor house on a steep slope of the Downs, almost in Wiltshire. From watercress beds and through elm trees it looks down to the Vale of the White Horse. Manor house (pp. 22, 23), Ashdown Park (pp. 44, 45). The church with stone dressings, has a roughcast tower. Except for the narrow fourteenth-century chancel, it is almost all Perpendicular, and its low, wide internal proportions suggest the large churches of Wiltshire. There is a vaulted south porch. The interior has been skinned and has pitchpine pews. Lately the chancel and north transept have been restored by Martin Travers. Decorative additions to the church are tablets of white marble on slate by Tarrants of Swindon, early nineteenth century.

Wayland Smith's Cave, a chambered long barrow of sarsen, is in this parish; and, on the Wiltshire border, the clunch and sarsen hamlet of **Idstone.**

ASTON TIRROLD and ASTON UPTHORPE [map 10]. Two villages side by side and almost joined, under the Downs. **Aston Tirrold** is a very pretty thatched village with cob, half-timber and tile-hung cottages, and racing stables, amid limes, chestnuts and elms. The two-storeyed Manor House is a Queen Anne house in brick with panelled chimney stacks and shell porch. There is another house of the seventeenth century with stone windows with mullions and transoms. The church is roughcast outside and has distinguished fourteenth-century tracery in the windows, an elegant priest's door and very early Norman font and north and south doors. The old nave roof, a Perpendicular pulpit and parts of the screen remain, but it is all the same a building to delight antiquarians rather than artists. There is an eighteenth-century Presbyterian church of brick, with leaded windows charmingly patterned, but the interior has been dully renewed.

Aston Upthorpe, to the west, is a place of cottages and a church among orchards, nettles and elders. The small church has a Victorian flèche and chancel added to what was a medieval building. Its best feature is its beautiful wooden porch, of the fifteenth century, on the north side. There is old woodwork in the pews.

AVINGTON [map 21]. A church, an old, rambling parsonage and a brick manor farm (1725), between the roar of Bath-road lorries and the rush of a Kennet weir. The towerless, aisleless church (p. 2) is plastered externally and patched with flint and brick. It was once richer and Norman, of the Iffley–Barfreston type, as the chancel arch (p. 3) and remains of—or beginnings of unfinished—quadripartite vaulting in the chancel of the dark and decayed interior show. The Norman font has figures under arches, and the south door is richly carved. The glass forms a Victorian mosaic of bright colour in the high, round-headed windows. With the presence of great cedars, holly, ivy and yew, and these old buildings all in a Kennet meadow, there is a beautiful and desolate melancholy about the place suggesting Goldsmith's *Sweet Auburn*.

BARKHAM [map 25]. In elmy fields near Wokingham. It has small brick farms and week-end cottages. The Victorian church is picturesque but architecturally undistinguished. It has a wooden effigy of *c*.1350. Near here, in a contrasting conifer district, is Longmoor Lake, constructed out of a bog in the last century by John Walter (of *The Times*). Near it is a collection of more than 700 bungalows and shacks, built in the between-wars period and known as 'California in England'. Every fancy style that could be constructed and decorated cheaply has been carried out by the owners.

BASILDON [map 17]. A chalk and beech-wood parish on the Thames-side slope of the Downs. **Upper Basildon** is a collection of old brick cottages, newer week-end houses, an iron church (1859) and a Congregational chapel, about 1810, with its original gallery and low benches, and a cottage attached. Tomb Farm, in a remote valley among flinty fields and groves of old yew trees, is a renewed house on an early site. Beside the gate to its yard is 'Nobe's Tomb', a ruined stone mausoleum in which an eccentric Quaker was buried in 1699. It is said that after his wife's death the door was locked and the key thrown inside. Late in the eighteenth century a man was transported for stealing the lead from the roof. Only a few moss-covered, squared blocks of Corsham Down stone now remain in position.

Two miles away from the high village, towards the river, is **Lower Basildon**, which has Victorian and later cottages by the main Reading–Oxford road and near the railway, and a church and church farm by themselves in fields beyond the railway. The thirteenth-century church has been nearly ruined by rebuilding in 1875–6. Its most attractive features externally, are the Decorated chancel windows (the east window is of the same design as that at North Moreton) and the eighteenth-century brick tower. It has an Early English south door, and a recessed, carved, Decorated tomb outside the chancel wall. Inside, there are parts of the old beamed and plastered roof, eighteenth-century brass altar rails, old altar table and chairs, and among the tablets one with a mourning figure with an urn, by Flaxman.

Dividing the two villages, and on the hill-slope here planted in the picturesque manner, stands Basildon Park, built in limestone (on the site of an earlier house) by Carr of York in 1767, in the Adam style. It has a large central block with recessed portico through the first and second floors, and a domestic block on either side, the whole composition held together by a rusticated ground floor. Carr of York probably also designed Castle Hill Farm, which forms a picturesque group on the south-east drive. In 1832 J. B. Papworth designed the baroque gate lodges on the main road, and so skilfully completed decorations and additions to the house itself, that it is almost impossible to distinguish which is the Adam style of Carr

of York and which is Papworth's (p. 65). The building is now (1949) in a state of decay owing to recent neglect, theft and mutilation.

The Grotto is a white, bowed house of *c*. 1810 on the river bank towards Streatley. It is backed by steep slopes wooded with beech and yew, and looks across the water meadows of the river gap towards the hills behind Goring.

BAULKING [map 4], is remote and beautiful at a dead end in open country in the Vale. Brick and chalk cottages and three farms surround an enormous goose green. The little stone church, of nave and chancel only, is almost wholly thirteenth century. The charm of the interior is a matter of atmosphere and texture. The seventeenth-century roof remains and there are traces of medieval wall paintings, overlaid with seventeenth-century inscriptions. A Royal Arms and a rustic church monument, gilded (1698), are on the north wall. The chancel is almost hidden from the nave by a stone wall pierced with a small thirteenth-century arch and holes on either side of it. There were evidently once nave altars below these. The chancel is, unfortunately, cemented. The pulpit is Jacobean. There is a large octagonal font. All windows but one are of clear glass.

BEAR WOOD [map 25]. This place was for long associated with the Walter family, of *The Times*, and their mansion with its grounds, lake and plantations of hollies, rhododendrons and great variety of conifers gives an exotic quality to the neighbourhood. The house, now an Orphanage, was designed by Robert Kerr in a French Renaissance style and was built, in brick and Mansfield stone, 1865–9. About this time, too, many cottages, an inn and a school were built as a model estate village at **Sindlesham**, nearby. Bear Wood church was designed in pretty and unlearned Middle Pointed by W. Good, junior, 1846. It contains most beautiful, rich glass by Wailes of the same date—as effective as any Victorian glass in the country. The window in the organ gallery is also by Wailes. The furnishing of the church is contemporary, and contributes to an attractive interior.

BEECH HILL [map 25] is a parish formed in 1868, partaking of the gravel and clay scenery of the adjoining part of Hampshire. Its two best architectural features stand together at a cross roads: Beech Hill House, a three-storey square brick building of 1720, now a nursery school; and the church, designed by William Butterfield, 1868, a pleasing essay in his rustic manner, using local brick, flint and timber. It has, like many a Butterfield church, contemporary glass by Gibbs.

BEEDON [map 15]. A remote downland place in flinty fields. Near the church is a magnificent collection of thatched timber barns (p. 47), set on a sloping site beside the manor house, and a brick eighteenth-century building, now a farm. The church is of about 1220, consisting of nave and chancel only, and is a beautifully proportioned building inside, graced at the east end by triple lancets, internally moulded and labelled, as at Chieveley. There is a huge open timber roof of the fourteenth century.

At **World's End** on the main road are entrance lodges taken from Hodcot, West Ilsley, to serve Langley Park, now demolished.

BEENHAM [map 23]. The village is a huddled collection of brick buildings on an eminence to the north of the Bath Road. A grey stucco Primitive Methodist chapel is in their midst. Poles and wires complicate the skyline. The church, H. Woodyer 1859, was added to an attractive tower of brick with stone pinnacles, of 1796. The superb carved tombstones (pp. 62, 63) stand beside the south porch. In a slight dip of elmy park-land above the Bath Road is Beenham House, a long, two-storey building of red brick with broad eaves, late Georgian. Its austere beauty is all in its proportion. Butler's Farm is an attractive old house towards Bucklebury.

BESSELS LEIGH [map 1], on the main Swindon–Oxford road, is surrounded by a dry stone wall, with a few stone cottages and many large elms. A very grand Renaissance house of the Lenthall's was destroyed in 1784. A seventeenth-century gate pier stands in a field where the house was, beside the church. The church, among the trees, is like a small Cotswold chapel of ease, stone-roofed, stone-walled, with clear glass and a bellcote. The little rustic interior is the least restored of all in Berkshire. The building is fifteenth-century; the furnishings seventeenth and eighteenth century. The plaster walls are pale yellow, diversified with inscriptions in gold and black on a blue background. There is a two-decker pulpit, a seventeenth-century roof with angels on it, a raised singers' gallery at the west end, and box-pews throughout, painted with oak graining. The little chancel has a family box-pew in it and a communion table covered with red velvet. There are Lenthall hatchments, slabs and tablets.

BINFIELD [map 19] is in a landscape of elm trees, farmlands and copses that was formerly an outlying part of Windsor Forest. Working and week-end cottages (brick and tile-hung) are glimpsed through trim and well-laid hedgerows, while the more imposing houses hide themselves, as a rule, in boscage. Among the older of these (but they are all much altered) are Binfield Place, originally a late medieval house, Binfield Lodge, Binfield Manor, an imposing classical house converted into flats, Binfield Court and The Grove. Billingbear Park to the west, is an old house-site with cedars. old oaks and cupola-ed stables, brick walls and new brick houses built of the old bricks. The house disappeared after a fire about 1923. South of the church is a newer community of buildings, with some large, early twentieth-century houses, and many smaller ones, shops and a church. The large houses here include what is now the Newbold Missionary College, an architect-designed brick mansion, castellated and with dormers, 1881 and 1910.

The old parish church, originally Decorated, has been heavily restored, and has old timber south porch, Jacobean pulpit, brass, floor and wall tablets. Its best feature is its glass. In one window there is fifteenth-century glass, in upper lights, of the Annunciation, St Peter, St Paul, St John the Divine, and St George, and there is a good deal of colourful Victorian glass; one window is a good example of A. Gibbs' earlier style. The church of St Mark is by Sir A. W. Blomfield, 1867. It is high-gabled, with lean-to aisles, and in red and black brick with stone dressings.

BISHAM [map 13], is a village of a few old brick cottages and new desirable residences strung along the trafficky road into Marlow from the south, between Quarry Woods and the river. Out of this are turnings to the Abbey and the church, which neighbour one another on the bank of the Thames. (They are well seen from the towing path on the Buckinghamshire side).

The 'Abbey' is set among lawns and well-grown trees, and its old walls present the variety of harmonious colours and textures of stone, chalk, brick, flint and plaster, the tower rising above a high-gabled roof of dark tiles. The entrance is through a fourteenth-century stone arch, plainly moulded in many orders, which, like the hall inside and certain other walls and fragments, were part of the medieval manor onto which the Hoby family built an Elizabethan house. The high hall has a minstrel's gallery. On the south side of the house, an oriel lights a large upstairs drawing-room, which was corniced and otherwise adapted in the eighteenth century. Over it, in attics, the early roof construction is visible. In a bedroom is some pretty Elizabethan plasterwork on an overmantel. But it is for the genial pictures it presents of weathered materials, set at odd angles, well-loved, and seen across mowed, riverside grass, that Bisham Abbey is to be remembered (p. 17).

The church, whose churchyard bank the Thames washes, has a tower of clunch of the twelfth century, of simple beauty. The rest of the church is a dull rebuilding, but contains the splendid Hoby tombs in the south chapel (pp. 24, 25). The east window of this chapel is full of effective armorial glass of 1609. There is a Tudor canopied monument of dark grey stone, brought from Anglesey in the early nineteenth century, curiously like one at Cookham. Also a large white marble figure of an Eton boy kneeling at a desk, canopied, 1904.

BLEWBURY [map 10]. A village under the Downs in their barest and most open section. Rolling cornfields surround it, and to the east is Blewburton Hill crowned with a camp that is, on this side, heavily ramparted. The village, owing to its open site, some old but unpretentious buildings, and its picturesque lay-out, has for long attracted refined and retired residents, but it also has some racing and many agricultural connections. There are several seventeenth-century houses in the main village street. A farm north of the church is moated and has old features, but the most distinguished building, apart from the church, which it is opposite, is the Malthus School-house, whose Queen Anne façade, with its casement windows and original roof, has a tablet with the date 1709. Cob and thatch walls (p. 49).

The church, plastered without, has a plan which will interest antiquarians. It was originally a twelfth-century cruciform building with a central tower, to which a north aisle was added in the fourteenth and a south aisle and western tower in the fifteenth century. At this time the central tower was demolished and the present Perpendicular west tower was built, and the timber roofs of nave and south aisle were made. The varying styles of the centuries may be seen in the internal mouldings, capitals, arcades and window tracery. But the church is beautiful as well as interesting, especially when seen from the west end. Great Transitional arches whose piers supported the twelfth-century tower, give a view of a long twelfth-century stone-vaulted chancel of two bays, the altar approached by flights of steps. This spacious long-drawn interior must have been the inspiration of Gilbert Scott's work at Bradfield parish church. The furnishings are mostly undistinguished Victorian. There is some old grisaille glass in the east window and a fifteenth-century wooden parclose screen. Brasses.

BOARS HILL, see WOOTTON

BOCKHAMPTON, see LAMBOURN

BOTLEY, see N. HINKSEY

BOURTON [map 7]. A village of pretty limestone cottages in the Vale of the White Horse, and near Swindon. Bourton House, now a school, is a stone building in early Victorian Tudor style. The Decorated Baptist church here, disused, was built in 1851 by W. Ordish for the Rev Baptist Wriothesley Noel and has a total immersion tank at its west end. The Anglican church, also Decorated, was built eleven years later by J. W. Hugall. It is a competent but uninspired little building.

BOXFORD [map 15]. Brick and half-timber thatched cottages and some larger eighteenth-century houses beside the river Lambourn in downland chalk and flint district. Its nearness to Newbury and 'civilization' makes this village, with its adjoining western hamlet of **Westbrook**, more self-conscious and trim than villages higher up the Lambourn Valley, such as East Garston and Eastbury. The prettily situated church, plastered without and having a brick and flint eighteenth-century tower, looks promising but it has had such a heavy Edwardian restoration within by J. Oldrid Scott and Sons, that it disappoints. There is a Jacobean pulpit amid much clean and hard Victorian and Edwardian work.

BOYNE HILL, see MAIDENHEAD

116

BRACKNELL [map 26]. A modern, main-road town of the Aldershot type in heathery country. The bright red brick houses are interspersed with shops, chapels and a thin and large Decorated-style church by Coe and Goodwin, 1851.

On the borderland between the coniferous country and the pastoral Windsor forest scenery is **Chavey Down.** Here is the girls' school of Heathfield which has an eighteenth-century shop-front let into one of its elevations and a small stone-dressed Gothic chapel by G. E. Street (c. 1850)—chancel 1900.

Bracknell is the dullest-looking town in Berkshire and it will be interesting to see whether the new town perhaps to be built here will be an improvement.

BRADFIELD [map 17], seen from the coppiced hills to the north, is a collection of red-tiled roofs in the quiet valley of the Pang and suggests a Kate Greenaway picture for children. On closer inspection it turns out to be not a medieval dream town, but mostly Victorian, and the large brick and flint buildings which dominate the village belong to the public school, Bradfield College. The school was founded by a Rector, the Rev Thomas Stevens, in 1850, and he used an eighteenth-century manor house called Bradfield Place to house the first boys. Tudor brickwork, dark, reddish-brown, may be seen on the corner wall by the principal entrance. This was originally part of a barn. By the churchyard, and part of the College, is a Tudor octagonal brick turret with vaulted interior.

In 1847 Stevens employed the ubiquitous Gilbert Scott to restore the parish church. Stevens was a man of strong personality who considered curves effeminate and insisted that his pliable architect built in the 'square abacus style' which he considered 'manly'. The vast interior of the parish church, until 1890 the school chapel, is virtually a rebuilding, and is in the Transitional style which Stevens favoured, all the columns having square capitals and all arches and vaulting being severely simple except in the chancel where decoration was permitted on the ribs of the vaulting. The interior, mysterious, grey and stoney, is most successful with its long, tunnel-like chancel approached by flights of steps, its vaulted vistas through aisles and transepts and its stern window tracery. Scott and Stevens spared the beautiful sixteenth-century tower built of flint and brick arranged in chequer-board pattern, though an incongruous Gothic window was inserted in its west wall, without which the long interior of the church would have been intolerably dark. This and other windows in the church were glazed by Wailes, about 1849. *The Ecclesiologist* rightly praised this glass, saying 'the drawing is good, the tinctures clear, the grounds light'. There are also windows in Powell's stamped glass. Scott was employed in 1850 on the school buildings, and very successful they are, using local brick and flint and timber framing. The timber-framed interior of the dining-hall has a window by Morris and Burne-Jones (p. 94). Among later additions to the school is an elaborate chapel (1892) by J. Oldrid Scott. The modern house was erected in a Georgian style (1899) in brick and stone, and the red brick Senior school (1887) and some laboratories opposite the chapel in a dashing free-Perpendicular style, one storey high, in glazed bricks with stone dressings, by C. Steward Smith (1913). The romantic open-air Greek Theatre in a wooded dell east of the College was opened in 1890 (p. 108).

In the parish are Bradfield Hall, a late eighteenth-century brick house with painted ceilings, and Victorian additions; **Southend,** a modern brick suburban hamlet with a dull flint chapel of ease (1835). At **Buckhold** is a large house, red brick and tile-hung by Alfred Waterhouse, standing in a beautiful valleyed park. Buckhold chapel of ease is a small stone building (1836), clear-glazed and candle-lit, with attractive flimsy Gothik at its east end. Near the large brick building of St Andrew's School is a wood of monkey-puzzle trees.

The whole area has an atmosphere of carefully preserved rusticity and shooting syndicates clashing with people on public footpaths.

BRAY [map 20]. This is a large village, which for a good many years has been in the throes of development and change, dependent as it largely has made itself on the popularity of the river as a resort, temporarily fashionable or in decline. A few large, old estates have been split up (Cannon Hill is among these) as housing estates, and some large Edwardian buildings have been adapted, or were built, as hotels. It is not easy to approach the river by road, and the village of Bray has very much the layout and appearance of a small and exclusive seaside resort. Bray Wick Grove, still a private house, opposite stuccoed Cannon Hill, is a seventeenth and eighteenth-century house. Jesus Hospital, founded in 1627, and mostly of that date, is an almshouse surrounding a gardened court. The white figure of the founder is in a niche over the entrance. Frederick Walker popularized Jesus Hospital by making it the background for his well-known picture *The Harbour of Refuge.*

There is a Chantry Chapel in the churchyard. The church house, or Chantry House (at the churchyard entrance), and two old inns, *The Crown* and *Hind's Head,* have some fifteenth-century woodwork. The parish church, except for its Perpendicular tower, has been so restored as to be almost wholly Victorian. A large vaulted Victorian porch is only less rich than the sumptuous Victorian interior restored first by T. H. Wyatt in 1859 and again by another architect in 1875. Standing at the west end of the nave with its two aisles of six bays, one appreciates the long-drawn vista ending in a narrow chancel arch and sumptuous chancel. The renewed windows have a big collection of unsigned purplish stained glass mostly of the 1860's. Brasses (p. 6, fig. 3), a painted monument to the Goddards (1622) and several modest eighteenth-century wall tablets. The vicarage beside the church is red brick, eighteenth century, and the living was a rich one before stipends for Maidenhead were taken from it.

On **Monkey Island,** nearby, the Duke of Marlborough built two pavilions, or banqueting rooms, that still remain. One, now a hotel, is built of wood blocks to look like cut stone. It has a painted room with very faded pictures of monkeys fishing, shooting, one sitting in a boat smoking, and so on. These are by François Clermont. The other pavilion, 'The Temple', is a residence. Originally, it was open below, like a market hall. The main upper room (a billiard room in Victorian times) has a magnificent stucco ceiling with Neptune, naiads, mermaids, shells, water sprites and other figures in high-relief plaster work. These may be by Charles Stanley or perhaps Roberts of Oxford, c. 1725. (Lady Hertford's diary mentions them as being there at that date.) Near the river, downstream, are Oakley Court, an enormous Victorian residence, and The Willows, an enormous Edwardian one, and Down Place, a Wyatt-like Gothic house, L-shaped, of about 1800. This is (1948) being repaired and altered.

Holyport is a pleasant Middlesex-like hamlet round a green.

At **Touchen End** is a little brick and stone church of 1864 by J. Turner, in a Woodyer-like manner, with well-thought-out tracery, like some medieval work at Old Windsor and Didcot, and with columns inside imitated from those at Winkfield.

At **Braywood,** on Windsor's fringe, is New Lodge, an elaborate Tudor-style house of the 'sixties by Cubitt, near a church of expensive design by Talbot Bury, 1867, in flint and well-laid stone. It has west tower, is transeptal and without aisles. The general effect is spacious and spindly, with good and rich stone-carving. It is a typical large Victorian Berkshire church. The scenery here is Windsor Forest's royal pasture, elms, thin oaks and rhododendrons.

The ground slopes down from Braywood towards the town and river. Ockwells Manor (glass: p. 8, fig. 3; house: pp. 16, 17) is in the parish of Bray.

BRIGHTWALTON [map 15]. A very pretty remote village in chalk undulations with many elm trees and oak woods, and consisting of scattered brick and cob cottages, almost all of them thatched. Some of the unmetalled lanes in this parish, leading to isolated cottages, take one back a hundred years.

The church (1862–3), replacing an old one which was demolished, school (1863) and rectory (1877) form a picturesque Victorian group all by G. E. Street and planted with conifers. The stone church with shingled spire and lean-to south aisle with clerestory above is one of Street's happiest designs. The mouldings throughout are big and decided, the internal effect is spacious, light and worshipful. As in all his churches, most light is designed to come in through the west window and the altar is visible from all parts. A low arcade with Purbeck columns shoulder-high, with huge flowered capitals, emphasizes the height and grandeur of the chancel arch. The open timber roofs of nave and chancel make a subtle contrast, and below a Decorated window filled with 1862 glass in well-arranged reds, yellows and blues, is an oblong altar piece carved by Earp, with mosaics by Salviati. The clean cream ashlar walls and other stonework of this interior give one an idea, as does Street's neighbouring church of North Fawley (p. 93), of how Victorian churches looked when they were first built. The beautiful window over the font is by Ford Madox Brown (p. 97). The Rectory, in brick and stone, is an original and clever composition, making decorative features of the brick chimney stacks which run down the whole length of the house. A tile-hung wing with leaded windows is a foretaste of the domestic architecture of England which prevailed until the nineteen-thirties.

BRIGHTWELL [map 6]. A remote but developing village in the flat meadowland between Wittenham Clumps and the downs. There are sixteenth- and seventeenth-century cottages, some of them thatched, one of them having wall paintings in an upper room. Old houses are Mackney Court, partly very early sixteenth-century, with a moat; the Rectory, with old portions; Small's House, near Mackney, a square, Elizabethan house of stone, for long tenements, burnt out, and now restored as a residence; Brightwell House, by the church, rectangular, brick, c. 1800, with some early seventeenth-century work at the back, and Slade End House, of brick, c. 1800. The slated church, well-placed and well-shaded, is a largely fourteenth-century building, with aisles and a late eighteenth-century west tower. It has plain but well-moulded arcades but was made rather commonplace by its restorer, Benjamin Ferrey. The Victorian east window, c. 1850, is colourful. Another window, in the south aisle, is signed by A. Gibbs, 1858.

BRIMPTON [map 23]. Brick cottages, a Victorian church with shingled spire and some Victorian almshouses stand on an airy gravelly ridge above the Kennet Valley which borders Hampshire. The type of farmhouse in this district is two-storeyed, early eighteenth-century brick with plastered walls and overhanging, steeply-pitched red-tiled roofs as at Shalford and Brimpton Manor. At the last named is a medieval chapel of flint with a Norman north door and carved tympanum and an elegant fourteenth-century east window. The chapel is now put to secular uses.

Brimpton church is a sumptuous flint building in the Decorated style of 1869–70 from designs by J. Johnson. Internally, the walls are of ashlar and the columns are of polished granite. The pulpit and cancellum are all of a piece with the design, and in the north transept is a three-light Crucifixion in stained glass by Thomas Willement. Down near the Kennet and Avon Canal is a decent Georgian-style Gothic Baptist chapel, built as late as 1843, with house attached.

BUCKLAND [map 4]. A golden-grey limestone village, stone-roofed, stone-walled, tree-shaded, on the Golden Ridge above the Upper Thames. Almost all the cottages are in excellent condition and there is no building out of scale or harmony.

Buckland House (p. 69) was built for the Roman Catholic family of Throckmorton in 1757 by J. Wood, junior, of Bath. It is of stone consisting of central block with attached pavilions, the eastern with painted ceiling being the library, the western with carved stone swags, once the chapel, now a dining-room. The library ceiling was designed by Cipriani. Two wings were most skilfully added to the house by Romaine Walker at the beginning of this century, exactly in the style of Wood. These wings altered, but did not spoil the proportions. The magnificently landscaped park with lake, winding walks and view across the Thames to the Cotswolds contains temples and grottoes. One of these is a domed peristyle protecting an urn containing the ashes of the Knight of Kerry whose widow was buried nearby. The urn and base were designed by Romaine Walker. Between the house and the church are the remains of a sixteenth-century stone manor house converted into stables in the eighteenth century and refaced on the west front in a fancy Gothic style of the period.

The church is a large cruciform building with a twelfth-century nave and thirteenth-century chancel and north and south transepts. The long interior is not improved by heavy modern glass in the east and west windows. The north transept retains some of its old charm while the south transept has rich mid-Victorian decoration in coloured tiles, reminiscent of Keble College Chapel, Oxford, with a south window by Clayton and Bell. The Roman Catholic church built from designs of J. Hansom in 1846 in the fourteenth-century style, has three windows by Wailes of Newcastle, but two of them have faded owing to poor firing.

Carswell House, now a school, in this parish, is a seventeenth-century stone building, redone in the Tudor style about 1840. Barcote House is a large Tudor-style mansion of 1884 in brick with stone dressings.

BUCKLEBURY [map 16]. The village was originally grouped round the church, where there is still a collection of cottages, shop, Elizabethan Manor and Manor farm, and a rustic foundry. Of the Manor only a small wing and old brick outbuildings (one now used as a theatre) and fishponds are left, the rest having been pulled down in 1830, after a fire. The village spread in the eighteenth and nineteenth centuries round five-mile-long Bucklebury Common, to the south, first in a 'squatting' manner, later in a more determined residential, but still 'free' way. Many small, desirable modern houses stretch on each side of the common from Chapel Row and the *Blade Bone Inn* westwards to Westrop Green. Green's Old Farm and a house at **Hawkridge** are representatives of sixteen-century half-timbered houses in this always-wooded area. The common has been cleared of its attractive birch and scrub plantations by the Army, and has lost all its old character. The Avenue, which runs for a mile eastwards from the *Blade Bone Inn*, is a roadside plantation of old oaks. Inhabitants have counted 268 footpaths in the parish.

The church, the centre of the old village, on the northerly, lower ground, has a pretty chevroned, late-Norman south door. The porch is of 1663. The fabric is largely Perpendicular, but the interior effect is that of an eighteenth-century church, sophisticatedly restored, with high pews, three-decker pulpit, west gallery, hatchments and tablets. In a window on the north side is painted glass of a sundial and a *trompe-l'oeil* fly, dated 1649.

BURCHETTS GREEN, see HURLEY

BURGHFIELD [map 24] is in low, Kennet meadows, elm-grown and unspoiled. Culverlands is a large, plain, late eighteenth-century building much altered in 1879, looking eastwards from high fir and cedar-planted grounds. Hill-fields (gabled, by Walter Scott of Liverpool, 1862) and Highwoods are large modern houses. The church is a curious, transeptal, Romanesque-revival building of 1843 by J. B. Clacy, who did better work at Dry Sandford, near Abingdon, and at King Alfred's school, Wantage. Its west front has an apsidal, arcaded ground storey, and an octagonal turret crowned with a stone cap. It is in blue bricks with stone dressings. It has been partly Gothicized later, especially in the chancel, and refurnished in an uninspired style. There are decayed alabaster tombs. A wooden effigy of a knight is the most beautiful feature, and may be compared with those at Barkham and Sparsholt (pp. 13, 14) in this county, though it does not compare favourably with the latter.

BUSCOT [map 3], in the Upper Thames meadowland, is in the extreme north-west corner of the county, within sight of Lechlade in Gloucestershire and with St John's Lock, the last upstream in the Thames, in the parish. The Rectory (p. 45) is added to an older building. The village was mostly laid out as a model settlement in 1897 from designs of Ernest George and Yates, with stone cottages, covered village well and parish hall. Buscot House, a plain Classic mansion, Adam style within, stands high in a picturesque park with two lakes. It was built in about 1780 and extended in an Italianate style by the first Lord Faringdon at the end of the last century. He employed Burne-Jones, staying across the river at Kelmscott, to paint the saloon (p. 103). In the 1930's the Italianization was mostly removed and additions, including lodges, in keeping with the original building were erected from designs by G. Hyslop.

The churchyard has on the south side some excellent carved headstones, in the Cotswold manner, of the eighteenth century. The aisleless church has a thirteenth-century nave and chancel arch, Perpendicular tower and thirteenth-century chancel altered in the eighteenth century. There are rich marble monuments of 1713, 1784 and 1788, a pulpit given in 1908 and made from a sixteenth-century Flemish triptych with painted panels said to be by Mabuse, showing the Adoration of the Three Kings and the Annunciation. The east window representing the Good Shepherd is by Burne-Jones.

CALCOT, see TILEHURST

CATMORE [map 9/15]. Most of the people in this very small and remote downland parish live in the hamlet of **Lilley,** a place of thatched cottages, an inn, a small disused church (c. 1870) of flint and brick, apsidal-ended, and a row of ill-proportioned new houses. The parish church stands on a downland slope among elms, with an old, tiled farmhouse beside it, a thatched pair of cottages across a field and a grassy platform north of the church where once stood a Tudor manor house.

This little aisleless church, roughcast without, is twelfth-century in origin and has Norman details on the outside north wall of the nave. Inside, the church is singularly imposing and stately for so small a building, thanks to an imaginative restoration in the Norman Revival style of about 1845 when the chancel and the chancel arch were rebuilt in that manner. The roof of the nave is magnificent, divided into five bays by four trusses of the braced collar type. Moulded braces, curved to an arch shape, support the collars, and pendants hang from their springings. This roof is dated 1607 and is, no doubt, an imitation of that at the neighbouring church of Beedon. The roof is ceiled in compartments. The walls are yellow with remains of seventeenth-century inscriptions. There is clear glass throughout and the floors are of old brick tiles. Candles fitted into wooden sockets fixed on circular cart-wheel hoops, hang down the middle of the nave.

CHADDLEWORTH [map 15]. An extremely attractive thatched and brick village in elmy chalk country with winding lanes. Most of the cottages are in a valley east of the church. Many of their gardens have hedges of box. The brick-walled garden of Chaddleworth House is south of the church and the house itself, a modest late eighteenth-century brick building, is on the east side of the church path. The church on top of the hill is largely Early English, but has a Norman door with chevron ornament on the south side and some other Norman features. The nave has Norman proportions, but to it was added a Victorian chancel (1851). One does not see at first the two family pews, like Transept Chapels, which open out from the north wall of the nave. The Blandy pew, the easternmost, was added in 1706, and the other, the Wroughton pew, in 1810. Both contain excellent eighteenth- and early nineteenth-century wall tablets.

Woolley Park on the western and downland side of the parish, is a large, plain, grey stone house designed by Jeffrey Wyatt (1799), rather like Denford, and stands high on a valley slope. Eastwards, its wide park is skilfully landscaped with beech plantations. Westwards, wood plantations dwindle to junipers and then to grass downs. On the estate are several eighteenth-century flint and brick cottages. Poughley Priory is entirely engulfed in Welford Aerodrome, where the erstwhile farmhouse which contains a few fourteenth-century windows is now the Commanding Officer's dwelling.

EAST CHALLOW [map 8]. A main-road village, almost part of Wantage, on a hill going down into the Vale of the White Horse. The village school, 1852, by G. E. Street, is built of chalk with stone dressings and forms a distinguished and picturesque group above the green with its set-back brick and tiled houses. There was a brickfield where is now an 1860 Classic stone building pierced by a high arch, now an ironworks. The disused Wilts. and Berks. Canal passes alongside it. The church looks odd because the tower, 1884, is much lower than the nave roof. Its interior is unexpectedly beautiful, considering that outside the church seems small and new. It consists of nave, chancel and south aisle. The chancel arch and nave arcade are graceful fourteenth century. There are fragments of old glass in two nave windows. The walls are white plaster. But the beauty of the church is first in its proportions, then in its fittings, the rich red and gold hangings of the high altar seen through the 1905 oak screen, the stone floors, the side altars and copper candleholders.

WEST CHALLOW [map 8.] A remote Vale village, lane-entwined, elm-surrounded, and stream-fed, on a level willowy site. North of the village is Manor Farm, a noble eighteenth-century house of red and blue-glazed local bricks with projecting central feature on its main front. The village itself has several timber-framed thatched cottages and tiled farms. The little church has roughcast outside walls and western bellcote. One of these bells is the earliest in England to have its founder's name, 'Povel Le Poter Me Fist, 1283'. There is a timber porch. The interior has been delicately restored by Frederick Etchells, F.R.I.B.A., and, though it lacks the boxpews, hatchments and old paintings of Bessels Leigh, is second only to that church as the most perfect hamlet interior in the county. There are a fifteenth-century chancel screen, Jacobean oak pulpit, fragments of fifteenth-century glass in the east window and eighteenth-century blue stone slabs in the chancel floor. The walls are plastered and the timber roof has massive tie beams.

CHARLTON, see WANTAGE

CHARNEY BASSETT [map 4]. The river Ock winds here towards Abingdon through flat meadows and corn among elms and willows. The village is of old limestone and thatched, or Stonesfield-slated, buildings, the most considerable of which is the Manor House, formerly called Charney Wick, once a Grange of Abingdon Abbey. It has small remains of monastic buildings of the thirteenth-century, including the chapel and a Perpendicular timber roof in the solar upstairs. For years a farmhouse, this is now a country residence, restored in a Cotswold style. The church looks diminutive outside, with its small, sixteenth-century stone turret (pp. 14, 15), but inside it is spacious, with cream washed walls and two-bayed north aisle and wide Perpendicular nave roof. It has a Perpendicular wood pulpit, a little fourteenth-century glass in the east window (otherwise clear glass), 1880-ish tiles and pitchpine pews. A Norman tympanum is built in the chancel (p. 3).

CHAVEY DOWN, see BRACKNELL

CHIEVELEY [map 15], in chalky upland shooting country north of Newbury, is a street of scattered groups of brick cottages with a few thatched timber-framed ones. There are also some gentlemanly late Georgian brick houses standing back from the road. The church is a long building with a Perpendicular west tower. The nave was rebuilt in 1873 by J. W. Hugall in the thirteenth-century style, and he so violently and clumsily restored, skinned, polished and reglazed the church that its only beautiful medieval feature is the triple lancet window at the east end which resembles Beedon's. Even this is much renewed. The wooden arch in the chancel is old and was used for suspending a veil in Lent. The new screen is by C. Birdwood Willcocks.

Curridge in this parish, among tidy copses, is a hamlet with old cottages and week-end hideouts and a pretty school of 1852, used on Sundays as a church.

Oare does not partake of the preserved shooting atmosphere of the rest of the parish. It is in a grassy sylvan valley, has a pond, Victorian brick cottages, several chapels, a Georgian farm and, on a slope, a correct little Tractarian church (1852), Decorated style, probably by B. Ferrey. The interior, nave and chancel only, has contemporary glass, light fittings, tiles, altar hangings, pews and pulpit. No hand crueller than that which occasionally wields duster and broom has touched its dim, religious interior.

Hatt or Hop Castle in Chieveley parish is a small flint folly house, c. 1790, with ogival windows and a dome.

CHILDREY [map 8]. Beech trees at a dangerous cross-roads on the Portway flank a fissure in the downland slope which descends northwards and opens into the Vale below to reveal a longish village of brick cottages with a few timber-framed ones, around a narrow green with a pond in it. Here are two dissenting chapels, one in rustic Victorian Gothic, several old houses of manorial dimensions, flint, brick, stone and red-tiled, hidden among trees. The Manor House itself, once the home of the Fettiplaces before they moved to Swinbrook, Oxon, has a fifteenth-century porch and mullioned windows and an old oak staircase. But it has all been much restored, as have the other large houses. Cantorist House has a sixteenth-century timber-roofed hall in it. The Fettiplace School of old red bricks is of 1732. The Fettiplace almshouses combined with schoolmaster's house and school are mostly rebuilt. There are also three 1912 almshouses.

The large cruciform church with western Perpendicular tower is prettily set among yews to the north of the village. Its low rambling exterior is spoiled by the removal of rough-cast and harsh repointing of the stone revealed. The interior (chancel thirteenth-century, transepts fourteenth-century) is spacious, but again the general effect has been spoiled by cementing of walls in nave and chancel instead of plastering, removal of original plaster from both transepts and by bad Victorian glass. So one looks for details, and these are many. There is a Norman south door and a Norman lead font. The chancel has elaborate stone-carved fourteenth-century recesses, on the north an Easter Sepulchre, on the

south piscina and sedilia, all beautifully carved with canopies and pinnacles. There is a canopied tomb of this date in the north transept with a broken effigy in it. In the chancel is the old screen and some bench ends. The north transept has a distinguished Perpendicular north window of six lights with bits of old glass in it. Medieval tiles are on the floor. The south transept, the Fettiplace chapel, has the family arms carried by angels on the roof, the arms are again on some of the old bench ends there, there is an early sixteenth-century altar tomb of Purbeck marble, and there are many well-preserved brasses, a dozen altogether. This Fettiplace chapel must have been beautiful once and still contains enough of its original fittings to give an impression of its former glory. The best of these is an east window with yellow and white fifteenth-century glass, not very well arranged in relation to the rest of the window, but with delicate drawing and detail. There is an enormous and handsome Royal Arms of George III.

CHILTON [map 9], all too near the spreading Harwell Atomic Research Station, looks lost and old indeed on the flat ridge of the Downs below the Ridgeway, yet above the Thames valley of Abingdon. The village is a happy mixture of timbered and thatched cottages with brick ones in a winding street, has a pond at one end and an old L-shaped farm. A new camp for heavy labour at Harwell, has been established next to the village. The church, roughcast, uneven and red-tiled without, with a high-pitched chancel and north aisle and fussy early Victorian tower added to a low, lead-roofed nave, stands in a girdle of beeches. The interior is full of white, uneven atmospheric charm—clear glass windows, mostly Perpendicular except for a violent east window designed by J. F. Bentley and executed by Nat Westlake (1873); open benches; Norman proportions to nave; Transitional chancel arcade of three bays and chancel arch; and gilded white marble tablets to the Knapp family, 1713.

CHILTON FOLIAT [map 14]. The Kennet Valley village and church are in Wiltshire. In the Berkshire part of the parish, standing on a chalk slope of the willow-bordered river so full of trout, is Chilton Park. It is a noble, square, ashlar-faced house with pillared south portico, built in 1800 in the Adam style by William Pilkington. It was added to, and the south terrace built (spoiling the effect of the south front, as seen in an engraving in The Beauties of England and Wales) by Sir A. W. Blomfield. A house on the Wiltshire and western side of it, by Sir John Soane, has disappeared. The old red-brick-walled garden of Chilton Park is near the river below the house where the road passes the eighteenth-century estate village of Leverton (p. 100).

CHOLSEY [map 10] is a rather commercialized village with railway sidings in rolling open arable. It is seen at its best from the railway, whence the well-proportioned church and an immense range of barns to the north of it, set in wide fields, are more prominent than the ill-assorted and debased Victorian and modern habitations of the largish village. Lollingdon Farm has some sixteenth-century features. The very long, stone and flint barn near the church is a replacement, dating from 1815, of Cowper's Barn which was attached to Cholsey monastery and was, like this one, over 300 feet long. It has had its entrances renewed and takes its part in farm efficiency.

The church, with nave, chancel, transepts and central tower, has great presence, as well as architectural distinction. Its twelfth-century tower arches may be enriched adaptations of earlier ones, the tower being of Saxon origin. There are other Norman features, including the south door. The proportions of the interior are early and splendid. Beyond the heavily-moulded, round-arched tower crossing, the Early English chancel is well seen. Left and right it has triple, deeply-splayed lancets, with slender, detached shafts, and an east window of the same date, with plate tracery of original design. *Murray's Handbook* (1882 edition) remarked that the church was much in need of judicious restoration, having been 'greatly neglected'. 'Restoration' indeed followed, but it was not judicious, especially as to furnishing. Tiles and brass and dark woodwork too greatly dominate. Roofs and nave windows (except the west window) have been entirely renewed. The west gallery was removed in 1911. How badly, now, the church needs medieval grisaille glass, and the clearing of furniture! Its beauty is masked. In the churchyard is buried E. P. Warren, 1856–1937, the architect. There is a Baptist chapel of 1823.

CLEWER [map 20] is really now a suburb of Windsor, and the parishes of **Clewer Within** and **Clewer Without** trespass into Windsor town. A fifteenth- and seventeenth-century house called 'The Limes' and an eighteenth-century house of good, simple design are near the church. Otherwise Clewer is mostly of nineteenth-century development. Along the roads into Windsor are fine views of the castle, seen beyond modern bus-served villas. The parish church of St Andrew has heavy Norman arcades, but was darkly Victorianized in 1855. All the windows are stained, but not beautifully. Coronals have been adapted for electric light, and plaster saints have been built in.

All Saints, **Dedworth**, is a highly successful little brick church by G. F. Bodley, 1881, of nave, chancel, south transept and west turret. The glass throughout is by Burne-Jones and William Morris, and its effect in this unpretentious building is very happy. One or two panels, and the church itself, were damaged by bombs in 1943. St Agnes, **Spital**, is a small brick chapel of ease, worshipful but architecturally undistinguished.

(For Holy Trinity and St Stephen's churches, *see* Windsor.)

There is a large House of Mercy, founded in 1849, and built in the following years in brick, by Woodyer. The high-pitched roofs with their rows of dormers, and the arrangement of the several buildings are characteristic of his style. His chapel, of polychrome brick externally and internally, has a carved altar-piece and much contemporary stained glass.

COLD ASH [map 23]. A coniferous, sandy ridge above Newbury where late Victorian and Edwardian villas of health-seekers peep between the pine stems and above the rhododendrons. Here and there are humbler brick roadside houses, Aldershot retired-sergeant-major style. The apsidal-ended and still aisleless brick church by C. N. Beazley, 1864, is lofty and mysterious within. The east end, banded with glazed brick, the huge barrel of a pulpit inlaid with marble rose buds, the marble lectern and originally-designed font, all raise this building above the dull copy-book standard of the usual Victorian country church.

COLESHILL [map 3]. The picturesque and carefully preserved village stands on a westward-sloping hill, facing, across the river Cole, Highworth in Wiltshire. With its big house, church and limestone houses light ochre painted, all in a well-timbered landscape, it resembles north Wiltshire and Gloucestershire and is not characteristic of its own county. Coming from Buscot there is a view of the tall chimneys of Coleshill House in trees, framed between stone model cottages that flank the upper road into the village. But the best view of the house is through the gatepiers (p. 42) on the Faringdon–Highworth road. The 'modelling' of the village was done by the second Earl of Radnor, *c.* 1870. The Vicarage is a comfortable late Georgian house with imposing gates, patterned and rusticated. Coleshill House (pp. 42, 43), was built in 1650 by Sir Roger Pratt for Sir George Pratt, perhaps under the surveillance of Inigo Jones.

The tower of the church—grand Perpendicular, of Wiltshire, almost Somersetshire, type—was added to a Transitional and Early English nave, chancel and south chapel. There was eighteenth-century alteration, and Street restored the church in the nineteenth century. Box-pews in the large south transept hide a medieval effigy under a canopy. There are monuments of 1647, with two figures in white marble, recumbent, the hands especially being beautifully carved (this monument was repaired and altered, 1831); and a monument with medallion portrait and cherubs by Rysbrack, 1768. The east window, a large quatrefoil, has a Nativity in foreign glass of the sixteenth century, brought from Angers in the eighteenth century. Tombstone (p. 63).

COMBE [map 21]. Sunk in bare and spectacular downland scenery that belongs geographically more to Hampshire. The downs descend to coppice country from this still high area of unploughed hills and lanes with no telephone poles, lean brick farms and small thatched, brick cottages. The church, beside a farm, is surrounded by a flint churchyard wall with a gazebo. An orchard garden slopes above the church, which has patched walls and a brick porch dated 1652. Some big stone table tombs dominate the long-grassed churchyard. The interior of the church is respectable but lacks sensibility. There are yellow-washed nave and chancel walls, some parquet and some tiled, some green glass and oil lights, a plain narrow Transitional chancel arch, some respectable wall tablets and black marble floor ledgers with deep armorial carving.

COMPTON (or COMPTON PARVA) [map 16]. A Government Agricultural Research Station has increased the population of this small downland village, in a dip where the river Pang rises, and has changed its character, imparting 'utility' and 'efficiency'. But a cluster of pleasing chalk, brick and half-timber cottages, thatched or slated, survives up a lane. The church was rebuilt in a hard style in 1850, except for the plain Perpendicular tower, and retains only traces of medieval work. There is an eighteenth-century pulpit with carving, and an early tub font.

COMPTON BEAUCHAMP [map 7] is the most attractive and unspoiled place in the Vale of the White Horse. It lies close to the downs among elms, a grand avenue of which leads across fields and the road, past a disused 1820 Gothic school, to Compton Beauchamp itself, a moated Tudor building with an eighteenth-century stone entrance front of three storeys. The older part of the house, small old red bricks reflected in the moat, may be seen by a tall person over the churchyard wall. He will also see the clipped boxes and yews and terraced lawn sloping from a wooded downland valley to the house. A picturesque Victorian Vicarage by H. E. Kendall & Son, 1849, in clunch with limestone dressings, forms a tall, compact and picturesque contrast in some trees to the south-east of the house. Some modern cottages built by private enterprise in a harmonious style are to the north.

The church, hidden from the road by house and trees, is almost all of white clunch with stone roofs. The little stone-capped tower has a marked batter, as though it were pressing itself together for fear of falling apart. In the churchyard are decent eighteenth-century headstones and an early nineteenth-century stone altar tomb has been freshly repainted in grey, white and black, as was the custom in these parts. The church has a high, narrow nave whose distant roof is painted white, narrow transepts and wide impressive chancel stencilled with vines by Miss Lawrence in 1900. It is cleared of stalls, and has a golden altar by Martin Travers, who also designed the east window (except for its exquisite fourteenth-century figures of the Annunciation in the top lights) and the lofty pillared font cover, regilded the rich seventeenth- and eighteenth-century monuments in the nave and designed the altar to St Placidus under the tower arch. Most of the windows are clear so as to show sky and elms outside. It is indeed an unusual and uplifting church.

Up the hill to the Portway is a square-built, two-storey farmhouse of about 1840, with low-pitched slate roof eaves and well-spaced windows. It is one of many to be found in North Berks, a serviceable well-proportioned design which fits into any setting. Older thatched barns are across the road beside it and beyond these, down the hill slope among elms, are the old clunch and brick thatched cottages of the undisturbed hamlet of **Knighton**. Hardwell Farm to the east, is the remains of a moated manor house. It, too, is built of clunch and has some mullioned sixteenth-century windows and stone roof. Odstone Farm to the west, north of the Portway on the road to Ashbury, is a high seventeenth-century building with steep-pitched roof and brick-dressed walls, a farm version of Ashdown Park.

COOKHAM [map 13] is a riverside place that has for long been favoured by artists, writers and others as a place of residence and retirement. The river here divides into several separate channels, forming islands, and has hanging woods above it. The bridge is of original design, of wood and cast-iron. The village has not lost its old character, as have some Thames-side resorts. The main street of irregular architecture (a much altered sixteenth-century house, the Church Gate House, and an imposing Georgian brick house opposite, are features of it) opens out westwards on to a large green, 'the Moor', and thence a road goes to the station, where is modern development. Farther west, on rising ground, are **Cookham Rise** and **Cookham Dean**. Moor Hall and Cookham Grove have eighteenth-century features. Formosa Place, which was a beautiful Gothic house of 1785, backed by the Cliveden Woods, has lately been destroyed.

The church has been somewhat heavily Victorianized and some of its best features are blocked by a big organ. It was Early English and still has proportion, possessions, and a sense of style owing to its flint and chalk construction in diaper work. The original work inside is all of hard chalk. There is a Perpendicular altar tomb of dark grey marble, with brass, very like one at Bisham (the latter is said to have been brought from Anglesey), a family kneeling at a desk with entablature and arms, 1561; an elaborate seventeenth-century tablet with sculptured fruit; other brasses and other mural tablets. Among the last is a moving one by Flaxman, 1810, to Sir Isaac Pococke, showing him being 'suddenly called from this world to a better state whilst on the Thames, near his own home'. The glass in the east window is of c. 1840, rich-coloured and beautiful. The faces have pink complexions.

Cookham Dean is a desirably residential place on high ground among orchards and woods. Here is a church of 1844–5 by R. C. Carpenter—a wide and untidily planned building with a plain but rather successful interior. It has glass of c. 1850, early pre-Raphaelite style.

GREAT COXWELL [map 3] is a broad street of limestone, stone-roofed houses and old cottages standing on a limestone spur which juts south from the Golden Ridge into the Vale of the White Horse. At the southern end, surveying the elms and hunting country of the Vale, stands the low stone church with western tower, nave and chancel. It is a blending of Berkshire and Cotswolds. The fifteenth-century gargoyles on the tower are obviously Cotswold work, while the timber-faced north porch with stone walls and benches within it, is Berkshire style in its timber work. The church inside is dark and restored in 1882, the thirteenth-century nave having windows, doors and other details of later medieval dates. There is a Jacobean pulpit. The narrow thirteenth-century chancel arch and dark trussed wooden roof of the nave are effective. But architecturally the most impressive thing in the village and for miles around is the Tithe Barn (pp. 18, 19) adjoining a sixteenth-century farmhouse at the north end of the village. The ugly

council houses, out of scale and texture with everything, are, fortunately, some way from the village street.

LITTLE COXWELL [map 3]. A greyish-yellow hamlet consisting of decent farmhouses, a small new country house, Cotswold style, and a street of limestone cottages—new and old and all harmonious—a pond, some box hedges and a little church. This, with its model thirteenth-century bellcote and stone roofs, had a shocking late Victorian restoration. The screen was taken down and some bits of it worked into a west gallery, the old hourglass was removed and its stand turned into a lamp-holder, the seventeenth-century table was shoved into the vestry and the present altar and inappropriate east window put in the chancel, the old windows were glazed with dim cathedral glass. A fine candelabrum, 1729, hangs in the nave.

CRANBOURNE [map 20, near Winkfield]. Cranbourne was formerly in Winkfield parish. Cranbourne Tower, among trees, on the high ground to the south-west of Windsor Great Park, is a tall, mellow brick fragment of the ducal hunting box, Cranbourne Lodge (1688). This is an area where several large houses stand in well-fenced parks. Fernhill Park was built about 1700, but has been greatly altered. Other residences are Cranbourne Hall and Cranbourne Court. The flint and stone church was designed by Benjamin Ferrey, 1850. The South transept was added in 1866.

CROWTHORNE [map 26]. Windsor Forest and Bagshot Common contribute their characteristic scenery. Straight tarmac roads run between Wellingtonias, deodars and rhododendrons, disclosing views of red villas and quieter-toned houses here and there, and again of the towers and cupolas of Wellington College and the high walls of the Broadmoor Mental Hospital. The nucleus of the village began only in the eighteen-sixties. There was at that time a proposal to call it 'Albertville'.

Wellington College (pp. 1, 102) is a most successful Renaissance (Louis XV) building (1856–59) by John Shaw, jnr, who succeeded his father as architect to Christ's Hospital. In its architecture it anticipated much that was to be done afterwards; the later work of the architect's namesake, Norman Shaw, for example, owing it some debt. The main building has ten dormitories, hall, museum, library and chapel. The last two were built from Sir Gilbert Scott's designs, in Italian Gothic. The chapel has an apse and a slender spire and is elaborate, but has none of the originality that belongs to Shaw's work here. Sir A. W. Blomfield added a north aisle, and there have been other additions to the chapel. In the grounds is a double avenue of deodars.

Broadmoor Mental Hospital was opened in 1863, and designed under the direction of Major-General Sir Joshua Jebb, G.C.B. Crowthorne church, in the village, and well set in a sloping churchyard, was designed by Sir A. W. Blomfield, 1873–89, in polychrome brick—outside and in. It has a bellcote over the chancel arch.

CUMNOR [map 1]. The Oxford side of the parish consists of rows of modern houses in every style, from Cotswold to Jazz. On Cumnor Hill, through a deserted brickfield, one may reach the first clump of **Cumnor Hurst**, which has the best view in this part of the county—eastwards to Oxford, south-westwards to the Downs and north-westwards to the Upper Thames. The old village has staved off encroaching Oxford suburbs. It consists of limestone cottages and a tithe barn, a church house and an old stone inn with gabled wings and moulded window openings, the 'Bear and Ragged Staff'. Only in the sloping fields to **Bablockhythe** and around the limestone hamlet of **Eaton** may the 'lone homesteads' of Matthew Arnold be found. The eastern part of the parish is overbuilt. There are no considerable remains of Cumnor Hall. Cutts End is a small L-shaped stone house on the road to Appleton, well restored early in this century.

The church stands on high ground, amid eighteenth-century tombstones. It is remarkable because it retains the shape and many details of a Transitional late-twelfth-century building despite so many later additions in the form of aisles, transept, parapet, battlements and clerestory. These early features are seen in the tower, corbel tables within and without, and chancel arch. The north aisle arcade, like the chancel, is Early English. Inside, the church is white and electrified, and its most prominent and handsome object is neither the chained bible (1611) nor the Purbeck Forster monument in the chancel (1572), nor even the Georgian communion rails, nor poppy heads in the chancel, but the wonderful circular, oak staircase behind the tall tower arch. This staircase was built in 1685.

DENCHWORTH [map 4]. In flat Vale of the White Horse country; partly brick boxes of the eighteen-sixties and partly timber-framed, thatched cottages. Denchworth Manor is entered from the village street by a wide arch, and is a two-storey, sixteenth-century building of stone with brick chimney stacks. It was beautified in the eighteenth century with a front door and shell porch, and inside is work of both dates—panelling, cornices and fireplaces of the manorial kind. South-west of the house is a large out-building with Berkshire type windows of the seventeenth-century, a hipped roof and wooden eaves, dated 1708. It was once a wool store. The stone village school, 1851, is by G. E. Street. It is remarkable for the skilful and, at that time, original way in which the architect used the chimney stacks as prominent features in the design.

The old, irregular-shaped church has stylistic examples of all dates from the thirteenth to the sixteenth centuries. Internally, it was restored by G. E. Street in 1852, who left well alone. He paved the church throughout with simple black and white tiles, and put rather too many pews in nave and chancel, but he allowed the low, rambling building to retain its medieval character. The old roof remains and the plastered walls are washed yellow. In the chancel are some fine tablets with urns and Ionic columns, unsigned, late-seventeenth- and eighteenth-century; and a rather nice east window like an old-fashioned lantern-slide in red, blue, green and purple. There is a village library at the back of the organ, mostly of theological books, locked, behind wire.

DENFORD [map 21, near Hungerford] is all in private property where are an austerely beautiful Classic house and fancifully contrasting Georgian Gothic church, both by Sir Jeffry Wyatville, 1832. They stand on a hill near Hungerford and the house is above a finely landscaped hollow which slopes southward to the Kennet valley. The church inside is a disappointment since almost all the Georgian fittings have been taken away. Two wings were added to the house in 1939, by the late G. P. Banyard, in similar stone and style to the old centre.

DIDCOT [map 6]. Didcot at present is neither town nor village. It lacks any centre. The railway junction to Oxford, together with the windy station, were opened in the 'forties. Later the G.W.R. built the large provender store north of the line. But the only railway part of the place is the row of Victorian brick cottages on the hill from the station to Northbourne. The large building estates along the Walling-ford–Wantage road mostly house people connected with the Ordnance Depot at Milton, which was started during the 1914–18 war. At the west end of the town, to the north of the main road, is one well-designed estate in brick, the Georgetown Garden City, 1926, in the East Acton manner. Later developments have been less happy.

Northbourne, once in Hagbourne Parish, is the part of Didcot south of the main road. Here is a very plain church of 1890, surprisingly chapel-like for the date. At the western end of Northbourne, a large timber barn has been cleverly adapted as a combined social hall and chapel of ease.

Old Didcot survives as a medieval village on an eminence above the railway station. The grassy approach to it by foot has been defaced with army huts. The village consists of brick cottages and brick- and timber-framed houses, a farm with a yard of fine thatched, timber barns, and a large rectory in Tudor style (H. J. Underwood, 1851). The church has a shingled spirelet, on a timber frame inside. The nave has lean-to aisles and lead roofs, and a disproportionate Decorated, Victorianized chancel (largely of 1865). Though the building is old and full of atmosphere inside, its most distinguished architectural feature is a late Gothic window (p. 11), a lovely example of local moulding and design. Some of the glass is by Hardman.

DONNINGTON, see SHAW-CUM-DONNINGTON

DRAYTON [map 5]. Modern bungalows flank the Abingdon–Newbury road, but the old village east of it is another world, with old brick and tiled cottages and half-timbered ones among elms and orchards. The Manor House, south of the village street, has an early eighteenth-century brick front grafted on to an Elizabethan building, and a walled garden with eighteenth-century gatepiers. The church looks old on the north side and new on the south. Inside it is very much renewed. It contains the well-known alabaster reredos, now looking lost in the south transept, of the fifteenth century, which was dug up in the churchyard. It shows, from left to right, the Assumption, Annunciation, Nativity, Betrayal and Scourging, and there are traces of gold, blue and white painting on it. The east and west windows were designed by J. F. Bentley and carried out by Nat Westlake, 1872. There is also a colourful window with much blue by O'Connor, 1853.

DRY SANDFORD [map 1, near Wootton] is almost entirely a large colony of modern bungalows, stretching to Wootton, at the foot of Boar's Hill. A few limestone farmhouses remain near the church and at the hamlet of **Cothill.** The church, designed by J. B. Clacy, 1850, is a most original little building, in plan and execution, consisting of nave and apsidal chancel. The walls are of brown ironstone. The bells in the turret over the chancel arch are rung from outside the vestry on the north-east corner. The chancel arch of the high, thin nave is flanked by an elaborate stone-canopied pulpit on the north and a stone reading-desk on the south. A long chancel diminishes into a stone-vaulted apse, with rich and enormous bosses. The glass is Powell's Improved.

EARLEY [map 18, S.E. Reading]. On the Reading–Wokingham road, with modern villas eastwards towards Wokingham and classy Reading-suburban houses down the hill towards Reading, and large estates now mostly divided and built upon. Whiteknights, once a large eighteenth-century Classic mansion, was pulled down in 1840, when the present Gothik house was built. The gardens, laid out in 1785, were the most famous in the south of England. Of them, a lake and stone bridge over a canal, as well as the entrance gates on the main road, survive. But the park itself was sub-divided into five large properties with houses designed by Alfred Waterhouse—The Wilderness, Earley Whiteknights, Foxhill, Blandford Lodge and a house on the Shinfield Road. Further sub-division has gone on since, and the place now looks so cut up and trodden that it will never escape the atmosphere of evacuated civil servants, housed in Army huts. Also in the parish are Bulmershe Court, 1777, with its orangery, and Maiden Earley, a brick, pedimented Georgian house, embodying seventeenth-century parts.

The church, by J. Turner, 1844, plum-coloured brick with stone dressings outside, has a disconnected appearance inside because large transepts were added in 1882 by Francis Bacon. The interior is vast and greenly lit. There is a well-designed and light east window. But the interest of the church is in its successful history.

EASTBURY [map 14]. A valley village near Lambourn, full of streams and footpaths, with a brick and flint dovecote (1620) at the Newbury end of it and a large old red-brick manor farm with handsome brick chimney stacks and stone moulded windows at the Lambourn end. This has a panelled room with carved overmantel. Thatched cottages, timber-framed and brick; and, in the midst of them, the Victorian stone church, with a huge roof and double sanctus bellcote. Its interior is useful and practical, but not beautiful. It is by G. E. Street, 1867.

EASTHAMPSTEAD [map 6]. The country to the south of the village is a strange, unpopulated area of Royal Forest land, pine-planted, often in straight avenues. At one point, Lower Star Point, which is equidistant from Crowthorne, Bagshot and Sandhurst, eleven tracks converge. As F. G. Brabant says, 'the view of so many straight avenues, leading away in all directions through the silent pine woods, is most impressive'. Nine Mile Ride, an extraordinary straight road through the Forest, is cut into and crossed at intervals by other straight roads, and there are from it distant views of Wellington College, and occasional red villas and modern backwoods timber dwellings, characteristic of the neighbourhood. (For further references to this local scenery, *see* under BARKHAM and WOKINGHAM (HEATHLANDS). South Hill Park is a large, two-storey, Italianate house of early nineteenth-century origin, now turned into flats. Easthampstead Park, a large brick and stone house in an 1860 Elizabethan manner, was burnt out in 1945 and is being rebuilt.

The church was rebuilt in 1866-7 in a style that combines late thirteenth-century English, and Byzantine characteristics, from designs by J. W. Hugall. The result is (as Meade Falkner's revision of *Murray's Handbook* rightly calls it) 'pretentious', rather than original or successful. No doubt it shows an attempt on the architect's part to think in an impressive, personal style, but he surely thought too much and felt too little. Much Italian marble and carved oak are used in the heavy fittings. Pope's friends, Sir William Trumbull (d. 1716) and Elijah Fenton (d. 1732), poet and tutor in the Trumbull family, are commemorated by marble slabs, the tutor's having a rhymed epitaph by Pope, who says in one of his letters that Fenton died 'of indolence and inactivity'. The church's most beautiful feature is its east window, one of Burne-Jones's best designs. It shows the Last Judgment and St Michael. Angels, in small medallions surrounding the main circular panel, are modelled on pre-Raphaelite girls in wine-coloured dresses. There are four other windows by Burne-Jones in the church, and a window in the baptistry is signed by O'Connor. At **Priestwood** is a brick, apsidal chapel of ease, built in 1888.

EATON HASTINGS [map 3]. A still and willowy parish where the Upper Thames is almost a stream, where unmetalled lanes and grassy footpaths go under elms to wide and reedy meadows, and Gloucestershire and the cold limestone Cotswolds are near. It is a parish more than a village, with three groups of buildings each quite a mile from the other. There are the roadside cottages, expensive 1890 model estate houses with a Georgian style shop, all of Cotswold stone and by Sir Ernest George. These stand respectfully on the main Faringdon–Lechlade road where it runs through those two miles of well-kept plantations of Buscot Park. Almost opposite is one of the turns to Philip's Farm and thence by footpath to **Eaton Weir**, where a decent brick inn looks upstream and a footbridge crosses to William Morris's limestone manor house at Kelmscott (Oxon) among its high walls, clipped yews, willows and wild roses. Another turn goes to Eaton Hastings church which stands on a bank above the Thames, with an old stone cottage with thatched roof, and a plain 1840-ish stone Rectory beside it. The church, tower, nave and chancel, is clean and late-Victorianly expensive inside with creamy cemented walls, coconut matting, green kneelers and two Burne-Jones

windows in the north wall (p. 96). There is an old and simple timber roof to the nave, a low chancel arch and long impressive chancel, at present cluttered with stalls, terminating in a Clayton & Bell east window. Some thirteenth-century details will please the antiquarian and there is one graceful little wall tablet by Gould of Swindon, 1816.

ENBORNE [map 22]. This scattered place with narrow lanes has brick and tile-hung cottages, some of them of mellow colour and irregular outline, among beech and oak copses between the Kennet valley and the downs. It is on an old sheep drove from the great sheep centres at Weyhill, Yarnbury and the west, to Newbury and to the famous fair at East Ilsley; the route being over Woodhay Down, through North End, Gore End, Holtwood and over Wash Common. Some of the houses on this route, now among the older private dwellings, were inns. Enborne Lodge and Cope Hall are Victorianized houses of earlier origin. Near Cope Hall are some cottages called the Hospital, where King Charles visited the wounded after the Battle of Newbury. The church is neighboured by the trees of Hamstead Marshall park, and from its churchyard looking south is a Surrey-like view, with barns and tile-hung cottages among undulating fields and small plantations. The church is a neat, an over-neat, restored and cemented little Norman and Early English building, with two heavy Norman arcades with carved capitals. There are traces of wall-paintings, and of early timber benches. And there is one of the oldest bells in England.

ENGLEFIELD [map 17]. Miles of flint and good oak fencing, an estate saw mill, a deer park, a lake, then a well-conditioned red-brick model Victorian village with a Georgian house (probably for the agent), a stone rectory by P. C. Hardwick in mid-Victorian Tudor, a school, a big walled garden with acres of glass, a well-kept drive swirling past exotic firs and rhododendrons to a spired church, and finally an enormous stone house—a sort of condensed Longleat—almost entirely rebuilt on its terraced slope, in the middle of the last century. All this has the overwhelming and firmly established atmosphere of the great country house of Trollope's novels, which continued into Good King Edward's reign. It is the last of its kind in the county and worth seeing as a compact, well-run example of benevolent private ownership still holding out against occupation by orphans, R.A.F., the Army or evacuated departments of Government.

The church, approached through an artistic Edwardian lychgate designed by E. Swinfen Harris, though medieval in places inside, seems to be almost wholly Victorian, being restored in 1857 by P. C. Hardwick and in 1874 by Sir Gilbert Scott. The result is a flint building with yellow stone dressings—an unhappy combination of textures without; a high, dark, pinched cavern within, aisled, chapelled, over-pewed, screened, picture-hung and, as the eye gets used to the dimness, rich and full of details from the manifold Victorian mouldings of the chancel arch to the refined Greek tablet to Milburg Alpress, 1803, and the unsigned composition in marble ascribed to Sir Robert Taylor (pp. 70, 71). North of the encumbered chancel, is the sixteenth-century Englefield chapel, a beautiful building, blocked by the organ. It is still possible to see the fine coloured sixteenth-century monuments to the Englefields in this chapel. In the south wall of the nave are a thirteenth-century stone effigy of a knight in armour and a fourteenth-century wooden effigy of a lady, each under a stone canopy and each obscured from view by pews. The south nave arcade and the triple lancet in the east wall of the south aisle are thirteenth-century, renewed by the restorers.

FARINGDON [map 3]. This is an almost entirely limestone town at a junction of secondary main roads. It is a hilly place and its houses are mostly eighteenth and early nineteenth century, modest and agreeing to differ from one another in a gentlemanly way so that the whole effect is of variety within uniformity. There are no masterpieces of architecture except Faringdon House, Sudbury House and the Church which stand aloof among high trees. The seventeenth-century Town Hall, raised on Tuscan columns of stone and with steep stone roof, *The Bell* and *The Globe* Hotels, a seventeenth-century teashop and saddler, and flattish late Georgian houses with shops and banks below the sloping market place—all make a modest and charming country town composition. More than any town in Berkshire, Faringdon seems remote from London and really in the country at last. This is partly because of its being the only limestone town in the county and partly because the biggest roads come from Oxford and Swindon, not from London; and partly because it is still the natural market centre for the farmers of the Vale of the White Horse. The streets are at present lighted with charming nineteenth-century gas standards. There is a nice little Tudor-style branch railway terminus (1864).

Faringdon House was built about 1780 and stands on the edge of the Golden Ridge looking northward to a private lake, the Upper Thames and far-descried Cotswolds, southward up terraced grass to the great church beside whose north wall walks the headless ghost of Hampden Pye ('Hamilton Tighe' of the *Ingoldsby Legends*). The house is as charming an eighteenth-century stone house as may be seen in England, square, three-storeyed, with stone attic hidden by a parapet and a curved screen wall on its entrance front (p. 69). There is a double staircase and much Bath-style plasterwork within. The agriculturalist and poet laureate Pye (immortalized in *Sing a song of Sixpence*) built the house and is said to have planted the fir trees on the hill known as Faringdon Folly on the Oxford side of the town. The tower in the midst of these was erected in 1936 at the expense of the fourteenth Lord Berners from designs by the eighth Duke of Wellington. It is the last purely decorative building to give landscape pleasure to be built in England. From the observation room at the top of the tower is a wonderful view in all directions, for the Golden Ridge, though not high itself, rises out of flat country in a basin of distant hills. Sudbury House outside the town is a two-storey, stone-roofed, Regency building with curved bows and an exquisitely-proportioned horizontal design. Wadley, farther out on this road, belonged to the Untons (*see below*) and has panelled rooms and a seventeenth-century oak staircase.

The large cruciform church has many well-carved Georgian headstones in its graveyard. Thirteenth-century Transitional Norman and Early English styles predominate, though a west window, a north aisle and a north chancel chapel all in light Gloucestershire style of the late fifteenth-century let in light to the many-vistaed interior. The spire was knocked off the thirteenth-century tower in the Civil wars. The south door has thirteenth-century ironwork. The interior has far too many pews but it is a stone-carver's paradise, for in no other church in the county is there such original and beautiful deep carving of the thirteenth century as on the flowered capitals of the nave arcades and on the capitals of the many orders of the four supports of the central tower. The chancel is as wide and spacious as that of an abbey church and its tall triple-lancet east window has becoming glass of 1854, medallions on grisaille ground. The Unton north chapel has four seventeenth-century Unton monuments and the kneeling lady in the north transept is taken from the tomb of Sir Henry Unton (1596). The marble monuments to the Pye family are rich eighteenth century. Indeed, as a museum of monumental sculpture, Faringdon church is only equalled in the county by Bisham and Hurst. The Victorian north transept and south aisle (1853) must be pronounced gloomy failures. The south aisle is made a little less gloomy by Wailes' glass of the eighteen fifties.

FARLEY HILL [map 25]. This is a hamlet of Swallowfield on a ridge along the base of which curves the river Blackwater. It has a chapel of ease and three houses of beauty in separate small parks, or grounds of their own. Two of these have changed their names. They are called Farley Castle (formerly Wragg or Ragg Castle), Farley Court (or Farleyhill Court), and Farley Hill Place (formerly Farley Hall). Farley Castle is a Gothik-folly red-brick house of about 1830 on the hill-top, with round turrets and crenellations, not elaborate or expensive in design, now an hotel. At Farley Court lived in 1820 a friend of Miss Mitford, Mrs Dickinson, author of *Old Court Life in France*, and there is a description in *Our Village* of watching a sunset from the round room in this largely eighteenth-century house which has plaster decorations in an Adam manner—the sun 'lingering longest on that long island of old thorns and stunted oaks, the oasis of B[ramshill] Heath, and then vanishing in a succession of gorgeous clouds'. Farley Hill Place was built for John Walter about 1730, and is a long, low house of brick facing down the slope of a terraced and landscaped park westwards to a lake. Mr Hussey has tentatively ascribed house and gardens to the landscape gardener, Charles Bridgeman. Inside the house is some beautifully carpentered woodwork and the painted ceiling (p. 66). Below Farley Hill, slightly east, at a crossroads, is a farmhouse with a mellow, corniced brick front of the early eighteenth century.

The church is a red-brick building of 1891, on the hill, with a semi-detached, tiled spire on the south of the chancel. There is a triple chancel arch, a ribbed ceiling of wood and a parquet floor inside.

FARNBOROUGH [map 9]. The highest village in Berkshire, 720 feet up in downs, fast losing their character through cultivation. There are some brick cottages, two farms, a church and a rectory. The last, well set among beech trees, was built in 1749 of blue-glazed and red bricks in local Wantage style (pp. 56, 58). About a century later a projecting central feature with a bellcote was added in a harmonious style which gives the elevation great architectural distinction as seen from the road across a large lawn (p. 58). Beside the Rectory is a magnificent crescent-shaped and thatched barn with brick walls. Internally, its wooden roof-supports rise on piers, Great Coxwell fashion. The small church, of tower, nave and chancel, has some plain Norman windows but it was almost rebuilt in a heavy-handed manner in 1883-5. The plain fifteenth-century tower with its pronounced moulded courses is its grandest feature (pp. 14, 15).

FAWLEY [map 8]. South and North Fawley are a mile apart, high in unspoiled downs, eastern border hamlets of a vast area of racing gallops, juniper thickets and springy turf. In South Fawley are a few brick cottages and lonely stone manor house built in 1614, three-storeyed, gabled, with Renaissance entrance porch, brick chimney stacks, mullioned windows and several panelled rooms. As it was for many years a farmhouse and was partly demolished on the north side, it lacks its former grandeur, but it is finely sited above a grassy hollow. At Whatcombe, farther south, are Norman remains of an old church built into the farm. Yews and box and garden walls give a sense of former state. North Fawley with ponds, new council houses, brick and thatched cottages, a rambling Victorian rectory, is in a tree-sheltered cup of the downs. The magnificent stone church, a bit hard and red-roofed outside, was built by G. E. Street 1865-6, with tower, north aisle and vaulted chancel (p. 93). It replaced a more modest medieval and seventeenth-century structure whose old churchyard is to the north.

FERNHAM [map 3]. This village, on a hill slope looking south across the Vale to White Horse Hill, is a compromise between the limestone style of the Cotswolds and the cob, brick and thatch of the Vale. The cottages almost equally are in one style or the other. Stone tiles were taken from many of the roofs for the new Cotswold-style house called Ringdale Manor (1937) by Cole & Partners. Fernham Manor is brick mid-Victorian Gothic. There is a dark red-brick Congregational chapel 1830. The nave and chancel church (*c.* 1850), by H. J. Underwood, is a conventional nave and chancel job in limestone with roofs of too steep a pitch for the stone tiles upon it. Some lancet windows have stained glass by O'Connor, one of which is dated 1863.

FINCHAMPSTEAD [map 25]

FINCHAMPSTEAD [map 25] is in broken country to the south of Wokingham, on the Hampshire border; sands, clays and Bagshot beds alternating as subsoils and varying the scenery in smallish areas. Plantations of huge Wellingtonias, pastoral Blackwater scenery, copses of oak and hazel, with narrow and winding but well-traversed roads, are within the parish. The church is on a rise of plateau gravel, which material, in conglomerate form, has been used as a local building stone. The names of a few private houses in the parish best indicate the landscape here: Edge-of-the-Hill, Birchenholt, The Nook, The Triangle, Rhododendrons, the Coppice, Wheatlands Manor. Breezy Finchampstead Ridges are National Trust property. A straight avenue of giant Wellingtonias leads towards Crowthorne. A small red-brick house called Banisters is dated 1683. West Court Manor House, another seventeenth-century house, which was altered in 1835, has tall ground floor windows in a mellow brick front, and inside are carved wood fireplaces and panelling. Also several panels of thirteenth- and fourteenth-century glass, placed here in Victorian times.

East Court and Finchampstead Place are medium-sized twentieth-century houses; North Court is a slated Victorian gabled house. A ferruginous stream flows through the grounds of South Court.

The church, of nave, chancel, north chapel and west tower, is of Norman to Perpendicular development, and has been unified into an attractive whole by sophisticated and sensitive treatment. All the external walls, including the circular apse, have been covered with whitened plaster, which contrasts well with the early eighteenth-century (1720) brick tower. There are a few Norman features, including a piscina and a couple of windows (one over later arcade), and some decent simple tracery and moulding of later date, and there is much modern work, including most of the fittings; but all is well blended, even the recent 'art' glass. There are traces of wall-paintings (twelfth and fifteenth centuries) over the chancel arch, and later painted texts: plain tombs and tablets (seventeenth to nineteenth centuries); a Norman font with rope and chevron ornament; and some old woodwork worked into roofs, pulpit and elsewhere. The organ is in the seventeenth-century west gallery, which has slender balusters of good effect and new oak supporting posts. The organ supports a fine painted Royal Arms dated 'C.R.1660' (*sic.*). Floodlighting bathes the whole.

FRILFORD, see MARCHAM

FRILSHAM [map 16]

FRILSHAM [map 16]. In pastoral, wooded country on the river Pang. It is a brick-built village with a few small old houses. To the east, on Frilsham Common, is a newer assemblage of houses. Frilsham House is an ambitious building in brick with stone dressings, by S. Gambier Parry. The church, which stands in a circular churchyard, is a small nave and chancel building of Norman date, tripartite, and with north and south doors of this period. The chancel was extended eastwards in the fifteenth century. The tower is of the early nineteenth century. The interior has been lavishly restored in Art Workers' Guild fashion with irregular oak benches, Georgian style west gallery communion rails, white walls, metal lanterns and Nutgens glass. The east window is a vigorous early Victorian contrast in Hardman style showing a Crucifixion on a blue background. The old timber roofs, restored, are exposed. Handmade grizzle bricks were made here until the 1930's.

FROGMORE, see WINDSOR

FYFIELD [map 5]

FYFIELD [map 5]. A limestone village of Oxford character among elms (Matthew Arnold's 'Fyfield Elm' has been felled) at a crossroads on the Oxford–Faringdon road. The *White Hart Inn* with stone roofs is little spoiled, so are the limestone cottages of most of this village. Down a southward lane and looking over miles of cornland to the downs through clear panes of leaded glass is an 1860 Baptist chapel of brick, in style forty years earlier. Its interior is dull. The village north of the road has a three-cornered green, some limestone houses and a large manor among lawns and clipped yews. This is a stone, fourteenth-century building to which Elizabethan additions were made, Kelmscott style, with gables and mullioned windows. Inside are fourteenth-century and medieval features. It was 'restored' in 1864.

The churchyard has many late Georgian tombs and some distinguished table tombs with detached shafts (1844) and with remains of pink paint on them, signed A. E. Lock, Abingdon. The church itself has a south porch built about 1845 in the style of Uffington south porch, but curiously, and rather attractively, out of scale, and vaulted. The church was burnt out in 1893 and its interior, nave, north aisle and chancel give a genteel impression of 1890 newness with new brown oak screens and roofs, greenish glass and hard black and red floor tiles. There is a tomb to Lady Katherine Jordan (1537) in the chancel, of stone with Tudor stone panels and bosses. In the fifteenth-century Golafre chapel, north of the chancel, is a monument to Sir John Golafre (1442) with a recumbent stone figure in fifteenth-century armour and below it a frightening emaciated corpse in a shroud. There are some rich marble floor slabs to the White family (seventeenth century). **Netherton** is a limestone hamlet among elms, to the north.

GARFORD [map 5]

GARFORD [map 5]. A stone-built street of cottages with a farm all remote in wide, flat meadow country of the river Ock west of Abingdon. The little nave and chancel arch of the church is an interesting example of the later phase of the Gothic Revival when Perpendicular was no longer thought debased. The old church, an oil painting of which hangs by the south door, was demolished and a new one built in 1880 by E. Dolby of Abingdon, incorporating bits of the old. He added a north aisle but otherwise rebuilt the church to look as he thought it must have looked in the fifteenth century. He retained parts of the old screen and roof beams, added many pews and choir-stalls, lit it with candles and glazed the windows to give a dim, religious light. The result may be called a brown study in village Perpendicular and has strong late-Victorian character.

EAST GARSTON [map 14]

EAST GARSTON [map 14]. A collection of old brick and cob-thatched cottages in the Lambourn Valley into which new council estates have been intruded as though coming from a modern urban world. Over a level crossing by the single-line station (pp. 82, 83), is a handsome long, red-brick manor house of two storeys (early eighteenth century), the old tiles on whose roof are arranged in patterns. Inside there are panelled rooms. The cruciform church close by is of flint and stone, and the tower is decorated with bands of brick. This Norman and later church was restored, 1876–82, by G. E. Street and William Butterfield, when the walls were stencilled, particularly in the chancel, and windows filled with stained glass by Nat Westlake from designs by J. F. Bentley. Inside it is rather dark, though impressive. In the north transept is the seventeenth-century table and a baroque tablet to William Seymour, 1731.

GOOSEY [map 4]. An undisturbed village of scattered brick and stone houses and cottages round an enormous goose green in flat and pastoral Vale of White Horse country. The green is cut in half by a road. In the south-west corner, near a house with ball-piers at its entrance, is the little nave and chancel church with western, eighteen-ninetyish spirelet resting internally on a tiebeam of the nave roof. The church is roughcast outside and has windows with thirteenth-century and later mouldings. Inside it is tidy, artistic and restored, with red-tiled floor, no chancel arch and renewed oak roof with king posts and tiebeams, some fifteenth-century glass in a twelfth-century window in the north wall, a big Royal Arms of George III over the north door and a modern west vestry. The church key is thirteenth century.

GRAZELEY [map 24]. In the flat, near-Reading landscape, new Swedish-timber houses are prominent, but there is still a remoteness about the muddy winter (and dry, caked summer) meadows, and the tree-studded hedgerows, reminiscent of the quiet descriptions of Mary Russell Mitford, who for some time lived here. 'By 1802 we see the family not merely purchasing a Tudor house and seventy acres at Grazeley, but pulling the strong old place down to build a correct residence in the Georgian manner, named Bertram House, after the family castle. That year Mary left school, and by 1804 she and her mother, though not always her father, were settled in the new house. By 1820 the family were once more penniless.' (Sir John Squire). Bertram House has itself now been pulled down. The good Victorian orange-brick parsonage is Grazeley's most distinguished building.

The flint, stone-dressed church beside it, is an uninspired Middle-Pointed nave, chancel and west bell-coted building of 1850 by Benjamin Ferrey. It has a wide chancel arch, and some pleasing Victorian glass by O'Connor. The east window shows the Crucifixion and Evangelists on white grisaille, with coloured bands and patterns—a very good window. The date of death of the person commemorated is 1845, but the glass is of late 'fifties character.

GREENHAM [map 22]. A sandy southern outskirt of Newbury with a heather common, a few late-Victorian timbered residences on the Newbury side of it, a fine view of the Kennet valley, an adventurous golf course on the wooded slopes, a small flint and stone church by H. Woodyer (1875–6), north aisle 1888 (p. 99), and the famous Norman Shaw house of Greenham Court (pp. 104, 105).

GROVE [map 5]. In flat country, north of Wantage, a row of cottages, some timber-framed and thatched, others brick, more Victorian. A cob-walled Strict Baptist chapel (c. 1830) with clear leaded windows is attached to a cottage and has its own burial ground among yews. The *Bell Inn* has its name cemented into the brick wall with the ends of beer bottles. There is a camp here and many army huts and much churned-up mud. The church by P. A. Robson 1901 is a long, stone building, not beautiful, with a wooden eighteenth-century font from Pusey church.

EAST HAGBOURNE [map 10]. A long street of distinguished seventeenth- and eighteenth-century tile-hung and brick and timber houses and cottages (pp. 50, 51), in flat orchard country on the south and downland side of Didcot. Several of the cottages, including a farm near the church, have carved wooden corbels supporting their projecting upper floors. Many windows are leaded with lozenge panes and have wooden mullions and transoms, the transom forming a semicircle in the middle of the window. The casements have elaborate ironwork handles. At **Coscote**, west of the village, is an excellent example of the L-shaped style of seventeenth-century farmhouse, tile-hung and with windows as described. **West Hagbourne** has no church but contains several timber-framed and thatched cottages among orchards, on a winding lane with a pond beside it.

At the west end of East Hagbourne street is a restored fifteenth-century cross with Jacobean dial on top, and beyond it the church. This embodies fourteenth- and fifteenth-century additions to all four sides of a small fourteenth-century chapel. There are a fifteenth-century tower and timber-framed north and south porches. The interior is light and Perpendicular and spacious, with a fifteenth-century south and fourteenth-century north arcade, a fifteenth-century clerestory and wooden roofs throughout, a rich Perpendicular chancel with north and south chapels, some remains of fifteenth-century screen and pulpit, a large Royal Arms of George III, painted white, black and red. In the north aisle is some fourteenth-century glass showing Our Lady and Child and the Nativity. Outside in the churchyard are many eighteenth-century headstones as well as several external wall tablets. The restoration of this church in 1860 did little harm and, more than any church in the neighbourhood, it retains its medieval atmosphere.

HAMPSTEAD NORRIS [map 16]. A valley village where the small stream of the Pang runs between elms and chalk slopes and where the railway from Didcot to Newbury is throned above the houses. The houses are mostly brick and tile-roofed, as are those in hamlets in the parish. In the churchyard is a curious railed-in tomb to the Lowsley family (1855) arranged in steps with a cast-iron obelisk on top of it. The large aisleless church is venerable and plastered without, but within has been coarsely restored with cemented walls, tinted glass, pitchpine pews, flood-lighting and an over-large modern chancel arch. The seventeenth-century nave roof of wood and the 1768 font survive.

HAMSTEAD MARSHALL [map 22]. The park provides a beautifully planted landscape with small lakes on a low plateau to the south of the Kennet valley and the railway. On the Kennet and Avon Canal here is a group of stuccoed wharf buildings with a dwelling-house attached, of simple beauty. The canal was opened in 1811, and this group is of the same date.

Hamstead Lodge was first planned by Balthazar Gerbier, 1662 ('in imitation of Heidelberg') and, Gerbier dying (and being buried in the church) in 1663, it was probably completed by Captain Wynne, an Anglo-Dutch architect. It is known only from Kyp's engraving, since it was destroyed by fire in 1718. A large brick-walled garden remains, with terraces and eight pairs of entrance piers, which stand, some of them in the garden wall, others in the grassy park to the east (pp. 39–41). A ninth pair was removed to serve as an entrance to Benham Place from the Bath Road, near Stockcross. The present Hamstead Lodge, across the park towards Enborne and approached by an immense avenue across grass and bracken slopes, is a large stone two-storeyed house of 1720, with pediments and a pillared balustrade round the top. It has been much altered in the nineteenth and twentieth centuries.

The church, which was Decorated and Perpendicular, has had the taste of several subsequent ages lavished upon it. It was completely Jacobeanized, then Georgianized and was Victorian–Gothicized in 1893. The sophistication of the twentieth century (Sir Charles Nicholson's) has not quite pulled it together, but its Jacobean and Georgian box-pews, its panelling, gallery and carved three-decker pulpit, all in dark wood, give a pleasing effect in the pale-washed interior. And the stone-dressed old brickwork of the outside of the building, standing among elms above the Kennet valley, makes a mellow addition to the landscape.

EAST HANNEY [map 5]. Among willows and elms in a wide flat part of the Vale of the White Horse with huge fenceless, cultivated fields. The several lanes which make the village have timbered black-and-white cottages of the seventeenth century. The long and stately stone church, of nave and chancel only, is by G. E. Street, 1856. As Mr Goodhart Rendel says, 'It is remarkable for its date—just a barn with a few irregularly-placed windows entirely different from the Puginist type of nave and chancel chapel (e.g. Fernham and Littleworth). The stonework is well detailed, the woodwork stained and varnished, the trussed rafter roof a bit too thin'.

WEST HANNEY [map 5].

One of the Vale of the White Horse villages that keeps a great deal of its former agricultural-community character, in spite of modern developments. It has no big house, but several medium-sized ones and groups of stone and brick and plastered cottages, thatched, slated or stone-tiled, diverse in appearance yet homogeneous, and large enough in number to provide variety and contrast with the respectable new brick council houses that have been built in the village—some of them replacing old cottages.

The larger houses are The Priory, a late medieval stone house, altered and covered with stucco; the Dower House (of the Yates of Lyford) now the Post Office, a plastered house of the sixteenth century, by the churchyard; the Vicarage, a small red-brick Georgian house opposite; and the Old Rectory, now called West Hanney House, built about 1720 in a country Vanbrugh manner. Its rubbed red bricks and panels of greyish-purple bricks, its prominent keystones and curious symmetrical design give it a remarkable distinction (p. 58).

The church is cruciform, with a tower on the north side. The upper stage of this tower collapsed in 1946. A great deal of rebuilding has robbed the church of all but a few early features, the best of which are the Norman north door, the Transitional font, with vertical stripes formed of rosettes, the Decorated south aisle and the Early English chancel arch. Some fine eighteenth-century Commandment Boards are now set up in the south aisle. The chancel walls are pleasingly decorated by three simple wall tablets with urns on black backgrounds, 1830–50. There is early fourteenth-century glass; grisaille, and a censing angel. Among the Victorian glass is one early Clayton & Bell window.

The district is the headquarters of a fundamentalist sect called the Nazarenes, who have a camp meeting here once a year and use the brook for 'dipping'.

HARWELL [map 9].

A main street in a cherry-growing district of brick and timber houses, tiled, thatched and sometimes pargeted, runs above a little stream to which lanes descend, at the foot of a gradual and uneventful slope of the downs. In the middle of this street are Gearing's Almshouses 1723, with gabled wings and round-headed windows and a screen wall forming a distinguished one-storey group in red brick. There are three grand old farms in the village, Upper Farm, Middle Farm and Bishop's Manor, brick and timber-framed houses, and several houses of fair size, built in glazed purple brick of late Georgian times. On the outskirts of the village are modern bungalows of the mid-wars period.

The large church, with thirteenth-century tower, porch, nave, aisles and transepts and fourteenth-century chancel, stands on a high mound above the stream, among elms. The lofty interior was prominently reseated with pews and vigorously restored in 1867. The east window, with lovely Decorated tracery, has the arms of Piers Gaveston, Edward II's friend, in its top lights, and other chancel windows have pieces of old glass, all fourteenth century. The wooden chancel screen has fourteenth-century woodwork below and fifteenth-century woodwork along the top. There is a big brass chandelier in the nave dated 1766. The tower clock was made in the village in 1703. But the most enlivening objects in the church are the stone comic figures being bitten by dragons (fourteenth-century) supporting the chancel arch; there are other stone grotesques in the chancel.

Harwell Atomic Research Establishment (p. 112) is fortunately out of sight of this attractive village and much nearer Chilton, about two miles away to the south-west. 'We were given Harwell on a windy day of February 1946, on a flying visit from Canada' writes Sir John Cockcroft, the first scientist in charge. 'There was much transatlantic cabling on where we should establish housing sites. A start had to be made quickly and the only solution was to provide prefabs and to erect them on our own site where services and sewers were available and where the minimum of consents had to be obtained.' The result is a sudden muddle, worse than the Slough Trading Estate, and enclosed in a high wire fence, with a huge brick chimney, box-like factories and spreading prefabs and hundreds of buses waiting on acres of windy asphalt. It dominates the downs (and these were originally scheduled against building) for miles. Sir John Cockcroft admits that 'something might have been better done had we had more time for thought and less separation of space in the planning stage'.

On a moonlit night, the thatch and tile, stone and brick, elms and barns and farms of old Harwell village compared with the blue electric glare and bright sinister workshops of the Atomic Research Establishment form an instructive contrast betweeen the past and present.

HATFORD [map 4].

A few stone cottages, a pebble-dashed Georgian and earlier farm, a Victorian brick rectory and two churches on a breezy upland on the Faringdon side of the Vale of the White Horse. Some of the cottages were wrecked by German bombs in the Hitler war. The old church, beside the manor farm, has a picturesque roofless nave with a Norman south door and a roofed chancel. There are brasses (1614, 1629, 1687), floor slabs, Jacobean panelling and remains of thirteenth-century painting on the walls of the chancel which is now a mausoleum and funeral chapel. The new church, east of the old one, was built in 1873–4 from designs by W. Wigginton. It is in a thirteenth-century style with apsidal east end and western tower and resembles, within and without, a mission church in the potteries rather than a Berkshire village fane.

EAST HENDRED [map 9].

This village lies between the Reading–Wantage road and the downs, which are here bare and unspectacular. It had a medieval cloth industry.

It is a large and little-tampered-with collection of timber-framed brick and cob cottages of the late sixteenth and seventeenth centuries. It is largely thatched, but there are also old tiled roofs with bargeboards, and there are later houses that are not out of harmony. Well-grown elms and carefully-cut box hedges abound.

At a crossroads stands a disused and romantic stone chapel of the fifteenth century dedicated to Jesus of Bethlehem with a timber-framed Priest's House of the same date adjoining it. Opposite is a range of stone outbuildings of rather later date.

Grass-edged stone causeways flank the village streets, and form an attractive base and foreground to wooden barns and variously textured dwellings, irregularly grouped. One of the groups has herring-bone brick filling and panelled oak bargeboards on its gables. The Plough Inn, a farm house until about 1840, has picturesque tile-hung gables at the back facing across a shrubberied lawn and a well-planted garden.

The Manor House, low, rambling and many-gabled on its west side as seen from the village, has long been the home of the Eystons, a Roman Catholic family descended by marriage from St Thomas More. The east face is severe late Georgian, in the manner of West Hendred Vicarage, and probably by the same provincial architect. To enter the low, panelled Elizabethan hall, going thence to the high Georgian staircase hall and drawing- and dining-rooms, is to experience the extreme contrast of two styles of English domestic interior. But the strongly peaceful atmosphere of the house, and indeed of the whole village, radiates from the little thirteenth-century chapel of St Amand contained within the house. Architecturally, it is not remarkable, as it was extensively restored by C. A. Buckler in 1860: it contains some fifteenth-century glass, some seventeenth-century enamelled foreign glass, and some windows by Hardman of Birmingham. It also has, in the Sacristy, a medieval stone effigy from Poughley Abbey. This chapel was never desecrated and has been used for Mass regularly since the eighteenth century. In 1865 a larger Roman Catholic church, with more glass by Hardman, was built in the Middle Pointed style from designs by C. A. Buckler. It is connected by a covered way over the road to the brick Presbytery, the whole group of buildings forming a Puginesque dream come true. In the Presbytery are preserved—and used—much of Pugin's furniture and crockery, specially designed for his own use in his house at Ramsgate.

The parish church presents a pleasing effect in the village owing to its site and its Decorated and Perpendicular stone walls, lead roofs and handsome west tower. Its interior effect has been spoilt by Victorian restoration, but the carved capitals with heads and stiff-leaved foliage (pp. 10, 11) the pulpit (Jacobean) and reading desk, some fragments of fifteenth-century glass and some Eyston slabs and brasses may be noticed.

WEST HENDRED [map 9]. A hidden village at the foot of the downs with timber-framed and cream-washed and brick cottages, mostly thatched, a late Georgian vicarage, in stately proportion of whitewashed severity, standing in its own little park above a wooded stream with watercress beds. The church by the same streamside has a plastered exterior with lead roofs and stone porch. Inside it is the ideal village church with its plastered walls, symmetrical arcades, old glass fragments (including a well-drawn and coloured head of Christ and evangelistic symbols all, like the church, early fifteenth century) lovingly leaded into old-fashioned window glazing, and seventeenth-century font cover. This decent church was carefully restored by Philip Johnson in 1929.

HERMITAGE [map 16]. A collection mostly of small twentieth-century houses in a wooded valley where several roads meet and a railway runs, half-way between the moderate downland scenery of Hampstead Norris and the coniferous outskirts of Newbury. The small 1835 church has a pretty little vicarage in a late Georgian Perpendicular style beside it. But the church itself, of nave and chancel only, is in no particular style and has been filled with carefully dusted and polished modern fittings. The new lychgate with woodcarving is by C. Birdwood Willcocks.

NORTH HINKSEY [map 1]. The old stone village just survives among elms, willows and poplars, pressed between a useless by-pass of West Oxford and the Hinksey stream which borders the Oxford city boundary. Across the stream and flat meadowland of dykes and willows, a raised pathway runs from West Oxford. John Ruskin, when Slade Professor of Art, helped to make it with the aid of undergraduate disciples, including Oscar Wilde, in order to put into practice the doctrine of the dignity of manual labour. It is planted either side with poplars. West of the village and beyond the by-pass, climbs an elm-clad hill, now all too villa-sprinkled but saved in one place as a public park. From this the noblest view of Oxford's towers and spires may be seen.

The village consists of a row of modern red-brick cottages which suddenly stop and leave one in woody Matthew Arnold peace between dry stone walls, a few stone cottages and in sight of a little stone-walled, stone-roofed church. This seems to step down the hill eastwards from its western stone-capped tower in three short strides, of nave roof, semi-chancel roof and chancel roof. By the old stone porch is a broken churchyard cross and big yew and, to the west, overshadowing elms. A Norman south door opens onto an interior which is not disappointing, with a Norman revival chancel arch, a pretty modern west gallery, undisturbing glass and pews. The seventeenth-century Fynmore monuments in the chancel are all attractive designs and on one

is the inscription 'Reader, look to thy feet: honest and loyal men are sleeping under them'.

Botley, on the main road out of West Oxford, is now a suburb of Oxford. Islanded between roads are a few old seventeenth-century stone houses. Otherwise it is a place of twentieth-century roadside villas among buses and lorries, with a modernistic, enlightened County School in red brick, a shopping parade and a tin church and a brick Baptist chapel.

SOUTH HINKSEY [map 2]. The useless West Oxford by-pass on a hill-slope and the useful Great Western Railway from Oxford to Didcot east of it, leave a wide enough space of meadowland between them to insulate the village of South Hinksey. It has several old stone, thatched cottages and farms and an inn. But the lanes are interspersed with a few, but still too many, brick bungalows and villas. The little church is approached down an avenue of limes through a rather cemetery-ish churchyard. The nave has thirteenth- and fourteenth-century windows, has been spruced up and whitened and is quite attractive. **New Hinksey** across the river and railway, with a reservoir, a park, brick villas and a church by J. N. Comper, is now part of Oxford.

HINTON WALDRIST [map 4.] A village built round a triangle of roads on the Thames side of the Abingdon–Faringdon road. Cottages of an ordinary north-Berkshire character, of stone and brick, neighbour a church and manor house, the last being on a moated site and having a small castle mound in its grounds. The house is Elizabethan with many additions of 1698. It was early-Georgianized in 1933. It has a view across the upper Thames meadows towards the Cotswolds. The church was almost wholly renewed by the Victorians but the Decorated tower and a few other features were spared. There is a tablet with carving of 1701, and the interior is given some mystery and attraction by the rich glass in several windows of *c.* 1855. The east window shows the Cruxifixion, and in other windows are panels set in Powell's 'stamped' glass.

HUNGERFORD [map 21] has a High Street which climbs a southern slope of the Kennet valley and rises high above the river, trout farm, and main Bath Road at its northern end. The main-road addict never sees the town. As though to induce him to enter it, some public authority has lately disfigured the wide and climbing High Street with huge boa-constrictors made of concrete which dwarf the modest brick houses and hang over with a blue-green light at night like the wrath of God which takes all colour from the warm red bricks and tiles. The same sin has been committed at Wokingham.

Hungerford is mainly a Georgian town, despite the bold cast-iron Victorian railway bridge which crosses the main street and the tall, Italianate Corn Exchange and Town Hall (1870) in Bath stone and coloured bricks. At the Canal Bridge are attractive Georgian brick houses and farther up the High Street is the grand late Georgian shop front of Nicol's (p. 55), several well-designed private dwellings like Wilton House and one or two seventeenth-century inns and houses. As the High Street reaches the downs, here 400 feet above sea level, the houses take on a cottage character. The *Bear Hotel* in the valley and on the Bath Road, is a mid-eighteenth-century posting house, as are other buildings of coaching days to the east of it.

The constitution and customs of the town are so peculiar that it is worth departing for a paragraph from the strictly architectural character of this book to describe them. The government and manor of Hungerford, with fishing rights and commons, are vested in a Constable who is elected annually. On the Friday before Hocktide a 'Maccarini Supper' is held for tenants of town property at the *John o' Gaunt*. It consists of macaroni cheese and watercress and punch. At this supper the Constable for the coming year is tentatively suggested. His court is summoned by horn every Hocktide (the first Tuesday after Easter

Tuesday) in the Town Hall at nine o'clock and a bellman goes through the town ringing his bell and summoning the commoners of Hungerford. He wears a grey coat with scarlet facings and brass buttons and a tall hat with a gold band. Those not wishing to attend the court pay him a penny fine as he passes. At the court the Constable sits in a Portuguese seventeenth-century chair made of ebony. The Town Clerk (formerly seneschal) reads the Ancient Customs and provisions granted by John of Gaunt to the town. Two tithing-men or tutti-men start round the town carrying long poles with traces of gilt and colour on them and decorated with flowers and blue ribbons. They distribute oranges to the old people and to the schoolchildren and ask for a half-holiday. The tutti-men have the right to kiss every lady in each house they visit and then to hand her an orange fixed to the spike at the end of the tutti-pole. There is then a luncheon at the *Three Swans* in the High Street where special 'Plantagenet Punch' is drunk, and newcomers are shod with nails driven into their shoes, and oranges and hot coppers are thrown to the children in the street. On the following Friday the manor court meets. There used to be an evening dinner with singing. At midnight a horn (1634) was blown—there is also a medieval horn said to be presented by John of Gaunt—before the Constable as he was carried in his ebony chair to his house where his wife was expected to provide all officials with a coffee breakfast.

Down a lane west of the town for over a mile is North Standen Farm, a sixteenth-, seventeenth- and eighteenth-century building with the remains of a thirteenth-century chapel built into it, but invisible from the outside. East of the town, off the road to Kintbury is Hungerford Park, a domed late eighteenth-century house of two storeys, plastered, and with Victorian Italianate additions. At **Eddington,** a little hamlet of brick and flint cottages, thatched, north of the Bath Road end of the town, is a polychromatic brick church by Sir Arthur Blomfield, 1867. Eddington House more than a mile north of it, has pretty, modern wrought-iron gates between stone piers surmounted by figures of deer. They were assembled by the late Lady Hughes. Hopgrass Farm, to the left of the Bath Road going west, has a long range of thatched barns.

Hungerford parish church stands romantically by the Kennet and Avon Canal west of the town. It was built in 1814–17 from designs by J. Pinch in stone in the Perpendicular style (p. 88). It is a fine design, not merely a copy of late Gothic 'creditable for its time', but a piece of creative architecture in the Gothic style. The details of tracery and pinnacles may be Gothic, but the scale of mouldings, arrangement of stages of the tower, size of pinnacles and proportion of battlements on the aisles are wholly original. The slight curved bay at the east end is singularly happy and with no medieval precedent. The smooth ashlar facing outside is wonderful mason's work. Internally it was, alas, ruined in the 'eighties when the walls were skinned of plaster, galleries removed, pews cut down, chancel re-arranged, roof renewed, so that what must once have been an exciting Georgian church has assumed a green, dark Kempe-ish appearance. The original east window, half-enamelled and half pot-metal glass by W. Collins, the transparency artist, 1815, survives at the west end of the south aisle. The Whitelock monument, 1812, is probably by J. Pinch. There are three other chaste eighteenth-century monuments from the earlier church, one to the Stonehouse family, 1776 and 1779, signed by C. Harris of London.

HURLEY [map 13]. Between the noisy London–Henley–Oxford road and the comparatively quiet Thames (in neighbouring meadows, bungalows and caravans are only half hidden by elms and hedgerows) stand a church, the slight remains of a monastery partly incorporated in a modern house, a well-known inn and a few houses.

The inn, *Ye Olde Bell Hotel*, has sixteenth-century timber framing. It has been turned into a comfortable picture-postcard hostelry. Lady Place was a grand Tudor house built partly from the materials of the monastery, destroyed in 1837. Some of the monastic remains, Norman and Decorated, stand in the garden of the modern brick house near the church and, with the church, form a quadrangle; but across the road to the west, in a meadow, are two buttressed stone barns and a circular dovecote, also buttressed, which has six hundred nesting holes, L-shaped, in chalk. The date over the door is 1642, but the building like the neighbouring barns is of fourteenth-century origin. The larger of the barns has eight bays and has fine timber-work inside.

The parish church was the church of the monastery and is of Norman or perhaps pre-Conquest origin. It is barn-shaped, with a continuous roof, and was drastically recut and refurbished in 1852. It has a fifteenth-century bell turret. There is one good curvilinear window in clunch among the renewed Norman ones. The interior is a dark tunnel, with a stone screen-like reredos behind the altar, away from the east wall. Eighteenth- and nineteenth-century tablets crowd the walls, and there is an Elizabethan wall tomb with kneelers carved in chalk. Among the nineteenth-century tablets is an elegant one with an anchor and a furled sail, of 1866. In the churchyard are several delicately-carved gravestones of the early nineteenth century.

Hall Place, near the hamlet of **Burchetts Green,** was built 1728–35, on the site of an earlier house. It is a large, three-storey, east-facing brick house approached by splendid lime avenues, and with a flint Gothik lodge on the main drive. The large entrance portico is a nineteenth-century addition. The drawing-room is grandly decorated with plasterwork on scagliola (p. 64) and the doors and other woodwork are beautifully carpentered. There is also an oak-panelled room. Temple House, another large Classic building, by the riverside, was pulled down about 1910. A nineteenth-century paper mill, with attendant dwellings, stands near its well-planted site and the fringe of the park near the main road was developed as an estate of large middle-class dwellings between the wars. These houses are in a modern picturesque manner, reminiscent of Dinard or Paramé, and have wide eaves and roofs of pantiles or pre-fabricated thatch.

HURST [map 18]. This is a very scattered village, disposed about rural but used lanes, with elms in the hedgerows, leading among copses. Owing to expensive modern farming, the proximity of aerodromes and not-far-off Wokingham and Reading, Hurst is a country hide-out with a feeling of being very near civilization and the hub of modern life. In its village centre, round the church, it is picturesque and like a Middlesex village as depicted in the sketchbook of a Victorian artist. The Middlesex effect is increased by the old-fashioned wooden post-and-rail fence round the churchyard. This and several other villages in the neighbourhood are about as remote from London now as some Middlesex villages were in mid-Victorian times.

Cottages and farms are all of brick, slated or tiled, and several large houses in small parks are disposed about the parish, among them Hurst House, a many-gabled brick house of 1847 incorporating remains of a house of 1530, then pulled down; Hurst Lodge, with good early eighteenth-century brickwork and a pediment; Hinton House, square, of red brick of similar date; Hurst Grove, of stucco, and with an old tiled roof behind a balustrade; Haines Hill, a large, severe brick house of about 1780, which has rustic, lattice-windowed lodges with roofs of fish-scale tiles—these lodges are of later date, *c.* 1840; and Stanlake House, towards Ruscombe, a gabled Georgianized and Victorianized house of the end of the sixteenth century. Another brick house, Bill Hill, had fine iron gates, but they have been removed. Across the street from the church is a row of almshouses founded in 1664 and the Castle Inn, formerly Church House and the property of the Ecclesiastical Commissioners, a house of sixteenth-century origin.

The church, which has a late twelfth-century arcade, is a large, aisled building and has been much restored. The brick tower dates from 1612. It is remarkable for its woodwork, monuments, and an early window by Willement. The screen, which crosses nave and aisles, is carved and painted and is crested with the (Stuart) royal arms and Prince of Wales' feathers. (The lower part is of earlier date.) There is a Jacobean pulpit and iron hour-glass stand, and some spirited carved corbels adorn the north arcade. Monuments:—in north chapel: a large tomb with canopy and brasses, of stone and marble, of 1574; a magnificent seventeenth-century tomb—a mural version of the great tomb at Apethorpe, Northants—to Lady Margaret Savile, 1631, with figures holding back the curtains of a domed recess, and kneeling family in it; a large wall monument to Sir Richard and Lady Harrison with them kneeling, and a desk between them—a large rhapsody on earlier works of the type, by Thomas Stanton, 1683; two other brasses, one of them of 1600, representing a woman in a four-poster bed; two other tablets of the seventeenth century and one of the eighteenth; a white marble floor ledger with deep cut arms of 1678, and a black marble one. In the chancel: a monument to Henry Barker, 1651, in a recess up in the north wall, with arms and broken pediment above, at his head a chubby child holding books, and at his feet a skeleton with an hourglass; and, on the opposite wall, an elaborate wall tablet to Robert Palmer, a grey oval with delicate coloured marble decorations, including a draped urn at the top, by C. Harris, 1787. In the north aisle: a black marble ledger on a brick table tomb to Richard Bigg, of 'Hainshill' (see above), 1677. There is another black marble ledger on the floor, and there are other seventeenth- and eighteenth-century tablets.

At the west end is a three-light window by Thomas Willement, 1830—an early example of this artist's work. It was originally the east window, and was mutilated when it was removed. In the churchyard are some well-carved gravestones, some of them having black-painted ovals and scroll-surrounds.

EAST ILSLEY [map 9]. Within living memory, in the days of sheep farming when thousands of sheep were brought to the fortnightly market of this remote little downland town, it was a prosperous place with very many inns. Even to-day, when it is little more than a village at a road junction and a centre of training stables, there are five inns. East Ilsley climbs up a steep southern slope from a hollow in the downs and is near nothing but miles of grass. It consists mostly of brick cottages with tiled roofs and has a late Georgian rectory of stucco and, in Broad Street below the church, a handsome red brick house of the mid-eighteenth century with tall windows, wooden cornice and dormers in the attic above. Opposite is another house of this date. These are unexpectedly large houses for so small a place and still give it the character of a town.

The church, venerable and roughcast without, presides over the red-roofed village from the southern hill slope. It has a low western tower, long thirteenth-century chancel and south aisle, and an 1845 north aisle. Inside it is plastered and venerable with low square pews, simple three-bayed arcades, plastered nave ceiling and old timber roof in the south aisle. There is a Jacobean pulpit, one brass (1606), some pieces of old glass in the chancel windows, and the whole interior has a solid low-roofed country look as though built to withstand great winds.

WEST ILSLEY [map 9], seen from any of the unfenced grass roads which descend to it from the downs, is like a dream village with old red chimney stacks spouting blue smoke from an elmy hollow among hills of grass and corn. But the main street is something of a disillusionment, with its neat 1866 brick Baptist chapel at one end, its inn at the other and various half-timbered Lady Wantage style, 1880 buildings and modest brick houses and cottages between.

Hodcott House, a trainer's house south-east of the village, has classic stables to remind one of former eighteenth-century grandeur. The church in the centre of the village is still a small structure with western bellcote, though the nave received attention in 1850 and the north aisle, in an original style with dashing north door, all cusps and carving, was added by E. Dolby in 1874, who also renewed the chancel. The Archbishop of Spalato was rector here in 1616.

INKPEN [map 21]. Inkpen Beacon, 959 feet, is the highest point reached by the chalk in England. The river Enborne rises in the parish and flows into the Kennet at Aldermaston. The situation of the village under the bare down is romantic indeed. Walbury Camp and Combe Gallows are landmarks. (The gallows, several times renewed, still exists). Northwards across the parish the ground falls to 300 odd feet, and banks and knolls of the declivity form pleasant settings for brick and tile-hung farms and cottages, one or two of which have been re-antiquated or Georgianized. The church and Old Rectory are on a steep knoll. The Old Rectory was built about 1695 by Dr Brickenden, who afterwards became master of Pembroke College, Oxford, and he, at the same time, planted radiating avenues of beech and yew with a sidewalk of lime, leading to a point whence a fine vista of the downs is disclosed—a miniature, rustic and undulated Versailles. The house is a dignified, symmetrical Queen Anne house of brick, weather-tiled at the back, with careful details, including the original glazing bars (in front), the whole carefully preserved and tended.

The small church opposite the Old Rectory was thirteenth century and has a red-tiled bellcote supported on an oak structure inside. It is clearly a much and well-loved building, whose aesthetic character as we see it, dates from the end of the last century. It is a country version of Holy Trinity, Sloane Street. The woodwork and the heavy-handed oak screen and rood executed by Harry Hems from designs by Clapton C. Rolfe, 1896, are more prominent even than the brown stone, painted walls. There is a north aisle with an artistic modern chapel and much gilded wood about. There are two delicate-coloured eighteenth-century wall tablets at the west end.

KENNINGTON [map 2] is a long line of villas built between 1920 and 1939 between Bagley Wood and the wide water-meadows of the Thames opposite Iffley and Sandford in Oxfordshire. Breaking into the villas is a sixteenth-century stone manor house with mullioned windows and near it is a decent little Norman Revival church of stone (1828), probably designed by H. J. Underwood. It consists of nave and chancel only.

KINGSTON BAGPUIZE [map 5]. A main-road village with dangerous bends. The houses are of limestone, some of them not improved by brick dressings, and there is a small quota of main-road modern villas and army huts now used for housing heavy labour. The most distinguished building on the roadside is a stone house of the early seventeenth century, on the left going towards Faringdon, which has mullioned windows and stone roof.

Kingston House (p. 59) is in well-grown grounds and is of red brick with pronounced Cotswold-stone dressings and was built in the first quarter of the eighteenth century under the influence of Wren and Vanbrugh, possibly by a master mason of one of them—perhaps George Townsend of Bristol. The east and west fronts are identical. The east paved terrace was buried under a newly-made lawn (which cuts two feet off the bottom of the elevation) and the iron gates moved to their present position in 1865. The house contains a fine staircase and some Vanbrugh-esque fireplaces. The garden gazebo may be slightly earlier in date than the house itself.

The church (p. 78), a distinguished little building externally, was completed in 1800, from designs by John Fidel of Faringdon. It was refurnished and altered internally by Dolby of Abingdon in 1882.

Newbridge, which crosses the Thames into Oxfordshire in the north of the parish, is a medieval structure with cut-waters, at a point where the willow-bordered Windrush joins the main stream.

KINGSTON LISLE [map 8]. A small village of thatched cottages of chalk and brick at the fringe of a park whose beech plantations climb the steep slope to nearly 700 feet of downs. In the village is Thornhill House, a red-brick eighteenth-century T-shaped building of some magnificence. Kingston Lisle park is entered beside the church. It has a beautifully landscaped park and the house stands above a valley whose hollow is grand with a series of lakes, once fish ponds. The central part of the house is early eighteenth century to which wings were added in about 1840. One of these, with contemporary conservatory adjoining, contains a splendid Graeco–Roman entrance hall probably designed by George Basevi or C. R. Cockerell (p. 102).

The little church, roughcast without and with shingled bellcote, has seventeenth-century woodwork in roof and pews, pulpit and screen. The walls have large remains of late fourteenth-century painting and there is a piece of glass of this date in a window in the south wall of the chancel. But for all its fittings and paintings, this rich interior has a restored appearance which does not challenge comparison with an undisturbed church of like original character, such as Bessels Leigh.

The hamlet of **Fawler** on the Uffington Road has several timber and thatched cottages, a farm and a stone-roofed manor house (restored and enlarged in the twentieth century) with large clipped bushes of Scotch roses in the garden.

The *Blowing Stone* in a cottage garden up the hill on the Lambourn Road is a piece of Sarsen through a hole in which some people can, with great skill, blow a low wailing note.

KINTBURY [map 21]. Between Newbury and Hungerford, but a mile away from the Bath Road, Kintbury has preserved a large village character of its own and, though not picturesque, is not yet merged into impersonal modernism. It is a red-brick and slate-built place, much influenced by the railway and some small manufacturers, among which is that of whiting for tennis shoes. Wallingtons is a large and very much altered brick house of the seventeenth century, in the south of the parish, and Elcot Park, an early nineteenth-century stuccoed house with bows, in the north of the parish, beyond the Bath Road.

The church was rather damaged by nineteenth-century restoration. It has Norman, Transitional and later features, but they have been much obscured. Bodley and Garner were the most capable of several Victorians who exercised their taste in the building. From outside, the chequer-work tower is an attractive village feature. Inside, the monuments are the most pleasing things, but the Victorian painting of the roofs is successful. There are tablets, seventeenth to nineteenth century. Among the earlier ones may be noticed a white marble tablet surrounded by a black oval of 1678, and there are several eighteenth-century examples in coloured marbles in the transept. Here also (though originally on each side of the altar) are two pyramid monuments with marble busts to members of the Raymond family (d.) 1754 and (d.) 1767, by Scheemakers.

Christ Church, at **Kintbury Cross Ways,** to the south of the village, was built of brick with Bath-stone dressings and plate tracery by Talbot Bury, 1867. It has a strange and rather ugly tiled spire. The Puginesque interior is tall and flimsy, with German glass, carving, painting and gilding on altar and pulpit, and very original cast-iron cancellum. The church was evidently a rich Tractarian's whim.

KNOWLE HILL [map 19]. A main-road village with wide strips of grass and scattered Victorian cottages, houses, inns, farms and a small church by J. C. Buckler, 1840 (chancel, 1871), with grisaille glass in nave lancets. To the south are wide open fields, towards Shottesbrook and Waltham St. Lawrence; to the north is a curious area of closed country towards Henley, with two wooded knolls, and everywhere oaks, elms, birches, ponds and small commons, with tile-hung 1880-ish semi-cottages, barbed wire and very few cultivated fields. **Warren Row,** between the two knolls, is in the centre of the area. It has a corrugated iron church.

LAMBOURN [map 14]. The remotest town in Berkshire. In a slight valley, high up in the downs, it is almost entirely given over to the training of racehorses. The making of travelling horse boxes is one of the trades of the town. Lambourn consists mostly of brick cottages (shop: pp. 54, 55) lining four crossing roads with some parallel and diverging ones, with a church and restored market cross in the midst. A few larger houses are in an attractive local Georgian style, mostly with walls of sarsen stone with brick at the corners. Two of these on the Newbury road have moulded wooden porches; one in the street towards Hungerford is beautifully built of grey sarsens. The Vicarage, opposite the church, is of the seventeenth century at the back and early eighteenth century in front, of red brick. North-east of the church are Place Almshouses, 1827, a single-storey building with low pitched roofs, and Estbury Almshouses, rebuilt in 1852, in a scholarly diamond-chequered-brick, Tudor style, round a courtyard, from designs by T. Talbot Bury. Lambourn Place, designed in 1843, by Prof Donaldson, is now demolished. Its planted park remains, north of the church.

The town has one of the few grand medieval churches in the county. It was originally a late-Norman cruciform building, as may be seen from the west end, the nave arcades and the internal arches of the tower. To this were added transepts, three chapels and a porch in succeeding centuries. The last medieval additions are the most magnificent: the southernmost chapel and the upper stage of the tower, 1502, are the work of some distinguished architect with Gloucestershire Cotswold or West Country traditions. The rather dark interior, a good deal renewed, has fine proportions dictated by the Transitional arcades and tower crossing. From nave and aisles may be seen various vistas of the wide extent of eastern chapels. There is a Victorian Norman-Revival clerestory on each side of the nave. There are many fine details. In the north chapel is an alabaster tomb with effigies, 1558, and fragments of glass, 1532. The east window of the chancel showing the Last Judgment is by N. H. J. Westlake, 1876. Over the entrance to St Mary's chapel from the south transept is a fourteenth-century arch, and in a hollow moulding of this is spirited carving of hounds coursing a hare, and men blowing pipes. In the southernmost chapel is the Estbury altar tomb and brass (1508), sporting details (p. 6, fig. 1), and three windows are glazed by Thomas Willement (1849). In the south aisle is an alabaster plaque (1649) of King Charles the Martyr in a Victorian setting. It came from Lambourn Place in 1893. The chancel was restored by Street (1861). There are eighteenth-century tablets, including one to Edward Seymour of 1798, with verses by the Laureate Pye (*see* FARINGDON). There are also other brasses.

Upper Lambourn is a brick and thatch hamlet on the edge of the downs among training stables. It has a small red-brick church of 1868. At **Bockhampton,** down the valley from Lambourn, is a seventeenth-century house, with some late Georgian windows brought recently from Wantage.

LAMBOURN WOODLANDS, see WOODLANDS ST MARY

LECKHAMPSTEAD [map 15]. A scattered village in semi-downland shooting country, with a rich brick Methodist chapel, 1874 (at **Thicket**), a row of costly-looking council houses, a few brick and timber-framed thatched cottages, a 1914 War Memorial obelisk with a clock in it and an extraordinary polychromatic brick church, 1859, by S. S. Teulon (pp. 89, 90). The porch of this church has been partly constructed from a Jacobean screen taken out of the old church and painted plum colour.

LETCOMBE BASSETT [map 8].

Watercress, race-horse-training and agriculture are the industries which give life and character to this beautifully situated village (p. 1) in a deep elm-shadowed valley of the downs. Many of the cottages are timber-framed and thatched. The church, with fourteenth-century bricks in the tower, is largely thirteenth century, with Norman windows in the chancel and Norman north door, outside which are some carved seventeenth-century table tombs. The interior, except for the fifteenth-century nave roof and Norman font, looks new and hard with its pitchpine fittings, tinted glass and south aisle of 1862.

LETCOMBE REGIS [map 8]

is almost a suburb of Wantage, with an uncompromising entrance from that town past council houses and new brick walls, which suddenly relent, to display older brick cottages and some timber-framed houses. The Manor House by the church is eighteenth-century brick with modern additions. The small stone church is mostly Perpendicular but was very severely manhandled in 1863. But this 'restoration' left a few grand pieces of glass in the east window—in the centre light Our Lord seated, with blood streaming from his hands and side, is fourteenth century. The armorial glass and other pieces are mostly fifteenth century. There are a rich marble tablet in the nave to Alexander Fettiplace (1731), a mutilated brass in the vestry, and some slight remains of wall-painting in the nave. A Maori chieftain is buried in the yew-shaded churchyard.

LITTLEWICK GREEN [map 13, west of Maidenhead].

A collection of houses lying just off the Bath Road, three miles on the Reading side of Maidenhead. The small stone church is by E. J. Shrewsbury, 1893.

LITTLEWORTH [map 4].

A pretty limestone village on the Golden Ridge, east of Faringdon and off main roads. The little nave and chancel church was built 1839–43, in the Early English style, from designs by H. J. Underwood. The chancel was added in 1876. It was one of the first buildings of the Tractarian revival, and was erected at the instigation of Dr Pusey.

LOCKINGE [map 9].

A model Victorian village, 1860, in brick (p. 100) centred among miles of trim plantations stretching up to the downs and northward to the Vale. It is redolent of mid-Victorian benevolence, when Lord and Lady Wantage were landlords of the vast Lockinge estate. Their house, which had a famous collection of pictures, was undistinguished and large, and was demolished in 1947. Now, but lake, gardens and arboreta remain, at the edge of the village. The church in the park was not spared expensive rebuilding and refurbishing, and retains very little old work except the north aisle, which was the original church. There are tablets, seventeenth to nineteenth centuries, a 'desk-kneeler' of 1633. The east window was designed by Lady Jane Lindsay, and one of the brass candelabra came from Corfu. Barns (pp. 46, 47).

West Lockinge and Betterton are small hamlets. The latter has a timber-framed house, much modernized.

LONGCOT [map 3].

A village of many old stone cottages, some thatched, some stone-tiled, with the usual interruption, in this otherwise lovely part of the Vale of the White Horse, of ugly council houses out of scale and out of texture with their surroundings. The church is at the south end of the village from which may be seen the noble roll of White Horse Hill and the North Downs. In the churchyard is a tiny disused school-house (1717). The church, whose nave and chancel are mostly thirteenth and fourteenth century,

is roughcast on the north side and has a timbered fifteenth-century south porch and deeply moulded thirteenth-century doorway. The three-stage western tower, 1722, is a noble classic design, ashlar-faced and crowned with four stone urns. Though the interior of the church was skinned in 1897 and though hot water pipes are trained round the chancel arch like rambler roses, it is still an attractive building, long and gracefully proportioned. The pulpit is Jacobean. Hidden away in the tower is a lively Royal Arms of George II, much in need of repair and possibly a repainting of Stuart work. The rather badly fired mid-Victorian stained glass was brought from Newbury parish church in about 1935 and pleasantly modifies the light on the skinned walls.

LONGWORTH [map 4].

The southern part of this parish is flat market-gardening country merging into the large, almost treeless fields of this, the Charney Bassett/Lyford part of the Vale. At Southmoor in this part stands New House which is two separate houses, joined to one another and standing at right-angles, surveying miles of flat fields. Each building is a complete example of lesser domestic architecture of the county at its best. The older house facing east, is two-storeyed and yellow-washed, with white paint on its moulded windows, wide eaves and steep-pitched tiled roof all about 1710. At right-angles to it is a severe 1820-ish house of brick, facing south, again of two storeys, rectangular, with wide eaves and low pitched roof.

Longworth village is on the Golden Ridge and looks to the Thames meadows across slopes of elm, the whole country having here a park-like aspect because of the elm-topped circular Harrowdown Hill which here rises 300 feet out of the meadows. The village is limestone with dry walls to orchards and limestone cottages, some thatched and some tiled. It must once have been as pretty as Buckland, but ugly modern brick villas—of which the most glaring example is the smart new village inn—and clumsy electric light poles now spoil it. The church, in a wide acre of eighteenth-century headstones, stands high and apart above the Thames Valley. It has a venerable yellowish-grey roughcast exterior, battlemented tower and aisles, lead roof to nave and seventeenth-century clear glass leading to clerestory. The prevailing style is Perpendicular. Inside the church is light and uneven, a larger village building with cream-washed walls, lighting by well-arranged and enormous electric candles in white tin holders, much clear glass with some fragments of fourteenth- and fifteenth-century glass in the upper lights, nave and aisle roofs are plastered between the old timbers. Undoubtedly the most impressive fitting in the church is the early seventeenth-century chancel screen with its turned balusters and elaborate cresting. The chancel is, however, dominated by an Art-Nouveau crucifixion in stained glass, twisting through the Perpendicular east window. It is in memory of Dr Illingworth, the editor of Lux Mundi who was rector here and an inspirer of Archbishop Temple. The painted reredos in beaten silver frame is in similar taste to the east window, but less obtrusive. There are also in the church very splendid, City-church-style, seventeenth-century communion rails, Marten monuments and painted commandment boards in the north chapel—all of this date. In the north aisle are Royal Arms of George III and a white marble monument to William Bowles (1801) with elegant female figures in relief by R. Westmacott. There is a fifteenth-century brass of the shroud effigies of Richard Yate and his wife (p. 6, fig. 2).

LYFORD [map 4].

A remote limestone and brick village in flat meadowland among elms and willows beside the little river Ock. It is a hamlet consisting of four farms, a church, some cottages and a group of almshouses, the older limestone dominating the eighteenth-century brick. West of the church is the Manor Farm, a stone building with some original oak-framed windows and old chimney stacks, some of the chimneys being set diagonally. It bears the dates 1617 and 1621. The river forms a moat on the west of it. Another house, also now a farm, opposite the church, is dated 1717, and old stone cottages neighbour this. Lyford Grange is a quarter of a mile to the north-east. This was an old house, the mansion of the Yates family, but has been greatly altered. Here Edmund Campion, the Jesuit, was apprehended in 1581. The cottage-like Ashcombe Almshouses were founded in 1611 (p. 35). They were re-built in brick in the eighteenth century, and surround three sides of a quadrangle. There is a square 'prayer-room' under the clock in the centre of the west side. The church, which has a few Early English and later details, was re-stored in 1875 in an insensitive manner and had almost all its beauty removed.

MAIDENHEAD [map 13]. This town owes its importance to transport. There was a medieval wharf on the river here and there may, before that, have been a Roman road. Certainly there was a medieval bridge, the scene of a good many battles. The earliest building still standing in the borough is Smyth's Almshouses (1659) on the right of the Bath Road soon after crossing the bridge from London. It is dormered, two-storey, with delicately moulded brick. Coaching days brought posting-inns all along the main street and a few of these survive, together with some Georgian houses on the London side of the town. In 1772, the old road bridge over the Thames was rebuilt from designs by Sir Robert Taylor. In 1840 the Great Western came from Bristol to London and Brunel designed the magnificent two-arched railway bridge whose depressed brick arches are said to be the widest ever constructed in that material. Frequent trains soon turned Maidenhead into a country retreat for richer Londoners and suburbs sprung up to the north of the town, the best of all being that spaciously planned estate of **Boyne Hill** with its large red-brick houses and Tractarian polychromatic church by Street (*see* below). Bath Road villas (p. 83). In 1890 boating on the river became fashionable, the Brigade of Guards opened a social club for its officers close to the road bridge. Mothers of many daughters hired riverside houses for the summer on the newly-built estate of the **Fishery** in the Thames-side marshes by the town and watched for eligible bachelors from the shaven lawns of their mock-Tudor houses. The nobility settled in more permanent Georgian houses all along the river bank through Bray to Windsor. By 1920 the river had ceased to be so fashionable, but Maidenhead was saved from decay by the popularity of motoring. It was an easy run from London, and night clubs and restaurants sprang up. Gay little all-electric houses near the station and the Bath Road drew the newly-rich. The Victorian railway suburbs decayed and have never recovered their prosperity. Indeed, many of them have still the atmosphere of hurried 1939 war-time evacuation and most of the larger houses have been converted into flats in these quiet suburban roads. Maidenhead is now a suburb of London with its trainloads of commuters and the usual chain stores in its main streets and cafés and restaurants for passing motorists. The river seems almost to be forgotten.

The main street of the town was originally lined with inns and posting houses, fragments of which survive here and there, but not in large enough numbers or sizes to affect the predominantly modern, brick, irregular and yet stereotyped façades. Such old houses as there are lie modestly outside the town towards **Cox Green,** to the south-west.

The church of St Andrew and St Mary Magdalene at the foot of the hill where the Bath road rises out of the town to the west was built in white brick and stone from designs by Busby in 1825. Its chancel was rebuilt and interior altered in 1877-8. St Luke's is a more prominent, spired, building which stands away from the town centre, north-west of the bridge. It is in the Decorated style, in quarry-faced ragstone, and is a large and dull building. It has some late windows by O'Connor, including one of 1871, of the Agony, representing moonlight. The Roman Catholic church was built in 1884 from designs by Leonard Stokes, in brick and flint, in an advanced (for the date) Perpendicular style.

By far the most beautiful of the Maidenhead churches is All Saints, Boyne Hill, built 1854-8 (steeple 1865), from designs by G. E. Street. It is the Tractarian cathedral of an upper-class suburb, whose broad roads with detached brick houses among trees still keep a Victorian calm. To the south of the church, and forming a collegiate-looking community of buildings, are Street's vicarage and other buildings con-nected with the church. The interior is a rich example of coloured and cut brickwork. Though hardly any of the space is undecorated (a fatal habit of some merely decora-tive Victorian architects), the fine proportions and decided principles of the interior are yet easily taken in, owing to the feeling of masterful imagination in the composition. The decoration all keeps its place—it is busy enough as it is in the nave, richer still in the high chancel—and the effect is heightened by bright glass. The nave was lengthened westwards in 1911 by the architect's son, A. E. Street, and this extension unfortunately impaired the external pro-portions and spoiled the effect of the base of the tower by engaging it.

St Paul's, High Town Road, a chapel of ease to All Saints, is a brick building with imposing interior, 1887-9, by E. J. Shrewsbury, who also designed St Peter's, **Furze Platt**, in 1897, a brick apsidal church with, internally, a white wood roof and parquet floor. St James the Less, **Stubbings**, on the Hurley and Henley Road by the north-west fringe of Maidenhead Thicket, is a well-detailed little flint and stone Decorated-style church designed by R. C. Carpenter in 1850. It has a west bellcote and glass by Wailes and others.

MARCHAM [map 5]. In the meadows west of Abingdon, this is a village built largely of limestone, with some plaster and half-timber. An old stone barn and a dovecote, of the sixteenth century, in a field bounded by stone walls, are picturesque objects in the centre of the village (pp. 48, 49). Another building of the same date is the Priory, now an outhouse of the house called Marcham Priory. It has some original doorways and fireplaces. There are large houses to the north in small parks bordering Frilford Heath and Tubney Wood called Oakley House (Victorian, now a maternity home), and Upwood Park, towards Appleton. Marcham Park is near the village, the park wall adjoining the churchyard. It is a large, plain, late-Georgian Classic house of stone, its exterior walls having a 'batter'. The interior is without decorative features. It is planned round a large stone entrance hall and staircase (Adam style, from elsewhere). It is now a Women's Institute College.

The churchyard is approached from the south past the Old Rectory, an attractive building neighboured by a large barn which is dated on a cornerstone, 1646. The church was almost rebuilt in 1837 by Fisher of Oxford, who kept the plain stone thirteenth-century tower. The nave is a large rectangular space, Perpendicular or Tudor style, with two arches at the east end (the altar is placed against the central pillar—a not unattractive arrangement), and a flat hammer-beam roof. The two chapels at the east end have original features—their east windows, Early English and Decorated, and the Early English arch between them has capitals carved with knotted foliage. There are many unremarkable tablets and slabs, and a late brass.

On the road to Kingston Bagpuize, at **Frilford,** are two large early Victorian villas next to one another. One is Tudor, the other Italianate, both in stone and richly de-corated. They seem to have been copied exactly from a builder's copybook, even down to the planting of trees and arrangement of flower beds and are most attractive.

MARLSTON [map 16, near Bucklebury]. A big-estate village, with a small church rebuilt by William Butterfield in 1855, with a plain Norman doorway built into it. The two-light west window of the Annunciation is a dazzling composition by Gibbs, 1855, red and yellow predominating. The Palmers, of Marlston House, added the chancel in 1901 and a muddy east window by Kempe. Marlston House is an expensive, Norman–Shaw-style building in brick and stone, with a high, galleried hall, by Edward Burgess, 1896. Its design evidently owed much to that of Shaw's Greenham Court (p. 105). Its terraced garden has heavy, contemporary plantations. A row of estate houses by Burgess in the enlightened country-cottage style with white woodwork stands on a hill east of the church.

Between here and Cold Ash a road passes through open woodlands and through the earth ramparts of Grimsbury Castle. In the middle of the enclosure is an eighteenth-century castellated brick tower.

MIDGHAM [map 23] consists of a spired Victorian church, a picturesque feature across rising fields from the Bath road, a modernized Georgian Manor House in a dip, with an avenue through its park giving onto the Bath Road, and a few cottages disposed among undulating copses of oak and hazel. The flint and stone church stands well on its rise, and is approached by a long churchyard path through elms, oaks and rhododendrons. It was designed, like the church at Brimpton to which it looks across the Kennet valley, by J. Johnson, and built in 1869. It has south aisle and north transept. The columns are of Purbeck marble, one huge one at the south-west angle supporting much of the weight of tower and spire, with baptistry under. Small detached marble shafts rest on carved heads between the arches. The whole effect is decorative and rather sumptuous. Most of the glass is greenish, and all poorish.

MILTON [map 5]. Orchards of fruit trees carefully tended occupy a good deal of the south part of this parish, which rises from the village itself in the flat Abingdon country, across the mainline railway southwards towards the downs. Potash was once worked where orchards now flourish and the main village street is called Potash Lane. Milton Hill is a large Edwardian building in brick, now used as offices.

At the gates of the Manor House (p. 68) is the church. This was practically rebuilt in 1851 by Henry Woodyer. It has plenty of his curious, original mouldings and cuspings, and his wife is commemorated by attractive glass, soft and lemony in prevailing colour, opposite the south porch, 1852. Choirs of angels playing harps, in retiring half-circles, appear at the top of each lancet. This may be Woodyer's own design, or it may be by O'Connor who did the east window of the chancel, a window in the organ chamber and one at the west end of the north aisle. Another window in the organ chamber is by Thomas Willement, of St. Peter and St Paul.

NORTH MORETON [map 10]. In the flat agricultural country between Didcot and Wallingford, and within sight, across wide cornfields, of Wittenham Clumps. Here, an island of elms shades brick and tile-hung and half-timbered houses and cottages, about five of these, of sixteenth- and seventeenth-century date, being picturesque. North Moreton House, formerly the vicarage and before that a farmhouse, is one of these: it has a medieval doorway, brought from Little Wittenham, rebuilt into a garden wall, an old brick chimney stack and a neighbouring barn with herring-bone brickwork. Brick almshouses and Primitive Methodist Chapel, both decorative, were built in 1872 and 1874.

The church is one of the most beautiful of Berkshire's medieval buildings. Its corps is of late thirteenth-century date, but the south chapel, or chantry, south aisle and tower, with pierced quatrefoils in its parapet, were added a few years after, early in the fourteenth century. The Stapleton Chantry (p. 16) is of beautiful design and workmanship, in flint and stone, with tall geometrical windows and mythical animals carved along its outside cornice. The wide window in its east wall has all its five lancets full of original coloured

glass. The centre light shows the Scourging, the Crucifixion and the Resurrection. Other subjects deal with incidents in the life of the Virgin Mary, St Peter, St Paul and St Nicholas. The well-designed details in this chapel include a piscina with a corner shaft of original design and stiff-leafed carving on the capitals of the arch into the south aisle. Also, the high timber roof remains. The rest of the church is now rather bare, with a blue and red tiled floor; but the flat-footed Victorian wall paintings, done with the help of lantern slides, which were distempered over in 1947, did not enrich it beautifully while they existed. The early Decorated east window of the chancel is of the same design as the east window at Basildon, and no doubt by the same architect or mason. There is fourteenth-century glass in other windows, including the Crucifixion (pp. 8, 9).

SOUTH MORETON [map 10]. The main railway line runs between the villages of North and South Moreton and on each side of it is modern housing development, the houses being of varying architectural merit. The village of South Moreton lies to the south-east of this point, in flat orchard country with a small river, the Hacker brook, and its winding street has a Berkshire mixture of old plaster and new plaster, old and new timber, brick walls, old manors converted into country retreats of a cottage character (there are two seventeenth-century manors of this kind—those of Sanderville and Bray) and everywhere a feeling that galvanized iron is warring against art and that art, helped by cherry and apple blossom, is holding its own quite well. The church has distinguished Decorated tracery on the south side, but the interior is bare and unprepossessing, being curious only because of the two aisles that constitute the building are of equal width, divided by an Early English arcade. There is a plain, early door.

MORTIMER, see STRATFIELD MORTIMER

MOULSFORD [map 10]. A riverside place on the main road from Reading to Wallingford and Oxford with a wide Great Western viaduct over the river, a few roadside cottages of brick and timber, two barns restored as living places, and two hotels—the *Beetle and Wedge* (modernized) beside the ferry to South Stoke, with old brick boundary walls round a large garden at the back of it, and the *Moulsford Manor*, a Georgian yellow-gabled house beside the church. There is also a distinguished square brick house, Moulsford House, of about 1830, with stone dressings, a dentilled cornice and half-round dormers. The church was rebuilt by Sir Gilbert Scott in 1846, on the old site, a few old features being retained. It is a pretty enough feature from the river but not worth a visit. Inside, it has quasi box-pews, some out-of-key carvings and no beautiful features.

NEWBURY [map 22] is the red brick and tile-roofed capital of the Kennet valley. Its main old streets form the letter Y. The base of the letter stands on a ruled line to the north of the town, which is the main Bath Road. The top of the letter is where the Great Western main line from London to Westbury makes a rule across the top of the Y to the south of the town. The Kennet runs through the middle and is crossed by a narrow balustraded eighteenth-century bridge with remains of mutilated semi-domed pavilions at either end. As soon as wide Northbrook Street has narrowed and crossed the bridge, the road divides into two. Along these three old streets are most of the old houses, and all alley ways and courts off them are worth exploring for the views of the old and tile-hung backs of houses.

The Kennet valley at Newbury is broad. The northern slopes are wooded and ascend gently behind Shaw and Donnington commons and then to hidden and distant downs. The southern slopes are sandy, steep and fir-covered and have much peat on them and birch-clad dingles with

brown streams. The views from the steep slopes of the Newbury Gold Course at Greenham are worthy of the richest
water-colours of a Sutton Palmer.

Newbury is in history books because of a battle in the
Wars of the Roses (1460) and two famous battles of the
Civil Wars (1643 and 1644), but its history in building, still
clearly to be seen in its streets, is one of nearly five hundred
years of uninterrupted commercial prosperity. This prosperity began with the cloth trade when an apprentice, John
Winchcombe (d. 1519), married his master's widow, gained
favour with Henry VIII, employed one hundred looms in
the town and negotiated a trade agreement with the Low
Countries. He was known as Jack O'Newbury and his early
sixteenth-century house survives in part in a side alley in
the middle of the east side of Northbrook Street. It is of
half-timber filled in with herringbone brickwork and with a
wooden oriel window in it. Jack O'Newbury and his son
built the parish church, a large late sixteenth-century building of stone, all of a piece, with handsome restored pinnacles
on its tower, grand clustered columns of nave, 1932 roof
and clerestory. The church was restored in 1867 by H.
Woodyer and far too frequently after that. Its walls are
skinned, all its windows filled with greenish Kempe-style
stained glass so that it is dark inside and was expensively
furnished in late-Victorian times in the manner of any prosperous town church. Jack's brass is in the tower. But much
sixteenth- and seventeenth-century cloth trade architecture
survives in different parts of the town as at the Cloth Hall
off the market place, with an overhanging upper storey and
moulded wooden cornice. This building is now a museum.
East of it, by the bus terminus, is the long, low and galleried
seventeenth-century Corn Stores, cleverly transformed in
its ground floor into a picturesque row of shops. The biggest
cloth trade domestic building of all is Shaw House (p. 21).
The prosperous early Renaissance style survives in Northbrook Street in the beautiful seventeenth-century house
defaced by a modern shop fascia below it (p. 57), and there
is a humbler, tile-hung, gabled example at West Mills.

There are sixty almshouses in the town and the biggest
cluster of these is south of the railway. The Litten Chapel,
a thirteenth-century building in origin, now used for secular
purposes, and with a sixteenth-century wooden roof, stands
on the main road. It was originally the chapel of St Bartholomew's Hospital, a pre-cloth-trade foundation, and later
was used as an Edward VI Grammar School. This school
was rebuilt in 1886 west of the town. The Hospital revenues
were used for almshouses and north of the chapel is a gabled
almshouse dated 1698 with tiled roofs and projecting wings
called St Bartholomew's Hospital (p. 37). On the opposite
side of the narrow lane this brick front faces, is Bartholomew Manor, a home for retired nurses from the Middlesex
hospital. It was built in 1678 and was originally an almshouse. Across the main road is a plain block of almshouses,
called Raymond's Buildings. They formed a side of an
early nineteenth-century court of almshouses, destroyed by
the same stick of bombs in the Hitler war which demolished
Butterfield's 1860 brick church of St John's. But survivals
of this fancy Gothik may be found in a block of almshouses
(1826) north of St Bartholomew's Hospital and on the east-
ward face of the Hospital itself (1839). The most distinguished almshouse architecture in the town is Kimber's
Almshouses, 1795, on the Market Place, near the Post
Office. These are now abandoned, but the front remains, a
blue-glazed and red-brick composition with recessed arches.
There are numerous other small almshouses in the town,
such as Hunt's by the river near West Mills.

As might be expected of a manufacturing town which
prospered under early Renaissance merchants, Protestantism was strong. Jack O'Newbury was suspected of Luther-
anism by Wolsey, two Protestant martyrs were burnt here
in Queen Mary's reign and the Protestantism took architectural form in the seventeenth century. There were several
meeting houses down alley ways—Waterside Chapel, a

Presbyterian Meeting House (1697), later Unitarian, retained all its old fittings, including three-decker pulpit,
galleries and central communion table, until 1947, when its
furnishings were sold. Now only the picturesque exterior
with brickwork, steep-pitched roof and leaded windows
remains. The Congregational chapel, founded in 1662, was
rebuilt in 1822 in a chaste Grecian manner in brick, and
classicized in 1856 when the adjoining handsome brick
Classic schoolroom was built.

In the eighteenth century Newbury took on the look of a
main-road town connected with coaching. Along the Bath
Road itself arose several sizeable and stately brick mansions, the Dower House at the London end and several
houses towards Speen at the western end. In the town itself
much of the humbler, tile-hung architecture disappeared or
was refaced on the main streets. Cottages (p. 55). For two
centuries now there had been a high standard of brick
building and it is one of the pleasures of walking in Newbury to notice the varieties of moulded brick cornice and of
patterned brick—glazed and red—on the many old houses
which have been suffered to survive, above modern shop
fronts. One of the best of these is the large house above two
chain shoe shops almost opposite the gabled seventeenth-
century house in Northbrook Street already noticed (pp. 56,
57). The most complete building is the late Georgian
butcher's shop (Liddiard's) beside the bridge, clearly the
work of the distinguished local architect who designed
Kimber's Almshouses. A Newbury version of fancy eighteenth-century Gothic may be seen at Donnington Grove
(pp. 74, 75), and again in a house west of the Dower House
on the Bath Road. The stone entrance gates to Newbury
churchyard are the richest example of this style in the town.
Another Georgian relic is the theatre, now a warehouse,
on the London Road near the *Bacon Arms*: of this a decorated ceiling survives. Sandleford Priory (pp. 72, 73).

The high standard of building persisted until deep into
the nineteenth century. Smith's Crescent (1826) between
Speenhamland and Shaw is a long range of small houses in
red brick. Donnington Square on the Oxford Road is a
stucco range of Italianate and Gothic-style detached villas,
reminiscent of Leamington, but defaced by modern building.

Later Victorian buildings are curious and varied. Speenhamland church by G. E. Street, 1878, had an awkward and
ugly nave added to it by his son in 1911. The municipal
buildings in the centre of the town (1877) are in a local
Waterhouse style in brick. The Corn Exchange (1861–2) is a
last and noble gesture in the Classic style. A peculiar Swiss-
Mauresque corner building above a bicycle shop in Northbrook Street had multi-coloured tiles on its turret and has
much fancy balcony work on its first floors and barge-
boarded gables. (These adornments came from the Paris
Exhibition). South of the station is a lamp-post with cast-
iron palms wrapped round its shaft and an Ionic capital for
its head. In a park near here is a terra-cotta statue of Queen
Victoria, presented to the town by Lord George Sanger.

A good service of trains to London from the hard red
1900 Railway station in its cutting, has added a commuting
section to the population of Newbury. There are London
style suburban houses along the main roads south of the
station and a rich colony of neo-squirearchy towards the
Hampshire heights of Woolton Hill. Newbury itself has
new light industries of its own and the Bath Road to
Thatcham is lined with modern villas for factory workers.
This latest twentieth-century spread of the town has pro-
duced two churches, one a Neo-Romanesque brick Roman
Catholic church by W. C. Mangan (1928) whose campanile
rises beside the Bath Road and, on **Wash Common**, a
beautiful chapel of ease to St John, designed by the late
F. C. Eden with a white and spacious interior in a simple
Italian style with vaulted aisles and lofty nave and chancel.

Flat Racing at Newbury has gone on since the eighteenth
century. But the grandstand and other buildings connected
with the beautifully situated Racecourse east of the town,

are mostly red brick of 1905, when the course was opened. Canal (pp. 82, 83).

NORTHBOURNE, see DIDCOT

OARE, see CHIEVELEY

PADWORTH [map 24]. From heathery Hampshire commons and fir trees, the land slopes northward into the Kennet valley of Berkshire. The village of Padworth is the collection of houses around Aldermaston Station. The church and house are more than a mile southward up the hill. Padworth House (p. 67), a plain, three-storey plastered building puts its stateliest front to the Kennet valley and looks down through park and meadows to a little Gothic fishing lodge (p. 73). But this front owes all its beauty to the arrangement of windows. The house was mostly built in 1769 from designs by John Hobcraft. The entrance hall with stone floor, wrought-iron balusters, pillared passage and gallery above, with vaulted ceilings decorated with contemporary Adam-style plasterwork by Joseph Rose, is extremely elegant as are the main ground floor rooms. Beside the house is the church, which is wholly Norman, except for a late Victorian porch and vestry and five Perpendicular windows. It was built *c*. 1130 and is roughcast without, the stone window tracery being lime-washed in the old Georgian style. The interior, despite untidy modern furnishings, is overwhelmingly grand for so simple a building. A wide and high Norman chancel arch of two orders opens on to the semi-circular chancel which is semi-domed. Chancel, semi-dome and walls throughout are plastered and have the texture of ages, with remains of wall paintings on the east wall of the nave (south) showing St Nicholas as Bishop and again as restoring three students to life. There are several eighteenth-century wall monuments, of which the most splendid, to Christopher Griffiths, 1776, by J. Wilton, shows a woman leaning on an urn. There is a Royal Arms of George III. The Norman north and south doors are richly moulded. This and Avington are easily the most impressive Norman churches in the county.

PANGBOURNE [map 17]. The Great Western, a main crossroads and a spectacular reach of river, cliff-hung on the Berkshire bank, with tree-shaded meadows and distant view of woods on the Oxfordshire bank, converge here. The place is almost a town and the majority of its showier private and public buildings were designed for river enjoyment before main-road motor traffic had come into existence and spoilt its Edwardian remoteness. Its former appeal may be felt down by the river, the lock and lasher. Here was the home of Kenneth Grahame and here still is the atmosphere of *The Wind in the Willows* and the 'messing about in boats'.

In the centre of the village is a corner building designed probably by Leonard Stokes early in this century, as a block of shops, with fire-station included. It is gabled, tile-hung and solidly proportioned, an assured adaptation of local Berkshire style to modern commerce. It compares favourably with the more ornate 'Seven Deadly Sins' (1896) along the river reach (p. 110). Two buildings erected by rich late-Victorian magnates dominate the place. One, down by the river and just west of the railway, is Shooter's Hill House, by Leonard Stokes, 1898. It is a brick and tile-hung L-shaped building with a simple and stately picture gallery, now used as a Masonic Hall, at one end of it. The other, now used for the Pangbourne Nautical College, is large, towered and elaborate with brick and stone dressings in the Renaissance style, and much well-moulded panelling and vaulted passageways within. It was designed by John Belcher in 1898 and commands a wide southern view across to Hampshire. Various other late-Victorian and Edwardian small houses are settled behind firs and beeches in these steep chalk uplands above the village and were designed by Belcher and Stokes, with one, at **Bowden Green**, by Arnold Mitchell.

Bere Court once was a house belonging to Reading Abbey and there are still remains of this abbot's house and vaults of an abbot's chapel now bricked up. The present building is early eighteenth-century red brick, comfortably and squarely set out among lawns in a wooded valley. The fine walled garden is on a hill above. The entrance hall and staircase hall beyond are in the Adam style and one room has a Chinese wallpaper (1939), probably the last to come to England. Near is Maidenhatch, a half-timbered late-Victorian house by W. Ravenscroft.

Pangbourne Church has a pretty brick tower of the eighteenth century; the body of the church was rebuilt in a dull Decorated style in flint with stone dressings by Woodman, 1866. Concealed by the organ is an Elizabethan monument to Sir John Davis (1625).

PEASEMORE [map 15]. High up in chalk country where the downland scenery changes to arable and copses as it approaches Newbury. The village has many attractive brick cottages and barns, almost all thatched. There are also a few modern villas. The church was rebuilt in 1842 in a plain Perpendicular style and has a graceful stone spire rising out of the trees. Its interior was sumptuously refurnished later in the century and again in 1910. There is a brass to Thomas Stampe, 1636, and a stone tablet to William Coward, 1769, whose inscription asks grandeur to read and blush when it hears how much good he did with his small means.

PURLEY [map 17] is beside a beautiful winding reach of the Thames, but unfortunately the gap of hill in which it lies has had to accommodate the main railway and the main road, so that it is neither so rural nor so elegant as it might be. It has two large houses. The older, Purley Hall, is approached through an elaborate Gothik lodge in rusticated flint, with cobweb windows. It is a house of the early seventeenth century with many alterations carried out a hundred years later. It has much carved woodwork and some eighteenth-century painting. It is of brick and stone, and well placed in trees looking, from its north front, down hill to a rustic flint pavilion of the eighteenth century, beyond a small lake—Warren Hastings lived here while awaiting trial. Purley Park is a large, plain, white building in Wyatt's most severe Classic manner, and was built in 1795. Its park, stretching to the river bank, was ruined by the railway which divided it in two, and isolated the house on its wedge of high ground from the low-lying church which is now neighboured by a settlement where bungalows and wire are disposed about occupation roads.

The church was rebuilt by Street, 1870–7, who kept the seventeenth-century brick tower, dated on a plaque 1626, with the Bolingbroke arms, and also dated 1739—when it was largely refaced. The church is a simple building without strong marks of its author's hand. The monuments are collected at the west end, many of them under the tower, out of sight from the body of the church. A tablet with reclining figures is dated 1632, and there are some chaste eighteenth-century tablets. A Flaxman-like relief carving, dated 1818, showing several mourning figures, has distinction.

PUSEY [map 4]. The little limestone village is an estate dependency and its modest stone-roofed houses and cottages, almost all pre-Victorian, are on the edge of a large beech-timbered park. Beyond the church and last of the cottages a farm road goes to the huge oval earthwork of Cherbury Camp with its triple mound. Pusey House (1753), ascribed to John Wood of Bath, is a model house of its period, consisting of a large central block with low projecting wings. The public road curves through beech plantations arranged in clumps in the picturesque style of the early nineteenth century so that otherwise flat, dull landscape is given variety and vistas. And from the road may be seen the severe ashlar-faced entrance front of the house. The garden front is of such carefully dressed limestone that its effect is almost of white brick. It looks down to a lake with a Chinese bridge and circular temple and through a clearing to the distant downs. The interior has much Adam-style plasterwork. There is a forester's house at Pusey Common wood (p. 81).

The church is a strange little building looking rather like an Italianate villa (p. 78). The body of it was built in 1745 and the tower and present interior fittings date from about a hundred years later. It contains these objects of beauty: (1) A slab (formerly in the vestry) to Henry Doggett and his wife, 1399. This has incised drawing and inscription, is a rarity and is little known. (2) A panel of German, or Low Countries, carved woodwork, coloured, showing the Entombment, of about 1600. (3) Two seventeenth-century tablets to the Dunch family with cherubs and arms. (4) The Jane Pusey monument by Scheemakers (pp. 60, 61). (5) Moulded plaster (or Coade stone) Royal Arms. (6) Hatchments. (7) The glass: the east window (Crucifixion) is by O'Connor, 1848, and north and south chancel windows are by Wailes and of about the same date. All are good and colourful examples of their artists' work at the period. The south window is in Wailes' 'little-figure' thirteenth-century style.

RADLEY [map 6] is two places, between which is a railway station and cluster of new brick villas. One place is the old village of Radley, consisting of some old thatched cottages among streams by the Thames. Here is neither church nor inn, but the peace of a road which is a dead end and a view across the river of the woods of Nuneham Park. The other place consists of Radley Hall, now the public school Radley College, and the parish church, approached from Oxford by a long elm avenue.

Radley Hall still remains, an eighteenth-century brick house, large, square and of three storeys, on an eminence in a wide park and with school buildings near it. The house was started in 1727 and added to later in the century. The fine furniture which it and other parts of the school contain was imported by William Sewell, who founded Radley College in this house in 1847 and thought it would be good for the boys to be surrounded by works of art. Because the school was, and is, Tractarian, some of the best furnishings are in the chapel, itself a not very inspired building in a free Perpendicular style of brick and stone by Sir Thomas Jackson, 1895. Jackson also designed the large aisled dining hall, 1910. The other considerable additions to the College consist of a gateway tower and adjoining block by A. H. Ryan-Tenison, 1904, again in a free Perpendicular style in brick and stone beside brick buildings by E. Swinfen Harris, 1875–8. The school buildings are spaciously laid out and the conflicting styles of architecture—free Perpendicular, genuine eighteenth-century and ordinary 'school' architecture—harmonize because of their luxuriant park setting.

Wick Hall, off the road to Abingdon, is a rebuilding of 1889–90, with further old-world additions made five years later.

Radley parish church is a stone building with a collection of sculptured eighteenth-century altar tombs in the churchyard, a Perpendicular tower and rebuilt Decorated transept. All the rest of the church is late fifteenth-century, the windows being mostly square-headed Tudor. The interior is dark and lofty and the south aisle is separated from the arcade by wooden columns. As the visitor grows accustomed to the darkness, he realizes that here is the grandest collection of heraldic glass of the fifteenth and sixteenth centuries to be found in any parish church in Berkshire. It glows with amber, green and red. The arms of Henry VII are in the east window, and in one of the south windows of the chancel are the arms of Henry VI. In other windows are the arms of Henry VIII and Richard III. The west window contains a portrait said to be of Henry VII, and there are other portraits and scriptural scenes in the east window. Much of this glass, which must have been designed for elsewhere, is large in scale for such small windows. It was given

to the church in 1840 when Thomas Willement set it with armorial glass of his own—scarcely distinguishable from the original—in attractive and varied grisaille work which throws up the brightly coloured achievements. The seventeenth-century stalls in the chancel remind one of an Oxford college chapel and above the stalls are Gothic panelling and canopies. The medieval oak canopy of the pulpit is said originally to have hung over the Speaker's chair in the Houses of Parliament. One may well wonder that a small country church can bear the burden of so great an addition of old glass and woodwork. Yet there is no sense of over-crowding, but instead one of mysterious richness.

READING [map 18], (pp. 84–87). This, the capital of the county, is a much-maligned town. Too many people see it only from the railway and dismiss it as a modern place as they glide past a china orchard of electric transformers, the gay colours of Sutton's seed beds, Huntley & Palmer's biscuit factory and the castellated red-brick gaol (1833) where Oscar Wilde languished. Motorists horrified by the hideous villa-dom along the road from London after Waterer's Floral Mile, infuriated by the long traffic wait at the Grecian Cemetery gates (H. Briant, 1842) with Doric chapels among the tombs, are too upset to notice the noble lines of late Georgian terraces along the London Road (p. 86). They only recover in time to see the curious curve of villas on the by-pass to the Bath Road (p. 85). Even shoppers along Broad Street and Oxford Road, now the main shopping streets of the town, can hardly fail to be startled by McIlroy's fantastic building designed at the beginning of this century by Mr Frank Morris, an affair of stepped gables and corbelled balconies in red and yellow glazed bricks and granite all resting, apparently, on two tall storeys of plate glass. It was Mr Frank Morris who designed in yellow terra-cotta the even more amazing Pearl Assurance buildings in Station Road (p. 87). His hand may be seen in the new streets that run from Broad Street to the station and his gables appear above other commercial buildings in the town. Eventually, he became a follower of the Rev J. H. Smyth-Pigott and quitted Reading with his family to take up residence in 'The Abode of Love' in Somerset.

Thus with its railwayside industrialism, its miles of hard red suburbs and the weird commercial architecture at its centre, Reading at superficial glance seems hideous. Yet the space between the London Road on the south and the railway on the north is full of decent architecture as befits the capital of a county. It is mostly Georgian and early Victorian. No town in the south of England hides its attractions more successfully from the visitor. Its good architecture may best be described in terms of the history of the town, which divides itself sharply into halves.

Until 1539 it was ecclesiastical, for Reading Abbey, re-founded by Henry I in 1121, was one of the six great abbeys of England. It stands on a hill on the tongue of land between the Thames and the Kennet, which is the core of the old town. Kings and Queens stayed at the Abbey, an English Parliament was held in its great hall. The body of its royal founder still lies in Reading under the Roman Catholic Schools, north of the Abbey ruins. Reading, Colchester and Glastonbury alone of the Benedictine abbeys held out against the efforts of Henry VIII to dissolve them. The last Abbot, Hugh of Faringdon, was an old and pious man when that arch civil-servant Thomas Cromwell, Wolsey's tool, Henry's lackey and child of the Devil, condemned him to death without trial. The aged Abbot Hugh was executed with two other priests outside the Abbey gate near Forbury Gardens on a platform which, as the *Victoria County History* describes it 'was decked with the gallows for partially hanging, the knife for disgustingly mutilating the still living body, and the caldron of boiling pitch into which to fling the limbs when the quartering was accomplished'. The Abbey gateway of flint and stone, as seen at present, is largely the work of Sir Gilbert Scott (1861). Of the enormous Abbey there only remain dull and massive walls of flint with hardly any sculptured stones among them, for these were pillaged to build churches in more pious times and grottoes in the eighteenth century (e.g. at Park Place, *see* REMENHAM). Though a plaque tells one that the well-known 'Sumer is y-cumen in' was written hereabouts it is as hard to believe among the hooting of nearby trains and the hum of the biscuit factory as it is to believe that Henry I lies below the ground not a hundred yards away.

The medieval churches of Reading were violently restored by Victorians. The most attractive of them is St Lawrence's near the Abbey. Bombs in the Hitler war deprived it of its plenitude of Victorian glass, and now that most of the windows are clear-glazed one is able to appreciate the beautiful range of fifteenth-century square-headed windows in the north aisle and the old wooden roof to that aisle. The rest of the church is still very much an 1882 'restoration', except for a noble tower arch and some seventeenth and eighteenth-century monuments of which the best is that to John Blagrave, the mathematician (1611). St Mary Butts, in the centre of the town, is large and towny, with a chequer-board tower of flint and limestone seen at its best from Hosier Street to the west of it. The big, dark cemented interior, with dormer windows lighting the nave, has a painted monument (1635) to William Kendrick with kneeling figures, one panel of enamelled glass (*c.* 1810) in the south aisle and a pretty window in the north aisle (dated 1839). In the tower are many decent late Georgian tablets.

St Giles', in Southampton Street, was so enlarged in 1873 that it is practically all of that date. Its interior is impressive from its aisled and transeptal vastness. Greyfriars was a friary church put to secular uses until it was reconstructed in 1863 by that dull architect W. H. Woodman. He preserved its noble Decorated arcade, which is the finest example now left in stone of the great ecclesiastical history of Reading. The same architect designed the long red-brick range of Reading School (1870–1) on a hill above the University. This school is also a relic of ecclesiastical Reading for it was certainly in existence in 1486 near the Abbey and possibly was founded earlier. Archbishop Laud and Sir Thomas White, the Lord Mayor of London and founder of St John's College, Oxford, were two of its most distinguished pupils.

After Abbot Hugh's death, Reading's history is one of worldly success. With each wave of riches, the traces of the former wave have been overlaid, so that Reading's visible relics of earliest material prosperity are hard to find. This prosperity is founded on the town's geographical position. The two chief rivers of the county meet here and the Thames has for long been navigable to London. The main coaching road to Bath passed through the town. In 1716 the Kennet was made navigable to Newbury. In 1794 the Kennet and Avon canal was started, so that groceries and spices from the port of Bristol had no longer to come round by sea to London but arrived in the Reading shops probably earlier than they came to the metropolis. Four years earlier the canal from Oxford to Birmingham had been constructed and thus by the Thames to Oxford, Reading was connected with the Midlands. Its nearness to London gave it an advantage over Abingdon and Newbury, and this advantage was pressed further when the Great Western Railway in 1840 built Reading Station, in the form of one long platform, on its main line from London to Bristol. Trains ran every hour to London from 8.0 a.m. to 8.55 p.m. and fast trains accomplished the journey in seventy-five minutes. All this transport, instead of taking trade from the town, increased it, so that Reading, long chief town of the county by reason of its abbey, Royal and Parliamentary associations and its assize courts, has become also the largest town.

In the seventeenth century its two chief trades were cloth and brick and tiles. Reading's most benevolent clothier was John Kendrick (d. 1624), who left money for almshouses and schools and for the building of a large brick building round a quadrangle for the employment of poor spinners. This was nick-named 'The Oracle' and was demolished in the last century. Its wooden doors, early Renaissance style, are preserved on the Tilehurst Road. In the days when Reading broadcloth was famous, the town must have been mostly one of three-storey houses, timber-framed or of brick and tile-hung. The only considerable survivals are a house called Lynford in Castle Street with panelled interior, the *Sun Inn* almost opposite, the Phoenix Assurance Offices in the Market Place and, with its back to Hosier Street, an extremely picturesque brick building of late sixteenth century called Lady Vachell's House, now tenements. It has four tile-hung gables and ashlar and flint are mixed with the pink brick of its walls. The earliest brickwork in Reading is on the staircase turret (fifteenth century) to St John's Hospital, later Reading school, which may be seen at the back of the Town Hall.

By the eighteenth century the cloth trade had declined, but almost every other trade was carried on, pin-making, dyeing, tanning, bell-founding, stained-glass painting, to name a few. In 1723, the *Reading Mercury*, the third oldest provincial newspaper in Britain, was founded. In 1785, Simonds' Brewery was founded (that same firm which has destroyed so many old Berkshire inn signs, replacing them with tin signs of standard pattern with a red hop leaf in the centre) and in 1789 Cock's sauce factory (now in King's Road) was founded in Duke Street. This age may be described as coaching Reading. Castle Street and London Street are its earliest and most representative survivals. Its most handsome house is Holybrook House in Castle Street, a dark red-brick building of three storeys, with handsome baroque doorcase and with plasterwork inside. Many of the houses of various eighteenth and early nineteenth century dates in this street on Castle Hill (p. 84) which ascends westwards have panelled rooms and elegant brickwork, though none of this brickwork is comparable to that in Newbury. London Street is approached from the town centre by the narrow and elegant single-span bridge of Portland stone (1788) known as High Bridge, over the Kennet. It is wide and spacious, the handsomest street in Reading, with a pleasing variety of brick and stone buildings, mostly Georgian. But the impressive stone Ionic front of the Primitive Methodist church (1866) is one of the greatest adornments to the street. An earlier Non-Conformist building may be mentioned here, Castle Street Congregational chapel (founded 1837) with its pleasant interior of that date; though the earliest-founded dissenting chapels in Reading were King's Road Baptist (1640) and Broad Street Congregational (1672), both rebuilt.

The next and best phase of building may be termed Canal Reading (*c.* 1790–*c.* 1840). A distinct local domestic style in brick now appears. For the most part it is unadorned, depending almost entirely on the use of local pale red bricks with an occasional string course or cornice of stucco, and the subtle relation of window to wall-space. The brickwork of the old Town Hall (1786), which can be seen from St Lawrence's churchyard, is beautiful. Its interior was 'Italianized' in the eighteen-forties. Grey Friars Vicarage, ascribed to Sir John Soane, and built about 1810, is the beau ideal with its curved flanking walls with Soane-style doorways in them, its modest two-storey front and well-arranged chimney stacks. The stately brick building on the corner of Crown Street and London Street is also ascribed to Soane, and so are the noble pairs of villas at South Hill. It is likely, however, that this great architect, who was a local man born in nearby Whitchurch, Oxon, was emulated by Reading builders of his time. His continuous deep grooves round semi-circular-headed doors and windows, his bands of Greek-key-pattern ornament and his original and satisfactory severity all appear in many houses of Reading. The only building known to be his which survives in Reading is the Portland stone obelisk (1804) in the Market Place. But this is insulted by the stone ventilating tower of a public lavatory, erected just beside it. Prospect Park (or Prospect Hill Park) is an early Regency building that now serves the Public Recreation Ground. It has a pillared front facing downhill, with side wings set back with flat domes and first-floor verandahs. The well-proportioned rooms are featureless. A picturesque grotto (above ground) remains at one side. The longest range of canal Reading architecture is the beautiful Bath stone façade of Queen's Crescent, off London Street (c. 1830). The Dispensary (1802) in Chain Street is a fine building of this tradition. For a time in the middle of the nineteenth century, Reading seems to have favoured stone and temporarily to have thrown over brick except for its smaller artisan houses. The stone was carried by canal, and later by Great Western, from Box and Bath. The centre of the magnificent brick front of the Royal Berkshire Hospital (1839) belongs to this period (p. 84) and was designed, like the Cemetery, by the local man, H. Briant. Wings were skilfully added in the same Greek style by other architects later in the last century. Shortly before 1840 the Crown Commissioners sold Orts Farm on the east side of the town and some other fields on Castle Hill. On the first site the Greek-style houses of the King's Road were built and later Italianate Eldon Square (p. 85) and the unfinished Victoria Square later still, all of stone. The Castle Hill Estate has no buildings on it which live up to the grand baroque entrance piers to be seen on the left of the main road going west up Castle Hill. How beautiful this thriving town must have looked in late Georgian times may be judged by the numerous aquatints which artists made of it, and the best series is W. H. Timms' *Twelve Coloured Views of Reading*, 1823.

Though the two most famous Reading firms were founded in Georgian times, Sutton's Seeds, 1806, and Joseph Huntley's biscuits, 1826, the firms grew to their present size and celebrity later in the century. Both Suttons and Huntley & Palmers are associated with philanthropy. The intelligent botanizing family of Sutton helped to relieve the Irish famine of 1847, and later promoted the Seeds Adulteration Act by which it was made illegal to sell dead seed. In 1841 the Quaker George Palmer joined the Huntleys and invented a machine for cutting and stamping biscuits. Free trade in wheat greatly helped the business. By 1911 the Palmer family was rich enough to endow Reading University (started as a University Extension College in 1892) with £150,000, to which Lady Wantage, of Lockinge, contributed a further £50,000 and the Overstone Library. The University has wisely bought land near to Reading on Whiteknights Park (*see* EARLEY) and saved it from speculation; it has also admirably preserved some of the Georgian Terraces as part of its buildings on the London Road. Of the new buildings the men's Hall of Residence, Wantage Hall, in Redland Road by C. Steward Smith (1908), in a red brick of the Tudor style, is the pleasantest.

Late-Victorian Reading, the long lines of hard red-brick buildings one sees from train or motor-car, the greater detached residences, sub-Norman–Shaw or Maidenhead river style, which hide behind tree-lined avenues climbing to vast Victorian churches, the garish shopping streets already mentioned have undoubtedly given the town a name for ugliness which a superficial visitor might well continue to give it. Despite this glossy modern face, smeared with hard red, Reading has resolutely remained Reading and held out against the encroaching villa-dom of London. It is still very much a Berkshire town and its cattle market with brick Victorian Classic buildings is handsome and important. Prominent buildings of this later period are the Town Hall by Alfred Waterhouse (1875) enclosing the old one and the additions (1879–82) by Thomas Lainson. Though these are not beautiful they contain an excellent Museum, Library and Art Gallery. The most distinguished modern public building is the County Offices in Forbury designed by Newman & Hall (1911), a Wren-style building of brick and Portland stone, with elegant chimney stacks.

A curiosity in the gardens opposite is a lion made of cast-iron, said to be the largest statue of its kind in existence, sculpted by George Simonds and erected in 1886 to the memory of men of the 2nd Battalion 66th Berkshire Regiment who fell in the Afghan War at Maiwand in 1880.

Among the Victorian and later churches which served Reading's final expansion, the most distinguished are undoubtedly Woodyer's Christ Church, 1862–74 (p. 99) and William White's St Stephen's (Orts Road), 1865 (p. 87). St Mary's (Castle Street) (p. 86) has a Classic tower of 1798 and an attractive eighteenth-century Non-Conformist interior which has been Victorianized. St Giles' (Southampton Street), All Saints', 1866 (Downshire Square, north-west of Castle Hill), and St Luke's (Redlands Estate), 1885, are large churches by J. P. St Aubyn, lofty and elaborate (St Giles' was a rebuilding of 1873, keeping a few old features), but undistinguished. St Bartholomew's (London Road) is by Waterhouse, 1879, with a chancel by Bodley of 1898, and later additions. It has been spoiled by whitewashing the brick interior. St Saviour's (near Coley Recreation Ground), an unfinished, apsidal church by F. W. Albury, 1887, is not unimpressive, in a Pearsonesque way. St John the Evangelist (Watlington Street), by W. A. Dixon, 1874, is a ragstone, polychromatic building, thick and curly, with later Clayton and Bell glass. St Mark's (Prince of Wales Avenue), by Hoare and Wheeler, 1903, has rounded stone ribs crossing from the arcades against narrow aisles. St Agnes' is a brick, pantiled building of 1938 on a new estate to the east of the Basingstoke Road. St George's, Tilehurst is by S. Gambier Parry, 1884. The Roman Catholic churches include the Norman-Revival building in the Forbury Gardens, 1840, by E. Welby Pugin (with ambulatory and other additions by W. C. Mangan, 1925), which has a dark and impressive interior; and a pantiled, Byzantine church, also by Mr Mangan, 1926, in the Tilehurst Road.

REMENHAM [map 12]. Three hamlets, Remenham itself beside the river, Remenham Hill, and Aston Ferry, are in the wide loop of the Thames below Henley—with Temple Island (its pavilion is an eighteenth-century adornment of Fawley Court, in Bucks.) in the river opposite Remenham church, and Park Place up the river bank beyond Henley. The most prominent buildings in Remenham are the rectory, a large red-brick house of the 1860's, and the church, a Norman-revival flint and stone building almost wholly of 1870, with an apse, which is without architectural distinction, though pretty enough. A brass and a few recast features from the medieval building remain.

Aston Ferry, approached by riverside lanes and shaded by elms, has an inn called *The Flower Pot* and a few brick and flint cottages. Culham Court, beside it (in Wargrave parish but belonging topographically to Remenham) is a distinguished rectangular red-brick house with pediments, well set above the river. It was built in 1771, and restored, and had Victorian accretions removed by G. Hyslop in the 1930's. Beside it is a celebrated rock garden and across the park from it, set in trees on a riverside backwater, is a pretty Bothy with roughcast walls and Gothic windows.

Park Place is on a hill facing the river above Henley, on the Berkshire side. Its hanging woods with their walks and decorations of the eighteenth century, visited and admired by many eighteenth-century poets and statesmen, visitors to General Conway, still keep something of their plan and shape, but sad inroads have been made on them. At the top of the Happy Valley is a chalk amphitheatre, with tunnels running through it, flanked by artificial Grecian ruins, ascribed to James ('Athenian') Stuart, and the bottom of this grass ride between forest trees is crossed by a bridge of cyclopean rustic stones, brought from Reading Abbey, which carried the road from Henley to Wargrave. The engineer and adviser for the building of this bridge was the Rev Humphrey Gainsborough, brother of the painter. Elsewhere in the grounds are Gothic cottages, a picturesque half-timbered boathouse (nineteenth century), an obelisk formed of the top of the original steeple of St Bride's, Fleet Street, and the forty-five stones of a pre-historic burial chamber transported from Jersey in 1785, and re-erected on the lawn of a white brick house in the park called Temple Combe. Park Place mansion was rebuilt in a florid French Renaissance manner in the early eighteen-seventies. The garden decorations are celebrated in one of Horace Walpole's *Hieroglyphic Tales*. In the nineteenth century Park House had enormous lavender plantations.

RUSCOMBE [map 18]. A few farms and cottages of brick or half-timber, brick and plaster (one of these, Northbury Farm, is the remaining part of the seventeenth-century manor house) are disposed in low-lying fields near the main railway line to Reading. This, seen from the train from London, seems the first real country. The nave and tower of the church are of seventeenth-century brick (1639) and the chancel simple Early English with lancets in hard chalk. A fairly sophisticated restoration has retained some seventeenth-century woodwork in the interior, but there is nothing of real beauty, except the brickwork of the exterior.

SANDHURST [map 26]. On the Surrey border in heathery, military, Wellingtonia-planted surroundings, Sandhurst is almost entirely of nineteenth-century development. Scattered houses and shops occupy the centre, and lying apart are a few large Victorian houses with immense plate-glass windows and free Renaissance decorations (Sandhurst Lodge is one of these), and the church, by itself among quiet fields. This was designed by G. E. Street in 1853, and has a tall Surrey-style tower and shingled spire at the south-west corner. Characteristic of its architect, its exterior is most effective. It has nave and chancel, aisles and chapels, and the interior is darkened by late-Victorian glass by O'Connor and others. The lurid east window is by Ward and Hughes, and the late Victorian wall decorations by Heaton and Butler.

The Royal Military College, in spreading lawns, winding drives and trim plantations, has several vast blocks of military character of the early twentieth century, disposed behind the original Wyatt building (p. 78). The Royal Military Memorial Chapel, in a free Byzantine style, has a great wealth of coloured marble, stained glass and mosaic work of the early nineteen-twenties. There is a brick mission church in the village, 1889. For Wellington College, see CROWTHORNE.

SHAW-CUM-DONNINGTON [map 22]. These two villages, about a mile apart, are on the northern bank of the trout-stocked Lambourn river. South of that river along the roads to Newbury they become suburbs indistinguishable from the town—*see* Smith's Crescent and Donnington Square under NEWBURY.

Shaw has a mill and some old cottages and far more new ones. Dark yews, and old brick garden walls on the west of the village prepare one for the magnificent brick Elizabethan Shaw House, 1581 (p. 21). It is an H-shaped building whose principal entrance front is seen from the road to Shaw church. Dark red Tudor bricks, stone mullions and transoms to the large windows, stone Renaissance and contemporary porch, steep gables and stone quoins and strongly moulded string courses give it an appearance of lightness and symmetry. The north and west fronts have been spoiled by modern additions but the east front is the most charming of all. It has three gables. Below the central one is an effective arrangement of windows designed to show off the small classic garden entrance and flight of steps below it. Below the two outside gables are projecting windowed bays extending through first and ground floors. The weathered texture of the external stone and brick work of Shaw House is itself beautiful, but even this is eclipsed by the skilful arrangement of windows and chimneys and the satisfactory proportions of leading to mullions and transoms, and these in their turn to wall space. In proportion it is a Tudor

building with newly discovered Classic mouldings in the stonework. The house is now used as a county day school for boys. Its interior is mainly eighteenth century in character, with a fine oak staircase in the east wing. The house was built by Thomas Dolman, a successful Newbury cotton spinner. Shaw church, near the house, is a stone Norman-revival building of 1840 by J. Hanson with a chancel by W. Butterfield, 1878. It is awkward without and well-kept within.

Donnington is an old and insignificant village dominated by the large houses of which it mostly consists. Donnington almshouses on the Oxford road show a gabled front, a projecting porch with Queen Elizabeth's arms set in it and wealth of diagonally set, brick chimney stacks. The pretty square courtyard is cloistered. Besides Donnington Castle (p. 20), and Donnington Grove (pp. 73, 74, 75), there are in this parish Donnington Castle House of dark red brick and built in the seventeenth and added to in the eighteenth century; and Donnington Priory, a modest early nineteenth-century Gothic refacing an older house, close to the Oxford road. Some large Victorian and Edwardian country houses ascend the hill to birch-clad, heathery Snelsmore Common.

EAST SHEFFORD [map 14]. A large farmhouse, Italianized in the last century, a rectory and two churches, all in the Lambourn valley comprise this place. Away up the chalk slopes to the south is Oakhanger, a small Victorian house, now a riding school. The old church (p. 60), buried among weeds and willows of the Lambourn river is, externally, like what most small Berkshire churches must have been a century ago. It is white-plastered within and without, with brick eighteenth-century porch, dormer window, small wooden bellcote, sixteenth-century windows (one is Norman), and clear glass. Its interior is ceiled and contains an alabaster tomb of the Fettiplaces with recumbent effigies (*c*. 1450), another Fettiplace tomb of Purbeck with brasses (1524), a helmet and a Hanoverian Royal arms, but the old pews and woodwork have all gone and the floor is white with bat-droppings. The new church, beside the plain and stately late Georgian rectory, is an aisleless, apsidal-ended building in the Decorated style of brick and flint from designs by C. F. Hayward, 1870. Like the old church it is disused and locked. In one of the windows are some pieces of fifteenth-century glass taken from the old church, showing a mitred bishop and the Annunciation.

WEST SHEFFORD [map 14]. This crossroad village with a tiny station has a spreading inn, a prominent brick Methodist chapel, some old brick and thatched cottages, all in a narrow part of the Lambourn valley. The rectory east of the church is of pleasing plain late Georgian local type, two storeys, with low-pitched roof and wide eaves. A few yards south of it at a corner of the road is the manor house, now a farm. From the farmyard above the church one may see the sixteenth-century brick and flint work of the old house. It was much altered in the next two centuries and contains a sixteenth-century panelled room. The church was severely restored inside by J. W. Hugall in 1870 when it was re-roofed, re-pewed, re-floored and its stonework renewed. The Transitional tower arch, south door and font remain.

Shefford Woodlands is a crossroad hamlet southward, towards Hungerford. Its little church, once a Wesleyan chapel, was transformed to its present loved state over the years from 1910 by the late Captain A. C. Burmester, who did most of the wood carving himself. The Norman stoup came from Avington and the two altar tables (one Elizabethan) from the parish church.

SHELLINGFORD [map 4]. A small, limestone, elm-shaded village of the Vale consisting mostly of neat stone cottages rebuilt in a Cotswold style at the beginning of this century. The gabled Elizabethan house by the church was once a rectory. It has stone mullioned windows and a sixteenth-century oak staircase. South of it and beyond the churchyard are stone-walled gardens and sloping fields going down to the river Ock and wood beyond, all suggesting a former park-like grandeur belonging to the manor house which has disappeared. Kitemore House, north of the parish and near Faringdon, is a vast late-Victorian Tudor–Renaissance style building in stone with coniferous plantations.

The pretty church has a stone spire (rebuilt 1848) and several carved limestone tombs of the seventeenth and eighteenth centuries in the churchyard. The church itself was much altered in 1625 when the present porch and flat tie-beams were constructed and the nave rebuilt. The south doorway is rich late Norman and the chancel arch and priest's door in the chancel are of this period. In the nave a south window has many fragments of fifteenth-century glass. The chancel has large seventeenth- and eighteenth-century marble monuments. The best are Mary Packer (1719) and Sir Edward Harnes with portrait bust (1710), both in Baroque style. Simpler and equally elegant are the Adam-style marble monuments to the second (1780) and third (1802) Lords Ashbrook.

SHINFIELD [map 25]. The old village and church are in green clayey pasture between two main roads out of Reading. The village consists of new brick buildings connected with mechanized farming and dairying research. What were once country houses on high ridges down the main roads have gradually sold themselves to ribbon builders, and finally have been taken over by schools or service departments, the last bringing slums of nissen huts set on dry ground beneath Wellingtonias. The big houses have been deprived of architecture, the smaller ones never had any. Only Highlands at Spencer's Wood in the west of the parish survives uninsulted. It is a plain late-Georgian-style stucco building with a wide westward view. On the main road near its gate is a small, hard brick church of 1908.

Three Mile Cross is mostly modern main-road villas, though Miss Mitford's unimposing cottage survives. The quiet Berkshire of holly trees, fenced parks and deep, shady lanes she so beautifully described is hardly to be found today. Where there is a fork of the main road to Whitley Wood a mile nearer Reading, is a startling and attractive village school in flint with stone dressings by H. Woodyer, 1861.

Shinfield parish church has a beautiful red-brick tower, with some fanciful brick patterning of 1654. There are only a few medieval features in the rest of the building, and the interior is pleasing only because of these features: painted Royal Arms, 1660; hatchments; monument (late Elizabethan) of two children kneeling; seventeen-century Lewknor monument, with well-carved figures of girls holding back curtains; other seventeenth- and eighteenth-century tablets. Sir Gilbert Scott restored the church 1855-7, but there has been much alteration and much use of cement and oak, since.

SHIPPON [map 5] is some old limestone cottages with red-tiled roofs in flat orchard land near Abingdon, much disturbed by an enormous aerodrome. The little nave and chancel church of stone with crocketed sanctus bellcote is an early, well-proportioned, serviceable and unpretentious work of Gilbert Scott (1855) in his usual middle-pointed style. The stained east window is by Hardman.

SHOTTESBROOK [map 19, near White Waltham]. Shottesbrook Park (pp. 75, 76), a sixteenth- and eighteenth-century house, was transformed by Gothicizing in the early nineteenth century. It is cased in patterned brick, with turrets and plaster dressings. It was much altered inside in the first decade of the twentieth century by Dunn and Watson, architects, who at the same time glorified a small, old brick house and constructed its elaborate formal garden which flanks the south side of the churchyard.

The church, of flint and stone, is one of the most celebrated Decorated churches in the country (p. 5), obviously the work of one architect, and had a great deal of attention paid to it by Victorian restorers, one of whom was William Butterfield. But, though much of its texture was removed, it remains in proportion and design an unusually impressive building, in its main structure entirely of the late fourteenth century. The building is cruciform, with large transepts and north and south porches, the nave slightly shorter than the chancel, the gabled roofs high and tower and slender spire rising above the crossing. In many cruciform churches the tower and spire seem to oppress the cross below them, but at Shottesbrook the steep-pitched roofs are gathered up towards the slender ribbed spire and give the whole building a soaring effect. There is deeply-moulded curvilinear tracery in all the windows. The interior walls are white and some of the glass clear, so that there is plenty of light on the details. There is original coloured glass in some tracery lights. The sedilia (south of the chancel) and 'founder's tomb' crossing the north transept, with its miniature vaulting (p. 14), are delicate original details. There is an alabaster 'coffin' monument, some excellent brasses (including the knight and frankelein, p. 7) and some seventeenth-, eighteenth- and nineteenth-century tablets. The best of these are a bust in a curtained niche to Sarah Cherry, 1714, and a delicate plaque of a naval battle on a tablet of 1747. There are some prettily-carved tombstones by the churchyard path. William Butterfield published a book on the church, 1844, and Arnold Mitchell another book, 1885. Benjamin Ferrey reproduced the entire design of the building in his Kingswood church, Surrey.

The house and church have associations with the Non-Jurors in the reign of William III, when Francis Cherry, the pious and learned Jacobite, was squire.

SHRIVENHAM [map 7] has recently become two places. The larger and newer is a military college in Ministry of Works brick and stone Georgian, with a steepled canteen, erected from designs by another Government department. Estates of architect-designed red-brick villas, graded in size according to ranks of their inhabitants, adjoin it. This Shrivenham came into existence when Lord Courtown sold Beckett Park shortly before 1939, on whose land the present buildings were erected. Beckett Park was rebuilt 1831-4 in a picturesque gabled Tudor style in stone, from designs by William Atkinson. It is still surrounded by woods and has been allowed to retain its lake and late seventeenth-century summerhouse.

Old Shrivenham is on the main road from Oxford to Swindon. There are long and beautiful thatched rows of stone cottages at a corner of the road by the main entrance to Beckett Park and in a side road east of the church. Only wires and stout poles and tarmac disturb the spreading main street which consists mostly of modest stone, two-storey houses. Of these, the most distinguished is Elm Tree House, a late seventeenth-century building by the walled lane to the church, with steep stone-tiled roof, dormers and wide eaves, and moulded central door—as charming a small house as one could wish to see. The early Victorian Methodist chapel in stone, Gothik, is also on this side of the street. At the Swindon end of the place is a commodious stone-roofed and stone-walled War Memorial Hall in the Cotswold Tudor style. The railway station south of the village and near Bourton is the only station in the county to retain its original 1840 Great Western Tudor character. It is of limestone from Box, and the waiting-room has early Victorian furniture.

The large parish church is, like St Catherine Cree in the City of London, one of the last examples of late Gothic in England, and one of the first of Renaissance style. It was rebuilt (1632-40) in the form of a north and south aisled oblong (three bays west and two bays east) round a central late fourteenth-century tower. The window tracery is Tudor.

The columns are of the Renaissance Tuscan order with a very pronounced entasis. The interior, despite many beautiful furnishing and monuments, disappoints because the walls have been stripped of their plaster and repointed with cement, and too much money in about 1900 was spent cutting down box-pews, altering the woodwork and displaying heating pipes. There are, however, white marble and gilt monuments (Wildman, 1713; Barrington, not dated but of same period), these unsigned and in the Baroque style; grand inscribed slate floor slabs of the seventeenth and eighteenth centuries; a yellow and white marble monument to Anne Barrington, 1745, by T. Paty of Bristol; a white marble urn on a pedestal supported by an angel, to another Barrington, 1795, designed by James Wyatt, with sculpture by Richard Westmacott; a large tablet (Elizabeth Hale, 1721); armorial glass in the east window, 1505, 1607 and 178–, the last by Egginton of Handsworth; Jacobean pulpit and sounding board; Jacobean altar table in vestry; three eighteenth-century brass candelabras; 1764 Royal Arms in the porch and commandment boards of the same date; a hanging pyx in the form of a triple crown designed by J. N. Comper for the crypt of St Mary Magdalene's Church, Paddington, London.

SINDLESHAM, see BEAR WOOD

SONNING [map 18]. White and cream-walled and brick houses decorated with roses, honeysuckle, jasmine and clematis, carefully trained to climb over the corners of some of the old tiled roofs, line the streets of this rich river resort which is undisturbed by a main road and tinged (even on a grey day out of season) with an Edwardian holiday, or musical-comedy, gaiety. The bridge, of early seventeenth-century brick, is of mellow beauty. The Deanery Garden (p. 109), a brick house of genius by Sir Edwin Lutyens, set within an old brick wall which the architect preserved and used, gives distinction to the centre of the village. The house, which was built for the founder of *Country Life*, is very much in character in Sonning and in its picturesque solidity and its feeling of comfort in rich simplicity was a revolutionary essay which had an influence. In the short village streets are many seventeenth- and eighteenth-century houses, or parts of houses, including Falcon House (and The Red House), Sonning Farm, The Vicarage and Grove House; but the effect is that they have all been judiciously altered according to an agreeable kind of small, collective, Edwardian feeling for picturesque comfort: a character that is at once set, if one enters Sonning over the bridge out of Oxfordshire, by the black-and-white *White Hart* Inn (Leonard Stokes, architect). A doctor's house in white stucco is a chaste Greek-revival building in the midst of this cultivated village landscape, heightening it by contrast. The village schools are by Woodyer. Holme Park, now part of the Reading Blue Coat School, had a house of 1810 by Henry Hakewill, but this was rebuilt, 1881, in gabled flint with brick and terra-cotta dressings.

The Bishops of Salisbury had a palace here, which stood to the south of the church. Near the site of it is a comfortable inter-wars residence in modern builder's half-timber, called Bishop's Close. The church is large and has had much money lavished on it; but less sensibility than has the village. The outside walls of flint have been hardened and inside ones cemented, and there is a great weight of modern woodwork and decoration. Bodley stencilled and painted the chancel. The best Victorian window, among many colourful ones, is hidden behind the organ in the chapel: it is a Transfiguration by Wailes, 1853. The tombs include a desk kneeler, 1630, a large tablet with bust in oval, 1653, some figures from an Elizabethan tomb found in a vault at the restoration in 1853, and the Rich monument, 1667, under the tower. In this, four cherubs support a black marble slab like a dining table on which stand two enormous carved white urns. There is also a large Westmacott Jnr., with a mourning figure, 1780, and a spirited brass of 1836 on the south aisle floor to Lord Stowell, with deeply and richly-engraved lions and inscription.

SOTWELL [map 6]. Some picturesque cottages with thatched roofs or tiled roofs among winding, narrow lanes and orchards near Wallingford. One orchard with some extraordinary terraces marks the site of a manor house called Stonhouses (formerly Stonor Hayes). The small yellow-stone church with its spirelet and red ridge-tiles, by S. R. Stevenson, 1884, is one of those new churches of the date that pretended to be a restoration. A few old stones were built in. The architect showed up poorly.

SPARSHOLT [map 8] is one of the most countrified of Berkshire villages. A long elm-shaded street at the foot of the downs with scattered cottages and farms, some of them with half-timber and almost all thatched. The richest is Hall Place, with barge-boards and stone-mullioned windows. Sparsholt House, in a park, south of the high churchyard wall, is a plain brick building of 1722 and later. The church has some beautiful Transitional doorways—that on the north has beakheads and original ironwork on the door—but is, as a whole a well-proportioned Decorated building with flowing tracery in the windows, and some rich details in the chancel—sedilia, Easter Sepulchre and a recess with a panelled tomb and the effigy of a knight. Three wooden effigies lie in other recesses in the south transept (pp. 12, 13). The old roof, some Decorated and Perpendicular glass, an Elizabethan wall tomb with Renaissance details, a much-copied Decorated screen, several brasses, and the grisaille glass, 1847, by O'Connor, in a south chancel window, are other beautiful features. Gargoyles enrich the outside of the building.

SPEEN [map 22]. The Bath Road ascends here westwards from Newbury to a wooded hilltop where is an eighteenth-century monument to the second Battle of Newbury (1644), a Cromwellian victory. Many plain eighteenth-century houses survive from coaching days and some of them were inns. The high brick walls of Benham Park, farther west, flank the Bath Road. The farthest western gate piers came from Hamstead Marshall. The house itself is a large, stone, L-shaped Classic building of three storeys with balustraded parapet. It was built in 1775 and is ascribed to Capability Brown who laid out the finely landscaped park, with its southward view from the house looking across to a lake, for Lord Craven, the owner. On the north entrance front is a terraced garden.

Bagnor, in this parish, is a remote hamlet of brick cottages on the Lambourn river.

Hidden on a slope of trees south of the main road stands Elmore House, a brick early eighteenth-century building with wide southern prospect. North of it is the church which was rebuilt in an uncompromising Decorated style of flint with orange coloured stone dressings in 1860. The tower was added in 1871. Its interior is rich Victorian, in which can be discerned in the north chapel, by the faint light of fragments of old glass set among beautiful dark blue, purple and crimson early Victorian work, two Elizabethan tombs. One is an altar tomb to John Baptiste Castillon (1597) with armoured effigy upon it. The other, an armless effigy to his daughter-in-law (1603). In the tower are many chaste eighteenth-century monuments.

SPENCER'S WOOD, see SHINFIELD

STANFORD DINGLEY [map 16]. A brick-built village in the Pang valley. Its most distinguished building is the old Vicarage, an early Georgian red-brick house with a moulded Ionic door. The Mill House, of rather later date, is also attractive. The church has Transitional features, and the chancel was rebuilt in the eighteenth century in the prevailing brick of the district. The interior is interesting rather than beautiful since its restoration of 1885. There are wall paintings, some of them early thirteenth century but most of 1885, old tiles and brasses. There are old Spanish chestnuts round the churchyard, which is approached through a heavy, war memorial lychgate.

STANFORD-IN-THE-VALE [map 4].

A winding mile of houses of mixed materials, mixed styles and various dates in the elmy, brook-divided middle of the vale. Limestone from Faringdon parish and brick from eighteenth-century local kilns predominate. Most of the buildings are cottages. Starting at the western end of the village the most noticeable buildings are Coxe's Hall, 1690, of stone in the Vanbrugh-esque style used by Townsend of Bristol; farther east, on the right, a sixteenth-century house refaced in the eighteen-thirties but with some stone-mullioned windows; a bright and fancy brick Methodist chapel of the 'seventies; village school by G. E. Street of local stone (c. 1850); the road here bends north to reveal a yellow-washed house with sentinel yews before; a nineteen-thirties Romanesque front to the Congregational church; the parish church on the west of it, the last elm-surrounded; a rectory house—early eighteenth century, two-storeyed, steep-roofed in the manner of Buscot rectory (p. 45); north of the church is Manor Farm in similar style and with panelled interior; a large green is flanked on its north side by concrete and pretentious council houses, but east of them, by the road, is brick eighteenth-century Stanford House, three storeys spoiled by Victorian bays; the road then curves to the brook at **Bow** and some old brick cottages, and up an incline to Pusey.

Stanford Park Farm, in remote lanes east of the parish, is a two-storeyed late Georgian building with remains of an earlier and bigger house. Stanford Place, on the road to Faringdon, is a gabled stone building in the Elizabethan style of about 1840. Nearly opposite it is a square stone lodge, the eaves of whose stone-tiled roof rest on posts forming a verandah and commanding a wonderful view across elms and fields to White Horse Hill.

The parish church stands in a large churchyard on whose south side are many eighteenth- and early nineteenth-century headstones with well-carved lettering and designs. The church has old porches to Early English north and Perpendicular south doors, and western tower (pp. 14, 15), a north aisle, clerestoried nave and large Decorated chancel, whose tracery within and without is in a distinguished flowing style otherwise unknown to this neighbourhood. Inside, the nave has an elaborate Jacobean pulpit and font, the chancel has a brass on the floor to a rector (1398), fragments of glass of the fourteenth century, the same date as the Decorated windows in which it is set. On the south wall of the chancel is a Decorated piscina above which is an octagonal stone tabernacle, carved and crocketed, pinnacled and embattled. This was probably a house for the Blessed Sacrament. Fifteenth-century wooden roofs remain, that of the nave (rebuilt in 1756–57) resting on grotesque corbels. The walls retain their plaster, the Victorian restoration was extensive but inexpensive.

STEVENTON [map 5].

The Georgian and Victorian buildings of this large village line the main Newbury to Abingdon road, and stand round a big green, which this road crosses. At the station, originally called Oxford Road, and built before Didcot, are Tudor-style Company's houses used for board meetings, as this was about half-way from London to Bristol. At right-angles to this road runs a raised flood-path, The Causeway, roughly paved, bordered on both sides by old elms, on the north by a road and on the south by a series of beautiful seventeenth-century houses, all half-timbered and of brick and plaster. One of these has parget plaster work, another an oriel window and the date 1657, others again have stone-built details and all have tiled roofs. The main-line railway cuts through the Causeway, and west of it is one of the most beautiful of these houses (p. 53), also the church and the Priory, an E-shaped house with sixteenth-century features. The flood-path provides a good view of these old houses and also, in the other direc-

tion, of a large development scheme of raw red brick and tile.

The church, quite secluded from the village at its west end, is a picturesque limestone building with good external details and an old lead roof. There is fine Decorated tracery deeply moulded in the south windows. The bare interior has odd proportions and a ribbed barrel roof to nave and chancel. There is stiff-leafed carving on a capital which was no doubt done by the same hands as capitals at North Moreton and East Hendred. The pulpit and almsbox are Jacobean and there are some Perpendicular pews. Bits of Perpendicular grisaille remain in the east window of the south aisle. There are elegant seventeenth- and eighteenth-century tablets and brasses. There are three early windows by Warrington which provide colour and atmosphere in this church. The east window, 1833, has Old Testament subjects below and New Testament ones above, Oxford college chapel style (detail: p. 95). The electric fittings are clumsy.

STOCKCROSS [map 22].

Among conifers and rhododendrons north of the Bath road west of Newbury, this is a model brick half-timber-style village (p. 100) with shop to match, built about 1900 and later. The humble brick church in the Early English style of 1839 is surprisingly beautiful within. It was redecorated by J. N. Comper, who whitened the walls, designed the chancel east window glass and tracery, the alabaster reredos beneath and the superbly proportioned iron screen below the chancel arch. He also hung the nave with brass candelabra and in 1923 added a war memorial south chapel with parclose screen, altar and east window. The screen and chancel are part of a great scheme undertaken by Mr Comper for one of the Manners-Suttons of Benham Park (see SPEEN), which was never finished.

STRATFIELD MORTIMER [map 24].

Fir woods stretch away from Mortimer to the west and south-west into Hampshire, providing its most characteristic scenery. On the higher ground in this direction, **Mortimer Common** has developed since about 1860 into a residential town with shops and villas, in a Woking manner. Here is a brick church, built in 1881. Eastwards, facing pastoral Reading scenery is the older village, with late Georgian and Victorian houses in large gardens with shrubberies and small parks. Several of these are pleasant houses and none of them remarkable architecturally. The church was entirely rebuilt in 1869 from designs by R. Armstrong. It is the sort of church that was being built in expensive suburbs twenty years earlier, and with its broach spire and ragstone walls does not belong in character to this particular part of the country at all. The interior is very impressive in its Victorian way, with its huge scale, many enrichments in stone and marble and its array of glass by O'Connor and others. The additions to the west end were by E. Swinfen Harris, 1893. There is an inscribed Saxon tomb-lid, celebrated archaeologically. A window behind the organ is filled with old glass in a jumbled mosaic. A good deal of it is seventeenth century, but there are earlier fragments, including heads.

STREATLEY [map 10].

The Thames widens here and leaves an island, lock and weir and mill and overhanging woods, all to be viewed from a long bridge crossing to Goring and Oxfordshire. Brick houses and hotels, some of them old, but most of them tile-hung late Victorian 'Queen Anne-style', climb to the main Reading–Oxford road which narrows and roars across the western end of the wall-flowered village. At the crossroads here the road to Aldworth ascends a very steep chalk hill among beech woods. On the right is a picturesque thatched house of late Georgian date. The views from the steep hills on both sides of this road down the Thames Valley down to Reading and Windsor and up to Oxford are dramatic in their foreground and their distances. The hills, the green parklands, poplars and willows mark the winding river. From here what is striking about Streatley is its position, the arrangement of trees which mask or frame the houses and the church—and particularly the colour. Streatley church has a fifteenth-century tower but the rest of the building was rebuilt in a hard, middle-pointed fashion from 1864–5.

STUBBINGS, see MAIDENHEAD

SULHAM [map 17]. A Berkshire Selworthy village, under a beechy hill, which protects it from Reading. Cottages and lodge in the Swiss-revival style (pp. 80, 81) neighbour a spired Gothic church and the plain, Classic stuccoed house, all of 1838–40. The church is of flint and stone, prettily set in a sloping churchyard. A triple stone screen of pointed arches opens into an apsidal chancel which has wooden vaulting painted blue, with gold stars. There is rich 1850 glass, and the Wilder monuments include a beautiful medieval-style one with black outlines and lettering, and a half-figure of a woman drawn in black, 1845.

SULHAMSTEAD ABBOTS [map 24]. A few cottages and farms on coppiced uplands above the Bath Road. The church, beside a yew nearly as big as itself and carefully preserved thatched cottages, is a Surrey or Sussex building with a boarded bellcote supported on timber framing. Transitional and Early English features appear dimly in the Victorianized walls. The golden altar is by J. N. Comper. There is a Royal Arms of 1730.

SULHAMSTEAD BANNISTER [map 24]. Sulhamstead House stands white, Greekly Ionic and imposing on a landscaped southern slope of the Kennet valley. It was largely rebuilt about 1820 and expensively redecorated inside at the beginning of this century. The church of Sulhamstead Bannister, with its school and few brick and tiled cottages, is near the house but not in the parish. This small church (1914) of flint and stone in the Decorated style with western spirelet replaces an interesting building of 1815. A Royal Arms (1694) and hatchments survive.

SUNNINGDALE [map 27]. Served by the Southern electric and bordered on the north by the well-kept fences of Royal property, this is a far from medieval place. It and the adjoining parish of Sunninghill grew up around the large country houses built in the neighbourhood of Virginia Water and Windsor Park at that romantic period at the end of the eighteenth century when heathy tracts and artificial lakes appeared sublime, doubly sublime if they were also not too far, as these two places are not, from arable land and a Royal Palace and a race-course. Sunningdale was formed in 1894 from Old Windsor, miles away across the Great Park. Virginia Water, the largest ornamental lake in England, was made for the Duke of Cumberland in the middle of the eighteenth century. He was the Victor of Culloden and son of George II; founded Ascot Races and lived at Fort Belvedere on the Surrey border. The lake was designed by Thomas Sandby (1721–98), architect and artist, who arranged the Cascade. In the time of the Regent the ruins of a Roman temple from Leptis Magna, Tripoli, were erected by Sir Jeffry Wyatville, and a Swiss cottage was built and conifers were planted on the southern banks contrasting strongly with Sandby's oaks and beeches. The Surrey border crosses the middle of the lake north to south and Coworth Park with its woods on the southern Berkshire bank was a modest house of the mid-eighteenth century added to in late Georgian times in stucco Classic. Sunningdale Park, by James Wyatt (c. 1785), approached between high and winding banks of rhododendrons overshadowed by Scotch firs, sits four-square, severe and late Georgian, on an eminence. Other large houses in the parish are of less account, many of them late Victorian half-timbered. Smaller villa residences arose when the railway came, and motor-cars brought still more along the main roads where private parks were turned into building estates.

Indeed, in the last fifty years, the character of the place has changed from a Royal appendage with country retreats in it, to a place of lamp-posts, laurels and asphalt paths on heathy, sandy soil—Bournemouth without the sea.

The church whose broached spire rises above red Victorian cottages and Wellingtonias, replaced an 1839 building and has chancel, tower and spire all in red brick and stone by G. E. Street, 1861. His east end with separated chapels is effective. The west of the church was finished by J. Oldrid Scott, 1887–8.

SUNNINGHILL [map 27]. The general remarks describing Sunningdale apply here, though this is an older place whose late Norman church on a high hill was rebuilt in 1807 and 1827. Until the eighteenth century it must have been a remote hamlet. Burke, Chesterfield and Bolingbroke visited here. The Mount is a red brick eighteenth-century house; Sunninghill Park, now burned to a shell, was in the Adam style, and stands in a large grassy park with a lake. The park is sadly mauled by contractors at the Ascot end. Silwood Park was another Classic house, one of James Wyatt's grandest buildings; it was pulled down in mid-Victorian times and replaced with a large mid-Victorian Tudor building in red brick and stone with plate-glass windows. It is now an institution. Titness, which was designed by George Basevi in late Georgian stucco Tudor, was lately demolished, and only a picturesque eye-catcher remains. Harewood House is now a model farm. The Berystede Hotel has an admirable Victorian garden. For Buckhurst Park, see WINDSOR GREAT PARK.

The main street of Sunninghill is all Victorian red-brick villas with shops and an Art Nouveau public hall. Only in Sunninghill Park itself and in the lane to the church does one still have the impression that Southern electric London is far away. The church still has a Georgian Gothic exterior with its pointed windows and little battlemented tower. But inside it has been extensively and expensively refurnished.

SUNNINGWELL [map 1]. A limestone village at the foot of a hill, wonderfully preserving its rustic appearance, though Foxcombe Hill is above it, where fair-sized houses for Oxford dons nestle, and to the south and west are the villa-ed outskirts of Abingdon. Beaulieu Court Farm, on the hill east of the village street, is a stone Elizabethan house with eighteenth-century windows. The church is aisleless cruciform, with a square and dignified Perpendicular tower acting as north transept. Most of its architectural detail is fifteenth century, except for the heptagonal west porch, an Oxford college sixteenth-century blend of Gothic and Renaissance (p. 34). This porch, like the rest of the church, was cruelly glazed with tinted glass in 1902. Inside, despite the glazing, the church is very pretty, for a kinder restoration of early Victorian times has left its marks. The plain Victorian pews of the nave have fifteenth-century poppy heads, the nave roof is of the same date, the pulpit is Jacobean.

SUTTON COURTENAY [map 6]. The river Thames traffic uses a cut here, and leaves quiet the main stream which washes a small beach at Sutton pool, among willows and weirs and the lashers of a Victorian paper mill which has recently been pulled down. Most of the fine buildings of this large and delightful village are at the northern end of it where, near the church, the street divides into two and its verges widen into a village green. Sutton was a royal manor and also had connections with Abingdon Abbey for centuries, which accounts for the large early domestic buildings and the grandeur—for a Berkshire village building—of the church. The house, now called Norman Hall (at other times the Court House and Manor Farm), has a large stone hall with doorways of late twelfth-century date. Inside, it has Tudor woodwork and fireplace. The Abbey is a house of the fourteenth and sixteenth centuries, remodelled and covered with stucco later. It has a hall with an old oak roof, with arched principal supports. The Manor House is a plastered, gabled sixteenth-century house, full of panelling and other woodwork, some of it brought from elsewhere. There is a fireplace, with figures and inlaid panels, from the Priory, Steventon. Beside the churchyard, the Vicarage is a beautifully designed eighteenth-century brick house, with a shell porch, and elsewhere in the village are a gabled house dated 1631 and another eighteenth-century house of good brick work. There are also minor houses of beauty, such as the low range of brick almshouses (1818), and several early timber-framed cottages, the whole collection forming a museum of medieval and later domestic architecture. Most of the houses are small enough still to be in private hands. They stand back from the road in well-grown, shady gardens and are not easily inspected, even from outside, as are the stone houses of a town like Burford. There are modern buildings, which increase in numbers on the outskirts, but little in the centre to disturb the gradually built-up visual harmony of the village as a whole.

The church also has grown slowly into a unified whole, and has some work of every century from the twelfth to the twentieth. Its exterior is picturesque, the effect of the grey stonework, which has been well treated, being relieved by the warm brick of the sixteenth-century south porch, with its upper room. There is twelfth-century work, with great character in the mouldings, in the tower and one arch of the south arcade (which was probably originally the chancel arch) and the chancel is Early English, so is the pretty font. But the general interior effect—and it is a grand one, with the symmetrical arcades and wide nave wagon roof—is of a fourteenth-century church. A large and splendid painted Royal Arms surmounts the chancel arch. There are some medieval stalls in the chancel and some old pews in the nave. Eighteenth-century box-pews occupy the aisles. The chancel screen is Perpendicular and the pulpit (brought from elsewhere) Jacobean. Perpendicular glass remains in some windows, including Evangelistic symbols. There is an old stone (side) altar, and some chaste eighteenth-century tablets. Some colourful glass of about 1850 has beauty. The whole effect is somewhat spoiled by the glazing of the east window in a Burne-Jones manner which was done in the nineteen-twenties, and is out of key with everything else in the building.

SWALLOWFIELD [map 25]. Beyond the Reading villas, brick houses and inns lie off the main road to Basingstoke and form a short street that leads up to the lodge of Swallowfield Park. This lodge, like the school next door, is of glowing red bricks with black diamond patterns—decorative work of the 1860's. At the point where the main road crosses the Loddon is an old brick mill with a plain and elegant miller's house in brick with a fanlight over the porched front door.

Swallowfield Park is in its existing form a large Classic house of 1820 by William Atkinson, pupil of Wyatt, who more often built in the Gothic style as at (about this time) Ditton Park, Slough and at Beckett Park, Shrivenham. But he built Swallowfield Park round the remains of an existing house of about 1690, by Talman. Of this house there are remains about a courtyard, a beautifully-carved stone door with a rounded pediment serves as a garden entrance, and there are other details.

The church, which is picturesquely placed with a great yew on a southern-sloping bank on the edge of the park, is a bellcoted building of nave, chancel and large north chapel, much darkened and cemented by Victorians and keeping no untouched medieval features. Internal timbers support the bellcote. There is glass by Ward and Hughes and others. The best things are the Russell monuments, late eighteenth century, not to be admired for any decorative features, but for their simple and good proportions.

THATCHAM [map 23]. This main-road village, once a borough and the unsuccessful rival of Newbury, is chiefly distinguished for the beautiful little roughcast fourteenth-century chapel seen on the right as one approaches the place by the Bath Road from Reading. The tracery of its windows and the niches either side of its west door have rich fifteenth-century mouldings. The timbered roof inside is of this date. Having been used as a chapel of ease to the parish church, it became a Blue Coat school in the eighteenth century, and is still used for secular purposes. The old part of the village runs westward from it and turns a sharp corner which opens on to a green, tree-planted space, while the main road continues westward past more than a mile of modern villas to Newbury. None of the old houses of Thatcham, which are almost all two-storey brick with tiled roofs of the eighteenth and early nineteenth centuries, is distinguished, but round the market square in particular, away from the Bath Road, their effect is that of an old country town unvisited by 'progress'.

The large church stands south-west of the square on an unexpectedly countrified eminence above Kennet meadows. Internally, it shows every sign of the violent restoration of 1852, with new pews, new roofs, almost new chancel and general re-pointing and new vast Norman-style chancel arch to match the genuine Norman south door. There is a water-colour in the vestry of the church before restoration, and eighteenth- and nineteenth-century monuments are in the tower.

THEALE [map 17.] A Bath Road village that retains a flavour of coaching and early motoring. Irregular rows of brick shops, cottages and garages line the short street. The buildings are mostly eighteenth and nineteenth century, but none of them grand or pretentious. On the London side an inn, The *White Hart*, of about 1830, has an unusual and sensible plan. Its two small wings are set at a right-angle, so that windows look up and down the Bath Road from the site, on a curve.

The church is a wonderful early Gothic revival structure, architect E. Garbett 1822 (pp. 88, 89). It has a baptistry on the north side, now a vestry—an imitation octagonal chapter-house. There is an old chantry in the choir, moved here from Magdalen College chapel, Oxford. The chancel, 1892, is by J. Oldrid Scott, with decorations by Bodley.

TIDMARSH [map 17]. The most prominent buildings in the village are the picturesque cottages built along the main road, as estate cottages of Tidmarsh manor, which was itself partly pulled down in 1878, but has early eighteenth-century remains. The cottages were built about 1830, and are pleasant examples in half-timber and brick, of the medievalizing of the period.

The church has late Norman walls and proportions and a much decorated south doorway and arcaded font of the period, but it is given distinction by its six-sided apse of the thirteenth century, which has simple and beautiful vaulting and windows. These windows were glazed by Thomas Willement in about 1840, with purple and crimson hatchwork with medallions, but his work has been replaced by very poor late-Victorian windows. The timber framing of the bellcote, inside the church, was carved in imitation of Transitional stonework by an early twentieth-century rector's wife. There are slight remains of old paintings, a wall tablet with drapery, and brasses.

TILEHURST [map 17]. Lying between the diverging roads to Oxford and Bath out of Reading westwards, Tilehurst was, until the nineteenth century, a secluded village, but is now, on its northern side joined to Reading by late Victorian and later development. The village itself beside the church, and the undulating land to the south of it, is still rural, owing to the presence of Prospect Park, now a public recreation ground (*see* READING) and Calcot Park, now a golf club. Calcot Park is Tilehurst's most distinguished building. Of red brick with plaster doorways, pediment and cornices, it was built in 1755. Its entrance to the north is planned round a courtyard with an arched approach and with matching stables and outbuildings on each side. In the house are spacious rooms, two of them having scroll-moulded plaster ceilings. This main block has been somewhat spoiled by the later addition of a top storey. The park has fine trees and a lake, and two eighteenth-century lodges on the Bath Road of distinguished design.

The church was rebuilt by Street in 1855 but he kept the brick tower of 1731, crowning it with a rich stone spire. The rest of the building is in knapped flint. The interior is darkened by the Victorian glass, some of it effective (especially in the north aisle, east rose, and the south aisle, east window). An alabaster tomb with figures (1627) and some wall tablets (one with a kneeling figure by Gaffin) of the eighteenth and early nineteenth centuries, grace the interior. The churchyard has some delicately carved stones.

At **Calcot Row** there is some modern development along the Bath Road. Here also is a pretty group of almshouses, 1852, in red and purple patterned bricks with lattice windows.

TOUCHEN END, see BRAY

TUBNEY [map 5]. This is more a district than a village. **Frilford Heath** to the east of it, where there are Scotch firs, heather and small, new country houses and two golf courses, belongs geographically to Tubney, parochially to Marcham, Tubney Wood, north of it, is coniferous and shelters huts full of civil servants. Tubney was famous a century ago for the breeding of fox-hounds. The little church, a stone building of nave and chancel and western bellcote, stone-tiled, and stone-walled and Middle-Pointed is that unusual thing, an Anglican church designed by Augustus Welby Pugin. It has a Tractarian interior with rich chancel roof and Hardman east window, cream-coloured walls, coronals of candles and carved pews. With the little village school beside it, it forms a picturesque early Victorian group beside the Faringdon–Oxford Road.

TWYFORD [map 18]. The village grew up round the Bath Road crossing of the Loddon, and later round the main-line junction station for Henley. The oldest and most pleasing building is the group of almshouses, 1640. Now by-passed, the village street with its houses and hotels has an undisturbed late nineteenth-century atmosphere. There is a big cattle-cake mill, *c*. 1870, on the site of a silk mill, *c*. 1800, beside the Henley branch line. The undistinguished church was built (B. Ferrey, architect) in 1846, and its tower added in 1909 (Stallwood, architect). It has glass in one lancet by Willement, 1847.

UFFINGTON [map 8]. Despite a hideous colony of council houses at its east end and clumsily arranged electric light poles everywhere, this remains one of the loveliest villages in the Vale. It consists mainly of chalk-built cottages with thatched roofs (pp. 50, 51), sheltering under great elms and built along four roads enclosing a square of meadow traversed by a willow-bordered stream and footpaths. The long outline of White Horse Hill, looking large and near before rain and distant in hot weather, broods over the parish. Some of the prettiest chalk cottages are down footpaths. Off one of these is a simple brick Strict Baptist chapel (1832), and the best cottage group of all is south of the church corner near the chalk-built school (1617) between the churchyard and the road. Here 'Tom Brown' bothered the schoolmaster and boys and Squire Brown decided to send him to Rugby. The early chapters of *Tom Brown's School Days*, by Thomas Hughes, have vivid pictures of Uffington and the Vale. This school is now a recreation room. The present village school nearby is by G. E. Street (1872) and the Vicarage opposite, built of chalk with limestone dressings, is in a Gothic style designed by H. Kendall & Son, 1849.

White Horse Hill is undoubtedly the finest downland scene in the county and only by ascending the 856 feet does one get any idea of the vast bowl of 'the manger' and the grassy remoteness of the downs stretching away 'for miles in one vast, brown, rippling surface, with no sound to break their stillness [except a blasted aeroplane] and the Vale below', so dear to Tom Brown's heart, furnishing 'a delightful sunny panorama, rich with trees and water' to quote 'The Druid' in *Scott and Sebright*. The Horse itself is more like a Dragon (*see* cover of this book) and is now said to be of Iron Age date and to have been made in about 100 B.C. It and the Cerne Giant are the only two pagan chalk monuments left in Britain. It is so much older than the battle of Ashdown (871), when Alfred beat the Danes, that it cannot have been made to commemorate that event. It was more probably associated with magical pagan rites and many legends cling to it. The regulation walk for courting couples from Uffington is to White Horse Hill. St George is supposed to have killed the Dragon on the little knob below the horse, known as Dragon Hill. It has a bare patch on it where the Dragon's blood is said to have run out. A medieval mummers' play is still performed at Uffington, which has St George in it. Merrymaking occurred at regular intervals when the people of the Vale assembled to clean the weeds and grass off the horse, and a fair took place within the earthen ramparts of Uffington Castle on the top of the hill. This was known as 'The Scouring of the White Horse' and is fully described in Thomas Hughes' breezy book with that title. The last scouring was in 1857. Backsword fighting occurred with wooden staves with which Berkshire men bruised and cut one another, and cheeses were rolled down the manger. Professor Stuart Piggott's article in *Antiquity* (1931, Vol V, No. 17) gives the fullest facts about the Horse and an excellent book called *White Horses* by Morris Marples ('Country Life', 1949) relates this strange beast to the other hill figures of England. East of the horse, the downs slope steeply to the primeval-looking Uffington Wood, in a hollow of which are the beautifully placed brick and chalk buildings of Britchcombe Farm, below which and north of the Roman road called the Portway, the hollow continues into disused watercress beds. The Portway from Wantage to Wanborough (Wilts) is the most beautiful stretch of road in the county with a continuous view to the north of the Vale, while to the south rise the ever-varying grass slopes of the downs as the road twists and turns round grassy valleys and above the thatched roofs of old villages and farms.

Uffington parish church is an unexpectedly complete cruciform building of about 1150 with central octagonal tower. Originally the west end extended farther into the churchyard and the tower had a spire which crashed in the eighteenth century, knocking off the pinnacles of the south porch. In the seventeenth century some of the nave windows were given flat heads. Despite this, the church is as complete an Early English parish church as exists, retaining its pebble-dashed walls, rose window over blocked north door, three transept chapels with gabled roofs of stone, south-east porch (p. 4), moulded circles for consecration crosses, strongly moulded string courses round the whole building, original oak doors and ironwork. The only exterior features which are later than 1150, are the large Decorated (*c*. 1250) south window in the chancel and the eighteenth-century upper stage and pinnacles of the tower. Viewed from the *Craven Arms* on the Faringdon Road or from Grounds Farm, this is one of the stateliest churches in the county. From the deep precision of its mouldings and general excellence of proportion, one may infer that it was designed by an architect-mason, who probably worked on Salisbury Cathedral, some of whose nave, choir and transept mouldings are similar. Uffington church is more than a country builder's job. G. E. Street made a fairly harmless restoration in 1850, leaving the outside undamaged. The interior is now a little bare, though the walls are plastered. Most of the seating is in unvarnished pine and pleasing. In the north transept some pieces of fifteenth-century screen have been turned into bench ends. The long and stately chancel was re-roofed by Street, who finished the sanctuary roof with wooden vaultings on the lines of stone vaulting that should have been there. The south porch retains its stone vaulting and room above. The organ is in the west gallery. The finest features of the interior are the manifold mouldings over the arches at the tower crossing, especially on those over the nave and the transept chapels. There is a modern west gallery. In the south transept is a painted recumbent effigy to John Saunders (1638) and in the north transept are works of the old clock, a parish chest (probably fifteenth century), a mutilated monument to Edward Archer, 1603, and various decent eighteenth-century marble tablets. In the nave are well-carved floor slabs and a large Royal Arms of George III. The triple lancet east window (1850) is well suited to its Early English setting, better suited indeed than the later window by Gibbs in the north transept, the only other stained-glass window in an otherwise light and airy church. The churchyard on the south side has many headstones of eighteenth-century design executed quite late in the next century.

UFTON NERVET [map 24] is among beautiful oak plantations and primrose woods. Ufton Court is its only distinguished building. The church, beside a stuccoed and tiled rectory, is a spired grey stone, sandstone-dressed building of 1862 by R. Armstrong: its chief attraction is its colour. It has a restored tomb of 1615 with a delicate Renaissance surround behind the organ, and another with reclining figures under a canopy, 1560. There are also brasses. All these memorials are to members of the Parkyns family, who held Ufton Court, the most picturesque Elizabethan house in the county. It was built about 1568, but incorporates part of an earlier house. Great additions were made to it in the early eighteenth century and alterations to the outside in 1838 and again in 1900. The E-shaped north-east-facing entrance front today has dark ochre plastered gables, the upper storey projecting. The back, of brick, is largely eighteenth century. The family was a Roman Catholic one and recusant priests were harboured here. There is a chapel, an oratory and various hiding places in the attics, approached through apparently doorless plastered walls. The alterations of 1715 were done by Francis Perkins when he married Arabella Fermor, 'Belinda' of Pope's *Rape of the Lock*. There are Elizabethan doorways, pendant plaster ceilings with geometrical work—a kind of fan-tracery—a sixteenth-century staircase, panelling and several carved stone chimney-pieces. Pope, Steele, Arbuthnot and Bolingbroke stayed here, and Bonny Prince Charlie was entertained in the house in 1745. In front of the house at the end of the drive, is a very pretty early Victorian lodge with pierced barge-boards and a clipped yew with a passage through it in the garden.

UPTON [map 10]. Half-timbered cottages, thatched and tiled, dotted among winding lanes among orchards, compose this tiny village. There is a tile-hung Jacobean manor house, small and with eighteenth-century windows. The rectory is by J. P. St Aubyn in brick Gothic of 1864. The little Norman church, refaced externally and severely restored by Ewan Christian, 1885, preserves its Norman proportions and simple Norman chancel arch and font.

WALLINGFORD [map 11]. This is a very old town even though it is still a small one. There was a ford across the Thames here at a strategic point for all our earlier invaders. It is now replaced by a fourteen-arch bridge of various dates, the noblest three arches, spanning the river, having been rebuilt in Classic style in 1809. They are the newest part of the bridge. There are huge earthworks enclosing a square recreation ground to the west, between the old town and the little 1866 railway terminus. These earthworks are now thought to be Saxon. Hidden by houses and a forbidding park wall, and strictly private, on the north of the town, are the Norman earthworks of Wallingford Castle. Only a few walls of the castle remain and in the tree-planted enclosure is the ruin of St Nicholas Church with Perpendicular tracery in its windows. This place has now more the look of a romantic garden to an eighteenth-century house than the genuine article which it is—the earthy ramparts of an ancient and historic castle. The house in the grounds is small and unimpressive early Victorian Tudor.

Guarded by the Thames on one side, a castle on the other and the mounds which once included a Saxon town on yet another, no wonder Wallingford was a perfect site for a medieval town. Only one more side had to be fortified. So the old town still forms a parallelogram of streets though its southern walls have disappeared. Those who read old-fashioned history books remember that icy night in 1142 when the Empress Maud escaped from Oxford Castle. It was to Wallingford Castle she fled. Here she was besieged by King Stephen across the river at Crowmarsh in Oxfordshire and her son Henry came to rescue her. And at Wallingford he made the treaty in 1153 by which his mother Matilda gave up her claims to the English Crown on condition that Stephen recognized Henry as next heir, the future Henry II. In those days of private wars, Wallingford was a most important town. Kings stayed in its royal castle, the town had fourteen churches of which only three remain. The place was high in Royal favour and prosperous until 1285. Then through plague, and because other towns took its trade, it declined so that by Elizabeth's reign it must have been mainly ruins of churches and fortifications with a few half-timbered houses among them. Not even a brief time of importance for the castle during the Civil Wars, when Wallingford held out longest in the county for King Charles, revived its prosperity.

Consequently, there are few buildings, except the much restored churches, of a date even as early as the sixteenth century. The chief are St Lucien's, a three-gabled house on the river east of St Leonard's church by a mill stream, with pargeted walls: another three-gabled house of brick in the High Street. Both have been much restored. In the next century Angiers Almshouses (1681) on the Reading road were founded; they were prettily churchwardenized in Gothic, c. 1810. The Town Hall (1670) stands in the market place on an open piazza of Tuscan columns underneath with a grand oak staircase to the restored (1887) hall above. There are also old inns of sixteenth- and seventeenth-century date, and one has only to go down any courtyard and look back to see that houses with eighteenth-century brick fronts (generally a purple-glazed local brick which was popular in the town in the eighteenth century) are humbler and older buildings behind their façades.

The distinction of Wallingford today is its eighteenth-century architecture. Thames Street and High Street contain noble examples, of which an early one is Calleva House, Thames Street, three storeys high with brick pilasters and plinth and moulded brick corners. But the best range is that glimpsed along the river bank as one approaches the town from Oxfordshire. There is the delicate stone steeple of St Peter's church, close to the bridge (p. 71). The steeple, a Gothik version of Wren's City church of St Bride's, Fleet Street, was designed by Sir Robert Taylor (1777), who also designed the tower on which it rests. The rather dull church to which this elegant structure is attached was built in 1769, and is clearly not Taylor's work. Its interior has been deprived of Georgian charm by Victorian and later furnishing and by the addition of a chancel in 1904. Next to the church is a singularly noble, three-storey building, Bridge House, also by Taylor, late eighteenth-century stone on the river front, white brick behind. Beyond this is the graceful mid-eighteenth-century length of Castle Priory House, now an hotel. Sir William Blackstone (1723–80), the great historian of English law, lived here. He was Recorder of Wallingford and was instrumental in having the turnpike

148

roads from Oxford and Wantage brought through the town, thus bringing some prosperity to its ancient decay and causing, no doubt, the fine eighteenth-century refacings of some of the houses. St Peter's steeple was, as it were, a turnpike-side advertisement for the borough. Blackstone is buried in St Peter's under his arms on the floor of the nave and there is a tablet to him on the outside south wall. Thames Street, which runs past the backs of these river houses to St Leonard's church from St Peter's, is a charming vista of old walls with overhanging trees from gardens.

St Leonard's church has the most attractive interior of the three old churches. It is late eleventh century and in 1850 A. W. Hakewill built the eastern apse with its plaster semi-dome, the Norman-style south arcade, the rather dull aisle and clumsy west tower, and repaired the two large chancel and sanctuary arches of this characteristically Norman tripartite church over the middle section of which where are now choir-stalls may once have been the tower. Its interior, with whitewashed walls and mysterious east end, is impressive. The churchyard on the south side slopes to a mill stream and faces the timber-framed buildings of St Lucien's.

St Mary's church in the market place is almost wholly a hard, flint and stone 'restoration' of 1854, distinguished mainly by a marble pulpit with bronze panels designed by Onslow Ford (1889). The Congregational chapel (1785) in the market place is now a Roman Catholic chapel. Some of its charming churchwarden Gothic fittings and west gallery remain and the interior has been attractively redecorated in late Georgian style under the direction of Mr John Rothenstein. An ironmongery shop, also in the market place, has a pretty pillared early Victorian front and some Georgian coloured glass in its back premises.

The motoring age has brought its quota of modern villas and these are mostly on the western outskirts.

WALTHAM ST LAWRENCE [map 19].

This picturesque village built round a fork of roads has a half-timbered inn, *The Bell*, originally sixteenth century, a pound in the form of four rail-joined elm trees, some seventeenth-century brick and timber cottages, a church and the remains of an old manor house to the north of the church called Bury Court Farm. It has a fine barn, originally fourteenth century, tiled and with timber roof. The church is mostly Decorated. Chalk arcades divide the tall nave and aisles (plain Norman arches at west end, one on each side). There has been much modernizing, lighting, heating and cementing of inside walls—the last a great pity. A *priedieu* monument of 1573, a pulpit of 1619, part of the Decorated screen, several tablets from 1658 (an urn on a pillar) to 1809 (signed Richard Westmacott) and a fine Royal Arms of Queen Anne may be seen.

There is a small church at **Shurlock Row** by J. Sharp, ju nr., 1870. It is of brick and apsidal.

WANTAGE [map 8].

This red-brick market town is famous as the birthplace of King Alfred whose statue by Count Gleichen (1877) stands in the middle of the wide market square apostrophizing the three-storey houses with shops below them. Most of them are in the local style of red brick with blue-glazed bricks varying the surfaces between the windows; the best examples are the Bear Hotel, Barclay's Bank, Arbury's draper shop (with pretty pillared Victorian front below) on the same side, and the watchmaker's shop on the eastern corner of this side. At the eastern end of the square is the mid-eighteenth-century Post Office vaults, an attractive stucco building adorned with a Venetian window. Another good brick house, now a restaurant, stands on the corner of the Oxford and Faringdon roads. Opposite is the 1878 Town Hall in a tawdry half-timber style, and adjoining it the much more solid and satisfactory mid-Victorian half-timber refacing of an old building with shops below (p. 101). Other good brick houses in the town are Dalkeith, with two semi-circular bays, late

Georgian, on the Oxford Road; Messrs Adkins, Belcher & Bowen's offices near the King Alfred's Head Hotel, the early Georgian house in St Mary's School, Newbury Street, with its door of moulded bricks, the ranges of modest old houses in Church Street and Priory Road, and one or two old inns and cottages of an earlier age in Wallingford Street. There is also Stile's Almshouses in Newbury Street, a late seventeenth-century building, whose entrance floor is paved with the knuckle bones of sheep. But taken as a whole, Wantage appeals by its general effect more than by individual buildings and one must hope that no more buildings as jazzily discordant as the cinema will be allowed to insult its old streets.

Until the Great Western passed through the Vale of the White Horse in 1840, Wantage was a remote town indeed, known as 'black Wantage'. 'Alsatia', the slum area round Westminster Abbey, was cleared in the eighteenth century and the thieves who had sanctuary there are said to have fled to Wantage, so that the town was often visited by Bow Street runners. It is not surprising, therefore, that the old architecture of the place is more convenient than distinguished, though it has some pretty walks, particularly that along the little river Ock below the sloping gardens of old houses.

In 1846 the Rev William John Butler was appointed vicar. He is not to be confused with Bishop Joseph Butler (1692–1752) who was born in Wantage and wrote his *Analogy of Religion*. The Rev W. J. Butler was a Tractarian and put his curates into cassocks and top-hats, which excited the ridicule of Evangelicals. He founded the Wantage Sisterhood, which is now by far the largest order of nuns in the Church with daughter houses all over the world, and a big school, a convent, and two rest houses in Wantage. In 1850 the young Tractarian architect George Edmund Street settled in Wantage and designed the vicarage for Butler, a handsome stone building L-shaped, the Church school in Church Street, whose ceiling on the top floor he adorned himself with paintings copied from work by Overbeck, St Michael's Training School and Retreat House in Priory Road, a long, low limestone building, and the Convent itself (1854) on the hill on Faringdon Road. This last is of local limestone with steep-pitched roofs with dormer windows and a façade which is both varied and simple. As in the village schools of this area which Street designed, the chimneystacks are made into decorative features of the façade, continued, Tudor fashion, down the whole length of the building. Street's chapel (1866), with its original furnishings and glass, remains. The new chapel designed by J. L. Pearson later in the century, is tall and dark and vaulted in brick with stone ribs, all in the Early English style. Mr J. N. Comper has lately added a rich scarlet baldachin and hangings to the altar. St Mary's school for girls, at the south end of the town, is a mixture of brick buildings with a modernistic assembly hall by Sir Hubert Worthington, and an apsidal ended chapel of brick with a stone flèche by G. H. Fellowes Prynne (c. 1900), beautifully redecorated at its east end by Comper.

The large parish church, the source of all this building activity, is a cruciform building, late thirteenth century in origin, with a central tower. Aisles and chapels and clerestory and south porch were added in the fifteenth century. The chancel has carved fifteenth-century miserere choir seats with poppyheads on them, parclose screens and old timber roofs to the nave and south transept. The nave roof rests on lively grotesque corbels. The alabaster tomb to Sir Ivo Fitzwarren and his wife (1361) in the chancel, and the brasses now fixed into walls at the tower crossing are magnificent. There are some decent eighteenth-century monuments on the south wall of the nave. In the south transept is a pretty two-light window depicting the Annunciation by Thomas Willement. G. E. Street restored the church in 1857, putting in the large east window in a Decorated style filled with glass by Hardman of Birmingham, which is well designed for the tracery, but badly fired. Street skilfully extended the church westward so that one is hardly able to distinguish his work from the medieval except by examining the stone of the piers. In 1895 Kempe decorated the south chapel with screen, altar and windows, at the same time gilding the fifteenth-century oak roof—all in memory of the Rev W. J. Butler, who left Wantage in 1880 to become Dean of Lincoln.

Wantage Grammar School, an Elizabethan foundation, was renamed King Alfred's School in 1849, the millenary of the monarch's birth, at the instigation of Martin Tupper. Its 1850 building on the Portway is a charming piece of domestic Gothic in limestone by the talented architect J. B. Clacy (p. 101). The brick buildings behind are by W. Butterfield (1872), who also designed the much-altered chapel of ease, east of the town, at **Charlton**. Next to the Bear Hotel is the Victoria Cross Gallery (1865), which contains forty-five tattered oil paintings by the Chevalier I. W. Desagnes of people winning the Victoria Cross, including Lord Wantage, who presented these pictures in 1900 and won his V.C. at Alma. Here also is the fire engine. This must be one of the least known and most dilapidated art galleries in Britain.

In 1873 the first steam tramway in England was laid down between the town and Wantage Road station. It was the last to be taken up (1948). Its engines were even older than the line and 'The Shannon' (1857) is preserved through the initiative and generosity of Sir James Milne of the Great Western, and now stands in a shelter on the platform of Wantage Road station.

East of the town a huge settlement of two-storey prefabs, not uncomely in itself, has been built regardless of the former balanced structure of the town, on good orchard and agricultural land towards Charlton. It is to house workers of the distant Harwell Atomic Research Establishment.

WARFIELD [map 19]. On Bagshot sand, in back lanes between Reading and Windsor, but too near too many main roads for quiet. Hayley Green House has a moat, and is the oldest house in the parish of any size. Warfield Hall (white, Regency style) and Warfield Park are large modern houses in parks. At **Hawthorne Hill** is a racecourse. The church is Early English, Decorated and Perpendicular, and had much distinguished rebuilding by G. E. Street in 1876. Its most beautiful original feature is the east window with flowing tracery, and the chancel is altogether impressive. There are remains of the rood screen and loft across the north aisle. Delicate chalk carving with pattern work and foliate heads in chancel details on the south, some old glass (censing angels), three seventeenth-century 'kneeler' monuments and several eighteenth-century wall tablets are other features.

The son of the astronomer Sir John Herschel, Sir William, who invented the system of identification by finger prints, lived at the rectory.

WARGRAVE [map 18]. This riverside village, not quite so secluded or 'picturesque' as Sonning, but with a larger number of biggish houses in their own grounds, has many riverside houses with lawns stretching down to the water, and a boatbuilding yard, beside which the branch line to Henley (opened in 1900) crosses the Thames. Here, with a ferry, a towpath beside the meadows on the opposite bank, many side streams and an amateur Regatta, the river has moulded the character of the village. The Loddon joins the Thames here, and a willow-grown backwater runs below the picturesque road from the village street under the hanging woods of Park Place to Henley. This park-like road is a product of eighteenth-century taste which remains almost intact. The village street is narrow, and the houses, many of them white painted, have riverside character. The Woodclyffe Hall and, round a corner, the Woodclyffe Institute, are quaint buildings in art-nouveau style by Cole A. Adams, 1900. The Vicarage is a Queen Anne building of brick; the

Bull Inn has a fine stack of brick chimneys, and several middle-sized houses with pleasant features stand back from the street behind walls and fences facing the river. Beside the river and attached to the eighteenth-century house—Barrymore—formerly stood a fashionable theatre with ballroom and supper room. It was built in 1788 by the rake, Lord Barrymore, who entertained the Prince of Wales and other noble guests there. He was soon ruined, and the theatre (known from prints) was dismantled in 1792. Among more outlying houses, white-bowed Wargrave Manor (formerly called Wargrave Hill) with eighteenth-century features, looks grandly across the Thames from a height. Bear Place is an altered but stately brick house of the eighteenth century, white painted in a shallow valley to the east, Yeldhall Manor, near it, a tile-hung and half-timbered mansion built in 1874 in a conifer and elm-planted park and Woodside (at one time called Kingswood House), an imposing, midlands-style Tudor house in half-timber with symmetrical gables. Scarletts, near **Hare Hatch** on the Bath Road, is a small Georgian house of the kind that was built at the time to lie back from any coaching road. It has some armorial glass of 1838 in a side window. The old village schools, 1862, are picturesque; the new ones neo-Georgian. The church was burnt down in 1914, except for the seventeenth-century brick tower. It was rebuilt in a hard and expensive style in 1916. There are some churchyard tombs of beauty and a carefully designed mausoleum in brick and stone, of about 1910.

At **Crazies Hill,** on the high ground to the east, the façade of the old Henley town hall was re-erected and incorporated into a private residence when the new town hall was built in 1898. It is pale yellow, pedimented, and was designed for Henley in 1790. Here also are old brick cottages, and the half-timbered 'Horns' Inn. (For Culham Court, *see* REMENHAM.)

WASING [map 23]. The Classic, pedimented house in a well-landscaped park south of the Bath Road was burnt out in the 1939–45 period. Its stables and outbuildings to the west are an attractive Gothik castellated group and near them the church in roughcast stucco with stone dressings is an agreeable contrast. It has a yellow-painted bell turret, and presents as pleasing a Georgian exterior as Berkshire can show (p. 60). The dates 1769 and 1839 in exterior keystones show dates of building and repair. The chancel is Victorian and out of key, with its marble, glass and tiles. There is plaster strapwork round nave and transept windows, with angels and scrollwork, and a great deal of transparency glass, English and foreign, has been leaded into windows. Some is sixteenth century; other panels are dated 1629 and 1649. A rich, late transparency of Moses in the transept is dated 1839.

WATCHFIELD [map 3/7]. The remnants of the limestone village hold out against the encroachments of new houses connected with the Military College at Shrivenham nearby. The small bell-coted church was built by G. E. Street in 1858 and is a simple structure, on the lines of a great tithe barn, with steep stone roof and four buttresses at the west end between the northern pair of which is the picturesquely placed entrance door. The interior has lofty chancel and open benches.

WELFORD [map 15]. This is a secret and beautiful place in the Lambourn valley, almost invisible from the Newbury–Lambourn Road. The road from here to Wickham runs unfenced through a grassy tree-planted park; there are a few neat groups of thatched cottages with brick walls near the church. The great house of Welford Park hides itself in trees from public gaze, but its back is seen from the churchyard (p. 59). The front is adorned with brick pilasters between tall Queen Anne windows. Late eighteenth-century wrought-iron gates with stone piers guard an avenue of limes leading to the house from the main road. The church has round flint tower from which rises a graceful octagonal, late twelfth-century spire (p. 5). The body of the church, consisting of nave, aisles and chancel was rebuilt 1852–5 from designs by T. Talbot Bury. Outside it is flint and stone-dressed, hard and prickly looking and some old tracery that Talbot Bury cleared away is in the garden of the house. But its interior is rich, and light and lofty, richest of all in its long, narrow chancel. This is vaulted with chalk and stone, the columns in it are polished slates and marbles, the sedilia, though tooled over, are original. The whole chancel is in the Early English style of the spire. It is very early in the nineteenth century to find stone vaulting like this, so reminiscent of a later architect, J. L. Pearson (*see* SOUTH ASCOT). The pulpit is approached through the chancel wall (p. 91). The north aisle has Early English piers, the tower arch is Norman style, the south aisle has Decorated piers. These were regarded, in Talbot Bury's time, as the purest medieval styles and the church was no doubt rebuilt to illustrate them. The Rev William Nicholson, the munificent rector who provided much of this, is commemorated in a handsome brass in the north wall. There are also elegant eighteenth-century monuments to the Archer family, ancestors of the owners of Welford Park.

The hamlet of **Weston,** a mile up the Lambourn valley, has a charming row of thatched cottages (p. 50) and modest brick Methodist chapel.

WHITE WALTHAM [map 19] has been jolted out of its country character by an aerodrome, which spreads its level wastes north to the main railway line, and to Heywood Lodge, a Regency, three-storey house among trees. The *Beehive* and *Horse and Groom* inns are pleasant buildings of eighteenth-century origin. The church is one of Street's less happy rebuildings in its main outlines, but it has clean and bold mouldings and the tall interior, has enormous carved capitals to the arcades and very high tower arch (1869). Much of the medieval chancel was retained. Three windows are glazed by Mayer of Munich. G. E. Street skied the best monuments under the tower. They are plaques of architectural compositions, 1650–1807 (the last with mourning figure and urn), including a fine work, 'W. Palmer fecit', 1723.

WICKHAM [map 14]. The neat village of brick cottages, many with thatched roofs, is at a crossroads on a high chalky ridge between the Lambourn and Kennet rivers. The church is on an eminence south of the village. Its strange flint and mortar tower is late Saxon with little windows of the same date. The walls are immensely thick and the entrance seems to have been eight feet above the ground so that this tower may have been used for defensive purposes, as were the round towers of Ireland. The body of the church consisting of nave, aisles and chancel, was entirely rebuilt by Pugin's biographer and pupil Benjamin Ferrey, 1845–9, at the expense of the Rev William Nicholson, who was also rector of the adjoining parish of Welford. His rectory (now a private house) which stands east of the church, he Gothicized at the same time in a Perpendicular style, adding a conservatory and a stone spire higher than the church tower. In this conservatory were bits of the old church that Ferrey demolished. Recently the spire has been removed and the house stripped of most of its Gothic adornments, so that it has a Georgian look. The church is built externally of beautifully knapped flint, split and squared, and laid in regular courses, East Anglian style. The interior, dark at first entry by reason of the gaily patterned coloured glass, probably from Brussels (p. 94), is amazing; a complete early Victorian piece, whose strange beauty is mainly in its details. The arcades of the nave are a reproduction of the famous Decorated arcade of Stoke Golding church, Leicestershire. The wooden nave roof is adorned with large, pale angels made of papier-mâché. The same material is used for the huge coloured elephants' heads (p. 92) which support the roof of the wide north aisle, making it appear like a Burmese Temple. These last are said to have come from the Paris exhibition of 1862 and were presented by Lt-Col Nicholson, as was the Gothic font cover worked by Maoris out of wood. The table in the chancel, richly adorned with grapes, looks as though it had been worked by Maoris, too. Its top is covered with appropriate red velvet. Looking west from the chancel (the east window of which is the only inharmonious note) or north aisle (p. 92), the richness is great, what with the patterned glass, papier-mâché angels and elephant heads and the font cover standing against a background of white tracery before red baize in the tower arch.

Hoe Benham, in this parish, has a tiny mission chapel of brick. At Wickham Heath, farther west on an oak-planted hill slope, is a beautiful collection of thatched old cottages looking like a George Morland.

Near here, on the Bath Road, is **Halfway** where is a toll house (p. 76).

WINDSOR [map 20]. Here on the Surrey border is one of the most interesting and beautiful parts of the whole county. The beauty is mostly of the landscape order, depending on colour and light on distant pearly towers and red-tiled roofs seen from a foreground of oaks and bracken. Such scenery, ravishing to the eye in all seasons, is best depicted by colour and engraving; the camera turns it into the usual 'photographic study' known to railway carriages and travel brochures. Moreover, there is the Royal association of the district expressed visually in the beautifully run estate of Windsor Great Park with its miles of stout oak fencing in excellent repair, and expressed indefinably in the sense of the Royal ones, dead and living, likely to appear as ghosts or in the flesh, round every corner. Even the estates of the rich which stud the outer circumference of the Park and Old Windsor have something royal about them. Windsor is a kingdom within a kingdom and is best described in the five divisions into which it sorts itself. Old Windsor, Windsor Castle, New Windsor and outskirts, Home Park, Great Park.

Old Windsor was as far as the Saxon kings could reach by boat from London in order to hunt in Windsor Forest. It is a flat, riverside place, now mostly little new brick houses and 'bus stops on the main road to Staines. It is two miles south-east of Windsor. The original road was shorter and went straight through the Home Park, but Queen Victoria made a skilful and wise exchange of land with the Borough of Windsor and so secured for herself and her successors the inclusion on the south side of land more suitable for her enjoyment than the playing fields north of the road to Datchet. The quietest part of Old Windsor is down by the Thames where are the church and lock and manor house among trees and the noise of a weir. The church has a shingled spire, flint walls and chalk dressings and is Early English in origin. Its most graceful feature is a series of late Decorated windows in the south wall. These are square-headed with pairs of trefoils above the lower lights. In one of the windows is some old glass showing birds with necks enlaced. The church inside is dark, stencilled and 'restored'. Thomas Sandby and Perdita Robinson are buried in the churchyard.

The most attractive house outside the park in this parish is Beaumont, now a Jesuit school for boys. It is a tall three-storey building on a hill slope with wide views of the Thames valley. In about 1785, after it had been sold by Warren Hastings, Henry Emlyn of Windsor beautified the house with columns on its north and south fronts in a style of his own invention, the 'British Order'. These columns, most noticeable on the north front where they extend the whole height of the house, are meant to look like beech trees. They sprout into two a third of the way up, and the capitals are oak leaves with the order of the garter in between them. The frieze above is of the Prince of Wales' feathers, knotted, below the architrave with ribbon and acorns. The effect of these is that of tall men upside down with thin legs in the air and the cartouche with the order of the garter in it, where the legs divide, looks like a fig leaf. Inside the house are some fine Adam-style rooms. The chapel is tall and impressive inside, in its Italian way. It was designed by Joseph Hansom in 1870. To it J. F. Bentley added a new high altar and reredos (1876), and side chapels and Lady Chapel (1884). On the southern terraces of the house, against a background of tall trees, stands a vast and original open-air altar and Calvary designed by Sir Giles Gilbert Scott. A ditch running through the grounds divides Berkshire from Surrey and across on the Surrey side may be seen the turreted brick and stone Neo-Renaissance façade of J. F. Bentley's St John's Preparatory School (1888). Burfield Lodge has well kept-formal gardens and is in a Victorian French-classic style. Some other big houses in this parish are noticed under Windsor Great Park.

Windsor Castle (pp. 26–33) derives its name from Old Windsor. In plan, it is shaped like an hour-glass and slopes steeply up, so that even if enemies were to enter the lower ward, they would have to run up hill under fire from the Round Tower and through the neck of the hour-glass to reach the Upper Ward. The excellent *Official Guide to Windsor Castle* (price 1/-) gives a plan and a clear concise history of the Castle.

Windsor. The Borough of New Windsor grew up under the petticoats of the Castle (p. 26). Indeed, Windsor and its castle stand in relation to London rather as Potsdam to Berlin. Most of the king's soldiers at Windsor have barracks in the town. The Foot Guards, who provide the castle sentries, are in Victoria Barracks and the Household Cavalry in Combermere Barracks, St Leonard's Road. The smaller inns in the side streets are brick, with well-dusted and revered trophies of military exploits, and sets of cigarette cards showing uniforms or service medals are framed, along with portraits of the Royal Family, on the walls. A glimpse of the castle dominates almost any street in the town and the noblest view of all is that from the foot of Peascod (pronounced Pescot) Street, looking up the hill to the Round Tower. It is not an ugly town, despite the squalor of its western suburbs. The nearer it approaches the castle, the more respectable the architecture becomes, except for one late Victorian disaster, the turreted façade of the White Hart Hotel in Thames Street. Entering Windsor over the Thames from Eton one comes on a cluster of distinguished buildings at the traffic lights. The Old House, now an hotel, is said to have been a residence of Sir Christopher Wren. It is attractively decorated within. On the corner is a characteristic Lutyens design, two stone basins set on flattish plinths either side of a cenotaph, to the memory of King George V. The mouldings are bold and simple, the proportion graceful, with its insistence on horizontal lines. Just west of this crossing on the road to Datchet is Sir William Tite's Tudor-style terminus to the London & South Western Railway (1850) with Queen Victoria's private Waiting Room beyond it, now a Christian Science place of worship. Both these buildings are in red brick with stone dressings. Opposite to them is the house built to accommodate the Naval Knight of Windsor, now used by St George's Choir School. It is a long, low, late Georgian building with a stone colonnade and white brick above. In similar style and material is an extremely graceful house at the crossroads, known as The Brewery. It is three storeys high, of white brick, with central pedimented projection. The hill curving up under the castle walls is known as Thames Street and little harm has been done to the effect of Georgian façades above the level of the shops. Messrs Boots have built a sensitive modern façade in brick, designed by Morley Horder. The centre of Windsor is here at the top of the hill, where Castle Hill and Peascod Street cross Thames Street, which here becomes High Street. Many modest Georgian façades survive in High Street and here is the Town Hall (1687) ascribed to Wren, a small building of brick and stone

whose external effect has been greatly spoiled by the filling in of the open piazza below it with plate-glass windows. Queen Anne is in a niche on the north and there is a most delightful baroque statue of Prince George of Denmark, her little-known husband, on the south side, presented in 1713 by Wren's son. Up Castle Hill and opposite Henry VIII's Gateway is Windsor's show street, Church Street, a narrow cobbled thoroughfare with old houses, mostly late seventeenth and early eighteenth century, either side of it, some roughcast, some brick, some with Georgian bow windows and doorways and distinguished mouldings and cornices. Farther south, at the corner of Church Lane and St Albans Street and at the north-east corner of the churchyard, is the most distinguished of all these late seventeenth-century buildings, once the Free School (1707) and now a Masonic Lodge. It is of two storeys in dark red brick, with double projecting courses of brick between the ground and first floors, moulded brick cornice to the red-tiled roof, and chimney stacks turned into arched and decorated features on the blank sides of the building. The Parish Church in the High Street here has a Gothic tower of Bath stone designed by Charles Hollis, 1820–2, under Jeffrey Wyatt's supervision. Its outline is in simple romantic contrast with the castle. The galleried church was, alas, re-Gothicized and extended in a most commonplace manner by S. S. Teulon (1871) and further adorned with a screen by Sir Arthur Blomfield in 1898. The present effect is therefore only expensive, though there are some decent Georgian wall tablets and in the tower is a bust by P. Scheemakers to Topham Foot (1712). Opposite the church are late Georgian terraces with shops below and Messrs Savory and Moore's shop has a rich mid-Victorian interior. High Street at the next crossroads becomes Park Street and this quiet backwater terminated by Sir Jeffry Wyatville's Gothic gates to the Home Park is the most attractive street in the town. On its southern side it starts with a white brick and stucco late Georgian terrace, becoming pale red brick, with a narrow plaster intrusion of Strawberry Hill Gothik. The north side is wholly late Georgian red brick in effect, though some of the houses here have lately been rebuilt by the Crown Lands to harmonize with their neighbours. This street epitomizes the domestic architecture of Windsor which is partly Berkshire with its old red bricks, partly Middlesex and London, with its stucco and white brick.

Running south from the High Street, along the edge of the Home Park is Sheet Street on the east side of which is the tall, red brick, mid-Georgian Hadleigh House, three storeys high, behind a brick wall with ironwork entrance gates showing a flight of stone steps and Ionic-style front doorway. This street continues down the hill and displays, chronologically, every style of nineteenth-century domestic architecture. First there are, in Lower Sheet Street, modest white brick and stucco terraces in a Classic style such as Adelaide Terrace, 1831. Then, where the Home Park opens on the east side, we have Queen's Terrace (c. 1853) facing it and Frogmore. This terrace is in Prince Albert Tudor-style, made of red and black-patterned bricks with stepped roofs and latticed windows. Beyond is Osborne Road in white brick and stucco Italianate style (c. 1860), a sumptuous area of detached houses. Across the roundabout are some large red-brick neo-Renaissance mansions (1885) in the Fitzjohn's Avenue style (but not the work of Norman Shaw); one is now a Brigitine Convent, the other is still called Queen's Acre. There are some more houses which face the Great Park toward Queen Anne Gate and look as though they were built by late-Victorian friends of the Royal family. West of Peascod Street is a charming two-storey crescent of semi-detached houses (c. 1825) called Clarence Crescent and in its neighbourhood one or two broad roads of 1840–50 houses. All Saints' Church in Frances Road is polychrome Early English in the big-boned manner of Brooks and Butterfield by Sir Arthur Blomfield, 1868. Holy Trinity, by Edward Blore 1842, is islanded among Italianate white brick and stucco houses. The church externally is in flimsy, airy Early English of white brick with stone dressings and has a neat spire. Internally, it is much late Victorianized and military-looking. St Stephen's, **Clewer Within,** down by the gasworks and humble brick part of the town, is a vast Decorated and Early English white-brick building by J. Norton (1874). Its interior is lofty, dark and much used. St Agnes, in the south-western suburbs of **Spital,** part of the parish of **Clewer Without,** is a small early Victorian chapel of ease in white brick which has been cream-washed within and charmingly redecorated recently. The Roman Catholic church in Alma Road, by C. A. Buckler (1868), built of Kentish ragstone, is a spacious late Gothic-style building whose rich interior lifts the heart.

The Home Park is of 400 acres on the east side of the Castle (p. 26), a place of magnificent elms and wide pastures. The northern part of it is always open to the public, being the land which Queen Victoria exchanged with the Borough of Windsor in about 1850 in order to ensure the privacy of Frogmore and to give Prince Albert farming activity near the Castle. Frogmore is rarely open to the public, but on those few days in the year when it is visible, is even more worth a visit than the Castle. Enclosing Frogmore and within this park is Shaw Farm, approached by wide and weedless gravel walks bordered by grass and winding widths of flowering shrubs with sentinel Royal lamp-posts of handsome cast-iron design. The farm itself is L-shaped in the Osborne Italianate style, a spreading two-storey building with stone dressings and wide eaves supported on early wooden brackets. The Home Farm, half a mile north-east, is in the same style with a rather ridiculous clock tower and latticed windows in the cowsheds for the cows to look across to Frogmore. North of the Home Farm is Adelaide Cottage, a barge-boarded *cottage ornée* (1831) built by Queen Adelaide, the pietistic and kindly wife of William IV, out of the remains of George IV's Royal Lodge of whose associations she did not approve. But Frogmore is the chief glory of the Home Park. It was an early eighteenth-century manor house whose stucco-covered stables with their twin domes and weather-vanes still remain. In 1792 King George III made it a Petit Trianon for his wife Queen Charlotte. By 1794 James Wyatt had transformed it to its present simple, Grecian stateliness. Wyatt added wings and remodelled the interior and gave to the garden front its handsome colonnade of Doric columns. The interior, which is not shown, has an elegant entrance hall with delicate Adam style ironwork balusters to the stairs, a room with walls and ceiling painted by Mary Moser (*c.* 1794). The garden was laid out by Uvedale Price at this time. He was the great exponent of 'the Picturesque' and, by introducing an artificial river and skilfully placing his trees, managed to convey a sense of winding endlessness to the little garden. At this time, too, Wyatt added a Gothik Ruin by the waterside which Queen Victoria repaired and turned into a summer-house gaily furnished in red and blue and gold. No better site than this fairyland of a garden, with its weeping willows and winding walks—all beautifully kept up and planted—could have been chosen for the mausolea of Queen Victoria's Mother, the Duchess of Kent and of the Queen's husband, the Prince Consort. Whatever we may think of Victorian architecture, the Victorian age still knew about gardening and the vistas from the house are improved by the Circular Temple in Penrhyn granite designed by A. J. Humbert (1861) to the Duchess of Kent, high on its mound and the green copper roofs of the Mausoleum to the Prince Consort beyond it. Nor does Wyatt's cheerful stucco house clash in its Greek simplicity, with the Romano-German style granite and copper of the mausolea.

The Mausoleum to the Prince Consort who died in 1861, was designed externally by A. J. Humbert and internally by Professor Grüner. It is in the form of a Greek cross and the style is very German; the outside walls are of pale pink granite at the base, Portland stone above and the dome and roofs of Australian copper which has gone bright green. Age will not weather this remarkable exterior. Huge doors of gun-metal with elaborate grilles and a touching Latin inscription above, open into an unbelievable interior. One first looks up to the dome's octagon to see light percolating through yellow stained glass on to Sicilian marble arches below, on to grey polished granite columns with gilt capitals and gilt bases, canopied niches with statues. From the four transept arches hang gilt censers in threes, from which, surprisingly enough, sprout the chimneys of oil lamps. All the walls are covered with decoration, the drum of the dome is painted in imitation of marble, arches and niches are enriched with paintings and coloured marbles. Such a wealth of decoration, whose prevailing colours are red, dark blue and brownish-yellow, takes the eye off the main purpose of the Mausoleum, which is the tomb in the middle. Its black marble base stands on a marble pavement, above this is a square mass of dark grey Cairngorm granite at whose corners bronze angels designed by Baron Marochetti spread their wings and kneel. Above the level of the eye and best seen by mounting a wooden block nearby, are white Carrara marble effigies of the Prince Consort and Queen Victoria, whose bodies are encased in the granite below. One of the most curious white marble statues in the mausoleum is that by W. Theed entitled 'Allured to brighter worlds and led the way', depicting the Prince standing on a seashore, one of his arms round the waist of his wife who gazes towards him. With his other arm he points heavenward. The Mausoleum is said to have cost £200,000. The Queen's grief still sobs through its interior as though she had left her sorrow on earth to haunt this rich, forbidding temple to her loneliness. In a grass lawn outside it are buried some of those members of her family who did not become kings and queens of this or other countries.

The Royal Gardens at the Old Windsor entrance to the Home Park, display trim acres of plants enclosed in walls of warm old brick.

Windsor Great Park, unlike the Home Park, is open to the public in most places. But, except along the road which goes from Windsor to Ascot, motoring is not allowed. Consequently, many parts within its fourteen miles circumference are as wild and quiet as they were in the time of Alexander Pope, who spent part of his boyhood at Binfield and thus described Windsor Forest when he wrote of it in 1704:

> Where order in variety we see,
> And where, though all things differ, all agree,
> Here waving grass a chequer'd scene display
> And part admit, and part exclude the day;
> As some coy nymph her lover's warm address
> Not quite indulges, nor can quite repress
> There, interspers'd in lawns and op'ning glades,
> Thin trees arise that spurn each other's shades.
> Here in full light the russet plains extend:
> There wrapt in clouds the bluish hills ascend.
> Ev'n the wild heath displays her purple dyes,
> And midst the desert fruitful fields arise,
> That crown'd with tufted trees and springing corn
> Like verdant isles the sable waste adorn.

The order in variety we still see, because the Great Park is a model of competent estate running. Fences, as already mentioned, are uniformly good. Farming is carried out with efficiency but without the hideousness which modern insensitive materialists seem to regard as indispensable to 'scientific farming'. The Royal Estate is run on the principle that good houses for estate workers are wanted first. By the Prince Consort's Workshops, near the Ascot road, a model village has just been completed. It has its pond and a Post Office in Georgian style. Its houses, designed by S. Tatchell, of varying bricks and textures, are most cleverly landscaped round a green. This village must be one of the very few new housing estates to look like a village and not like a garden suburb. The Park itself owes its beauty to generations of foresters and landscape gardeners; not least to the present Deputy Ranger who has laid out the Valley Gardens and the Woodland Gardens in the Surrey part of the park, with an imaginative grandeur worthy of the best eighteenth-century artists. W. J. Loftie expresses things well in *Windsor* (1886): 'Everything is sweet and soft, green and grey, full of broad sunshine and deep shadow, full of old age and the echoes of long time, and full, also, of freshness and youth—young trees growing up to be to our children what the old ones have been to us'.

The first attempt at turning the Great Park into a park, from the wild forest for hunting which it once was, was made by Charles II. He planted the Long Walk in 1685 whose gigantic elms, almost all diseased, were felled in 1945. The avenue has been replanted with alternate plane and chestnut. The avenue will be thinned of whichever of the two does least well. The Long Walk belongs to the formal type of landscape gardening associated with Hampton Court. It is a straight line running from the south front of Windsor Castle to Snow Hill, a distance of nearly three miles. Queen Anne's Ride from Queen Anne's Gate, Windsor, to Ascot, is another product of formal gardening and also runs in a straight line through the park for nearly three miles.

But the present clumpy beauty of the Great Park is largely due to the good taste first of the Duke of Cumberland ('Butcher' Cumberland of Culloden), who was made Ranger in 1746 and appointed Thomas Sandby the architect and artist as Deputy Ranger, which he remained until his death in 1798. Sandby made Virginia Water out of a swamp, planted conifers in the heathy part of the Park at its Ascot end and arranged the exquisite clumps of oak and beech trees such as may be seen westward from Cumberland Lodge and in most other parts of the Park. Sandby believed that 'nature abhors a straight line' as much as she does a vacuum. He excelled in creating winding vistas and making hills seem to fold into hills by the skilful planting of clumps of trees and the use of sheets of water.

His principles were carried out by the next great beautifier of Windsor's Castle and Park, the Prince Regent, later George IV. One of his first acts was to take down most of the Charles II building, Cranbourne Lodge in the Forest (leaving only Cranbourne Tower which still stands) and to employ James Wyatt to redesign in Gothik style Cumberland Lodge, using some of the old red Charles II bricks. This house was much altered late in the last and present centuries when Prince Christian, then Ranger, occupied it. The Prince Regent also built a Fishing Temple on the shores of Virginia Water, planted more conifers in that area and had Roman ruins brought from Leptis Magna, Tripoli, which Wyatville re-erected. He also built himself Royal Lodge near Cumberland Lodge, in this most picturesque, beech and oak and sweet-chestnut part of the park. But Queen Adelaide all but demolished it (*see* Home Park, above). His present Majesty has rebuilt it in a plain style and its outer walls, washed pink, can be seen from some distance. The Prince Regent's greatest service to the Park was when in 1824, as George IV, he first employed Jeffrey Wyatt (later Sir Jeffry Wyatville) to remodel Windsor Castle. From the Great Park this remodelling appears at its best, for the boldly asymmetrical arrangement of towers and walls are seen, as they were intended to be seen, from glades and openings of the Park. George IV was catholic enough in his taste to appreciate the formal as well as the picturesque garden. He employed Richard Westmacott to design a statue of 'that best of fathers', George III, on Snow Hill, which crowns the end of the Long Walk as seen from Windsor. The horse was not finished until 1831 and it was so large that twelve of the workmen had their dinner inside it. It is now known as 'the copper horse'. Standing on its pedestal of rough stones, which are deliberately naturalistic in arrangement, it is a clever exercise in scale, for even from as far off as the Castle the group is recognizable as a horse and rider.

Other buildings in the Berkshire part of the Great Park are: Sandpit Gate, a plaster Gothic Lodge by James Wyatt on Queen Anne's Ride; Forest Lodge, near the Ascot gate of the main road, a beautiful red-brick building, mid-Georgian in the middle with its ground floor remodelled and wings added in 1793, probably by James Wyatt; All Saints Church, near Royal Lodge, a small bellcoted building with south aisle and flint exterior all in a dull Decorated style of 1854—its interior is unusual because all the Victorian woodwork has been pickled; the Prince Consort's Workshops, near the new village, in dark red-brick Tudor style, a small version of Queen's Terrace.

Finally, mention should be made of a modern building (1939) of great dignity and simplicity in the late Georgian style. This is the entrance gates, consisting of two pairs of white brick lodges, spaciously placed before the drive to Royal Lodge. Beyond them one can see the *cottage ornée* lodge built by the Prince Regent.

In the Surrey part of the Great Park are the superb Valley Gardens by Virginia Water, the Woodland Gardens and rhododendron walk and the Duke of Cumberland's obelisk with a pond below it.

WINKFIELD [map 20]. An enormous parish more than eight miles across—Winkfield Row and Chavey Down (*see* BRACKNELL) are hamlets. The grounds of Winkfield Place, Winkfield Lodge, Foliejohn Park, Fernhill, New Lodge and other large houses skirt Windsor Great Park, and well-laid hedges and expensive fences and the signs of careful planting and trimming are everywhere. Foliejohn Park has been neo-Regency-fied; Fernhill was a brick house of *c.* 1700, but is now large and stately, *c.* 1910; Ascot Place is a well-ordered symmetrical house of about 1850, Edwardianised and set regally in a park with a lake. The Rectory is a house of 1629, altered early in the eighteenth century; the *White Hart* a modernized half-timber and brick building. At the Windsor end of Winkfield Street was a spa with a covered-in physic well. The Pump House has been converted into three cottages.

The church has a brick tower, evidently of the date of the rectory house (1629). Inside, five wooden piers with arches (1592) divide the church into two. The effect is strange but not beautiful. The Victorian restoration—almost a rebuilding—was a poor one.

WINTERBOURNE [map 15]. The pretty little red brick and thatched village street is in a dry chalk valley. The manor house, a plain brick Georgian building, stands half a mile away with the church beside it. This has a plain Georgian brick tower with battlements. But the body of the church, originally twelfth and thirteeenth century, was violently restored in 1854 and later, and pitchpine pews, red and white tiles and organ case fixed into the squire's pew, are too conspicuous. The Victorian corbels to the roof show lively carving by some Jude the Obscure, of ivy, oak and hop leaves.

LITTLE WITTENHAM [map 6]. A lane bends round a shoulder of the northern Wittenham Clump and then downhill to vanish near the church, a large late Georgian farmhouse and Day's Lock on the Thames. There are some modern, model half-timbered cottages. The whole place is among elms and orchards, the old red sandstone tower of the church dominating it. The rest of the church was rebuilt by C. Buckeridge (very much in G. E. Street's manner) in 1861–3. It has a fifteenth-century altar tomb with brasses, a handsome alabaster monument with reclining figure of the seventeenth century, other tablets and other brasses.

LONG WITTENHAM [map 6]. Flat meadowland of the Thames valley gives Long Wittenham some of the character that first comes to mind when one thinks, in general, of a Berkshire village. If Sutton Courtenay is the prize village of this sort, Steventon and Long Wittenham would come next. The treatment by well-to-do restorers of several houses in Long Wittenham's long street has been fairly sensitive, and plaster, half-timber and brick provide pleasant contrasts in the irregular lines of houses. A house near the church has an overhanging upper storey. A fire destroyed much of the village in 1868, and the rebuildings of that period add rather a vinegary flavour. On the green west of the church is the site of a cockpit, and the original steps and pedestal of a village cross remain (south end of village street).

The church has a very attractive exterior. The timber fourteenth-century south porch is richly grey against the warmer stone walls. There is a Norman chancel arch but most of the work is Early English, and there has been a good deal of restorative work. There are some excellent details and fittings. A piscina in the south chapel, incorporating an effigy, with a trefoiled head with angel's wings continuing the lines of the trefoil above, is as attractive a thirteenth-century detail in stone carving as Berkshire can show. The small effigy of a knight in front is probably that of the chapel's founder. The lead font, of about the same date, is evidently of the same origin as those at **Warborough** and Dorchester Abbey (Oxon). There is old woodwork: pews, pulpit, some stalls and south chapel screen.

A late eighteenth-century incumbent, Stephen Demainbray, was Astronomer Royal before he came here, as his father was before him. He promoted the allotment system and wrote *The Poor Man's Best Friend*.

WOKINGHAM [map 26]. A good service of Southern electric trains to Waterloo has turned the rather coniferous neighbourhood of the town into one of detached new small houses and bungalows, while almost the whole seven miles to Reading is villas and bus stops. To find a comely old town in the midst of such country, and one in which bull-baiting occurred as late as 1821, is surprising. From the old parish church at the eastern and London end of the town are some half-timber cottages with projecting first floors and tiled roofs. The main road opens into a market place where roads divide and here one's first impression is almost wholly of the extraordinary Town Hall. It is patterned with black and red bricks with much ironwork and quaintly shaped Gothic windows and the shape of the building itself is quaint enough. It seems to be almost a parody of the stone and ironwork of Henry Woodyer, architect of St Paul's, Wokingham, and the polychromatic constructional style of William Butterfield. It is not by those Victorians but is the work of a Reading firm, Messrs Poulton & Woodman (1860). As a Victorian curiosity, it is unsurpassed in the county and, if only for the vigorous delight in brick and cast-iron and the unhesitating conviction that they were right, of its architects, it should be preserved as something preferable to the ponderous commercial baroque or spiritless committee-taste Georgian favoured for Council offices today. Opposite its western side is an elegant late Georgian shop-front with two bow windows, wisely and well preserved by W. H. Smith & Son. In the eighteenth century Wokingham was a town famous for weaving silk stockings. There was also much brick and tile making in the district as in all south Berkshire. Consequently, the main streets of Wokingham, particularly Rose Street and at the Reading end of the old town, have some handsome eighteenth- and early nineteenth-century houses of warm red brick with old red-tiled roofs. Lucas Hospital (pp. 36, 37), a mile south of the town, is built of some of the most beautiful old red brick (1663) in the county. Of the several large houses in the neighbourhood the most complete and handsome is comparatively new—Glebelands (1898), designed by Ernest Newton in a restrained Queen Anne style, making good use of a mellow red brick. It is now the Rest House of the Cinematograph Benevolent Institution.

The large parish church is old but was so extensively restored by Henry Woodyer in 1864 as to have lost almost all its ancient texture. Only a fifteenth-century timber roof in the nave, a clerestory and lofty arcades and font, all of the same date, remind one it was a medieval fane. The lean-to aisles look like a rebuilding and the chancel is by Woodyer. There is good glass by Heaton of Warwick. St Paul's (p. 98), at the Reading end of the town, with its lofty spire and highly original and effective north entrance, is also by Woodyer (1863). Wokingham's two churches provide an excellent example of how heavy-handed a great Victorian architect could be when 'restoring' an old building, how inventive and imaginative and skilful when building a new one. St Paul's is in the 'Decorated style of the fourteenth and fifteenth centuries' (as that best of Guide books, *Kelly's Directory to Berkshire*, puts it), but with what originality! Whoever saw medieval square-headed windows with tracery or setting like those in the clerestory (as seen from the inside of the church)? These are but two examples of the hundreds there are in this dark rubble-faced and Bath stone-dressed church, of Woodyer's artistic inventiveness. Woodyer delighted in medieval mouldings but his use of materials and proportion and detail went on *from* medieval. He invented a Gothic style of his own, which still remained Gothic because he was an artist in stone. The interior of St Paul's is large, aisled and lofty, and its east end, as in all Tractarian churches, is exceedingly rich, though not so effective as that of Christchurch, Reading. Its exterior is, of all Woodyer's Berkshire buildings, his most effective.

Heathlands was once a hamlet near the vast Pinewood Sanatorium (1901), nearly three miles south-east of the town. It seems at first glance remote still, as in 1864 when the little brick church was designed by W. Butterfield for the lonely heath dwellers who apparently had a form of worship of their own, to images. The Butterfield church was chastened and done up in a Perpendicular style in 1882, but a simple and original font by the architect remains, and a Gibbs east window is now at the west end. The remoteness of the place is, however, illusory. Uneven lanes reveal bungalows among the fir trees and heathery soil, a little to the south is the lakeland of Berkshire—Heath Lake, King's Mere and Queen's Mere (pp. 110, 111), and farther west, towards Finchampstead, the vast bungalow settlement of California in England, and finally, Longmoor Lake.

WEST WOODHAY [map 21] is among primrose copses, under the bare downs on the Hampshire border. Farms lie down long gravel drives. West Woodhay House was a beautiful mellow brick mansion built in 1635, until 1881 when it was greatly altered and enlarged. A year later the early eighteenth-century church nearby (the site of its walls marked by box hedges) was pulled down and the present hard and spiky church was built, farther from the house, from designs by Sir A. W. Blomfield. The glass in the east window is a very remarkable design by Burne-Jones of The Crucifixion. There are also single lancets by him on each side of the chancel. Morris's *Strawberry Thief* hangings beautify the sanctuary.

WOODLANDS ST MARY (or **LAMBOURN WOODLANDS**) [map 14]. On the Roman (ridge) road above the Lambourn Valley from Newbury to Baydon—otherwise, Speen to Cirencester. Inholmes is a large old house, greatly added to and dwarfed by a water tower. The small church by the roadside is an excellent little building by T. Talbot Bury, 1851, with a north-west stone spirelet of dashing design. The simple whitewashed interior (nave, north aisle, chancel, west organ) is enriched by glass by O'Connor and Gibbs.

WOODLEY AND SANDFORD [map 18]. An aerodrome, new bungalows, unfinished shopping arcades deface most of this flat district east of Reading. At Woodley is a tiny Congregational church of stone (1834) in the Gothic style, battlemented, with western spirelet, and clear-glass windows latticed with cast-iron. Its Georgian interior has open benches and hat pegs. The church nearby is a flint and stone building of great originality by H. Woodyer (1871). It has a triple bellcote, unexpectedly elongated and high. Its interior is lofty and graceful with a triple-arched screen with stone vaulting. The brick and flint school beside the church is also the work of Woodyer.

WOOLHAMPTON [map 23]. The village, which stands on the Bath Road between Reading and Newbury, was demolished on its northern side for road widening and two hotels, one neo-Georgian in brick and the other Dutch style, were built on its site. Up the woody hill to the north is Woolhampton Park, now a school. It has red brick Georgian stables and outbuildings, the house itself is mostly red brick Classic of 1858 by J. Johnson and the entrance arches at the Reading end of the park form a grand and extravagant composition in his brick Classic. The flint and stone-dressed parish church north of the park was designed by J. Johnson in 1857 and encases the old building. It has a wooden bellcote and south porch and a door in the north transept which, like the south door itself, has strangely original mouldings. The interior, with wide transepts, leads the eye to a big chancel arch on rich corbels, and a still richer chancel beyond, invisible from the transepts. The west window, by Thomas Willement, 1854, has armorial glass in its upper lights and Scriptural subjects below. It is one of the last and largest works for a parish church by this talented artist. The attractive brick vicarage is an early Georgian incorporation of a small Elizabethan building.

On the hill still further north is St Mary's Roman Catholic church, a modest little brick Gothic structure by G. J. Wigley (1848) with lean-to aisles, cowering below the red walls of Douai Abbey. The church interior is unsophisticated and shows what the Roman Catholics could do in Gothic without the aid of Pugin. The glass by Hardman is violent and vigorous, and the east window, blocked by an 1880-ish marble reredos (probably by F. A. Walters), with a Crucifixion, is richly beautiful. The aisle windows, with figures of saints, are bright and devotional. The red-brick gatehouse and entrance tower in a free-Perpendicular manner at the corner of the road are by F. A. Walters (1893–4) as is the main block (1885–6). These buildings were for St Mary's College. In 1903 Benedictines expelled from France by the Government re-established their boys' school and abbey here. Extensions were made in 1914–16 and 1927 by S. Pugin Powell. The most prominent and impressive building is the Abbey Church (1928–33), at present (1948) incomplete. It was designed by the late J. Arnold Crush, a pupil of Sir Giles Gilbert Scott, whose influence may be seen in its tracery and proportions. At present it consists of an eastern choir, with a high nave, two bays of which have been built. Externally it is of red brick. The lofty aisled interior is faced with beautiful white ashlar and is stone vaulted throughout. The whole effect is soaring and unmysterious and cries out for completion.

WOOLSTONE [map 7]. The only ugly building in this most perfect of Berkshire villages is a red and yellow-brick late Victorian folly, three storeys high and one room thick which was never completed and which time has mellowed. Otherwise it is a place of chalk, brick and timber-framed cottages, all thatched or stone-roofed in an elmy hollow under White Horse Hill, with its own church and half-timbered inn. Woolstone Lodge is an early Victorian two-storey building, L-shaped, beside a lake and waterfall. The little church, always a chapelry of Uffington, consists of nave, chancel and south transept with a Norman north door and leaden font and chancel arch. At a restoration in 1867 the walls were skinned of plaster and elaborate pitchpine pews were inserted.

WOOTTON [map 1]. An oasis on a lane that leaves the ribbon-development of the Cumnor–Abingdon road and climbs northward to oak the slopes of Boar's Hill. There are a few old thatched stone cottages (the best of which was once a forge) and barns, fine elms and a little church. The church has nave and chancel with western bellcote of wood, mostly early fifteenth century. Its interior is simple and charming, with chairs in the nave, old timber roof, black and white marble chancel floor, Comper altar and east window by Kempe. The vestry, entered north of the chancel, has lately been attractively furnished as a chapel.

A bit of gorsy common on the top of Boar's Hill surrounds the Jarn Mound, property of the Oxford Preservation Trust, from which there is a wide view to the Berkshire Downs across the city of Oxford to Shotover Hill. An engraved piece of metal, set up on the mound, indicates the sights to be seen. Youlbury, among conifers on this hill, a large red brick Edwardian house in a vaguely Queen Anne style, is where Sir Arthur Evans, the archaeologist, lived.

WYTHAM [map 1]. It seems odd that this Oxfordshire style and Oxford-surrounded village is in Berkshire. It is isolated from Oxford by the Thames and Seacourt Stream and a wide flood land of willowy meadows. Narrow country lanes from the Trout Inn and Godstow nunnery on the west and Botley on the south, approach it, while the beautiful oaks and elms of Wytham woods shelter it on the west. Wytham consists of the Abbey, a Tudor and Elizabethan house of stone, battlemented and with a gatehouse, but all hidden by dry stone walls and trees from the public gaze.

The church was largely rebuilt in 1814 by Lord Abingdon, who lived at Wytham Abbey, and used some of the materials of Cumnor Place in the building. These are the square-headed gate at the churchyard entrance with its inscription *Janua vitae verbum domini*, the Tudor porch, the tower door, and the late Decorated windows of the church itself. The church inside is a small nave and chancel building with west gallery, prominent floodlights, and a noble east window from Cumnor Hall with bits of seventeenth-century foreign glass in it and other windows, and also some old armorial glass. There is a memorial window in the Art Workers' Guild style by R. Anning Bell. The unspoiled village with its high limestone walls, stone-tiled and thatched houses and stone-built inn and cottage gardens (pp. 50, 51), is on a gentle slope from the church to Seacourt stream.

YATTENDON [map 16]. There are several very pleasant brick houses of the seventeenth and eighteenth century, including the Rectory and The Grange, to give distinction to this village, where Alfred Waterhouse, architect, and Robert Bridges, poet, were two distinguished residents. Waterhouse designed Yattendon Court, a large mansion on the east side of the village, which has been altered to a pretty half-timber replica style house by Mr Muntz, architect. The church, celebrated for its singing, and for its Yattendon hymnal compiled by Robert Bridges and Ellis Wooldridge, has been so expensively refitted that it has little original work to show. What there is, is Perpendicular. Screen, choir-stalls and other fittings are elaborate and richly tasteful. There is a large white tablet to Sir John Norreys, 1597. Part of the Perpendicular roof is original, and the seventeenth-century pulpit and reading desk remain.

INDEX

INDEX

The place name after the page number is the Parish under which the reference will be found on that page in the Gazetteer.

Buscot Rectory, 45
Butler, Bishop Joseph, 149 Wantage
Butler, Rev. W. J., 149 Wantage
Butler's Farm, 115 Beenham
Butterfield, William, 89, 115 Beech Hill, 126 Garston East, 134 Marlston, 141 Shaw-cum-Donnington, 142 Shottesbrook, 150 Wantage, 155 Wokingham

Calcot, 146 Tilehurst
'California in England', 115 Barkham
Calleva House, 148 Wallingford
Campion, Edmund, 134 Lyford
Cannon Hill, 117 Bray
Cantorist House, 120 Childrey
Carpenter, R. C., 122 Cookham, 134 Maidenhead
Carr of York, 115 Basildon
Carswell House, 118 Buckland
Carter's Pottery, Poole, 105
Castle Hill Farm, 115 Basildon
Castle Inn, 130 Hurst
Castle Priory House, 148 Wallingford
Catmore, 119
Causeway, 144 Steventon
Chaddleworth, 119
Challow East, 119
Challow West, 119
Charles II, 32, 154 Windsor
Charlotte, Princess, 153 Windsor
Charlton, 150 Wantage
Charney Bassett, 3, 14, 15, 119
Chavey Down, 117 Bracknell
Cherbury Camp, 137 Pusey
Cherry, Francis, 142 Shottesbrook
Chesterfield, 145 Sunningdale
Chieveley, 120
Childrey, 8, 120
Chilton, 120
Chilton Foliat, 120
Cholsey, 120
Christian, Prince, 154 Windsor
Christian, Ewan, 148 Upton
Christ's Hospital, Abingdon, 35
Church Gate House, 122 Cookham
Cipriani, J. P., 66
Clacy, J. B., 101, 119 Burghfield, 123 Dry Sandford, 150 Wantage
Clarence Crescent, 152 Windsor
Classic Revival, 78
Clayton & Bell, 118 Buckland, 124 Eaton Hastings
Clermont, François, 117 Bray
Clewer, 121
Clewer Within, 153 Windsor
Clewer Without, 153 Windsor
Cockcroft, Sir John, 128 Harwell
Cockerell, C. R., 132 Kingston Lisle
Cocks' Sauce Factory, 139 Reading
Coe & Goodwin, 117 Bracknell
Cold Ash, 121
Cole & Partners, 126 Fernham
Coleshill, 63, 121
Coleshill House, 43
Collins, W., 130 Hungerford
Combe, 121
Combe Gallows, 131 Inkpen
Comper, J. N., 88, 143 Shrivenham, 129 Hinksey South, 144 Stockcross, 145 Sulhamstead Abbots, 149 Wantage
Compton, 121
Compton Beauchamp, 63, 121
Cookham, 63, 121
Cookham Dean, 122 Cookham
Cookham Grove, 122 Cookham
Cope Hall, 124 Enborne
Copper Horse, 154 Windsor (Great Park)
Coscote, 127 Hagbourne East
Cothill, 123 Drayton
Cottages, 50–3
Cottages, Romantic, 80, 81
Coworth Park, 145 Sunningdale
Coxe's Hall, 144 Stanford-in-the-Vale
Cox Green, 134 Maidenhead
Coxwell Great, 18, 19, 122
Coxwell Little, 122

Cranbourne, 122
Cranbourne Lodge and Tower, 154 Windsor (Great Park)
Crazies Hill, 150 Wargrave
Cromwell, Thomas, 138 Reading
Crowthorne, 122
Crush, J. Arnold, 156 Woolhampton
Culham Court, 140 Remenham
Culverlands, 118 Burghfield
Cumberland, Duke of, 145 Sunningdale, 154 Windsor
Cumberland Lodge, 154 Windsor (Great Park)
Cumnor, 122
Cumnor Hall, 156 Wytham
Cumnor Place, 156 Wytham
Curridge, 120 Chieveley
Cutts End, 122 Cumnor

Day's Lock, 154 Wittenham Little
de Morgan, William, 105
Deanery Garden, 143 Sonning
Dedworth, 121 Clewer
Demainbray, Stephen, 155 Wittenham Long
Denchworth, 123
Denford, 88, 123
Desagnes, C. I. W., 150 Wantage
Didcot, 12, 123
Dixon, W. A., 140 Reading
Dolby, E., 113 Abingdon, 126 Garford, 131 Ilsley West, 131 Kingston Bagpuize
Dolman, Thomas, 141 Shaw-cum-Donnington
Domestic Architecture, 1870–1920, 106
Donnington, 141 Shaw-cum-Donnington
Donnington Castle, 20
Donnington Grove, 73–75
Donnington Square, 136 Newbury
Douai Abbey, 156 Woolhampton
Dower House, 128 Hanney West
Down Place, 117 Bray
Drayton, 123
'Druid', The, 147 Uffington
Dry Sandford, 123
Dunn & Watson, 142 Shottesbrook

Eagle House (or The Red House), 143 Sonning
Earley, 123
Earp, 118 Brightwalton
Eastbury, 124
East Court, 126 Finchampstead
Easthampstead, 124
Eaton, 122 Cumnor
Eaton Hastings, 97
Ecclesiologist, The, 117 Bradfield
Eddington, 130 Hungerford
Eden, F. C., 136 Newbury
Edward IV, 27
Egginton, F., 143 Shrivenham
Elcot Park, 132 Kintbury
Elmore House, 143 Speen
Emlyn, Henry, 73, 151 Windsor
Enborne, 124
Englefield, 71, 124
Etchells, Frederick, F.R.I.B.A., 119 Challow West
Evans, Sir Arthur, 156 Wootton
Eystons, 129 Hendred East

Falkner, J. Meade, 124 Easthampstead
Faringdon, 124
Faringdon House, 65
Farley Castle, 125 Farley Hill
Farley Court, 125 Farley Hill
Farley Hill, 125
Farley Hill Place, 66
Farm Buildings, 48, 49
Farnborough, 14, 15, 56, 58, 125
Fawler, 132 Kingston Lisle
Fawley North and South, 93, 125
Fenton, Elijah, 124 Easthampstead
Fermor, Arabella, 148 Ufton Nervet
Fernham, 125
Fernhill, 154 Winkfield
Fernhill Park, 122 Cranbourne